Rachael Roberts Joanne Gakonga Andrew Preshous

IELTS Foundation

Student's Book

Contents

Contents

Unit and topic	Reading skills	Writing skills	Listening skills	Speaking skills	Language focus and Vocabulary	Study skills
7 Globali-zation Page 78	Scanning Skimming T/F/NG Sentence completion Identifying the writer's purpose Guessing meaning from context	**Task 1** Describing a process Sequence and purpose	**Part 4** Multiple choice with more than one option Short answers Note completion Table completion Signposts	**Part 2** Identifying the topic **Part 3** Discussing issues related to globalization Identifying reasons for and against Balancing the argument	Non-defining relative clauses. Financial vocabulary The passive	Revising and recycling vocabulary
8 What's the alternative? Page 90	Classification Multiple choice Jigsaw reading Matching headings and note taking	**Task 2** Expressing your opinion Giving reasons to support your opinions Using adverbs	**Part 3** Multiple choice	**Pronunciation** Intonation **Part 2** Activities to keep fit or healthy **Part 3** Discussing questions on health	Medical vocabulary Real conditionals Avoiding repetition Unreal conditionals	Editing 1
9 Gadgets and gizmos Page 102	Skimming and scanning T/F/NG	**Task 1** Exemplification Drawing conclusions Describing how something works Infinitives of purpose	Listening for main ideas Note completion Multiple choice Information transfer – pie charts and bar charts Listening and writing simultaneously	**Part 2** Describing a machine **Part 3** Discussing technological developments	Present perfect vs. past simple Countable and uncountable nouns	Editing 2
10 The future of computing Page 114	Prediction Multiple choice Note completion Classification	**Task 2** Analysing the question Brainstorming ideas Balancing your argument	**Part 3** Table completion Flow chart Multiple choice	Discussing school memories **Pronunciation** Stress patterns **Part 2** Emails and letters **Part 3** Discussing the future of the Internet	Expressing the future: predictions and intensions Prefixes	Recording vocabulary
11 The art of advertising Page 126	Matching visuals with text Identification of beliefs or arguments Multiple choice Matching headings to paragraphs Note completion Multiple choice	**Task 2** Review of useful language	**Part 2** Classification **Part 3** Multiple choice	Discussion on advertising	Modals of obligation and prohibition	Finding useful language in reading texts
12 IELTS preparation Page 138	Y/N/NG Summary completion Top tips for the IELTS Reading module	IELTS Task 1 Writing checklist IELTS Task 2 Writing checklist Top tips for the IELTS Writing module	Short answers Note completion	**Pronunciation** Schwa in unstressed syllables IELTS Speaking module Parts 1, 2 & 3 Top tips for the IELTS Speaking module	Collocations – *make* and *do* Top tips for recording, remembering and using new vocabulary	How to revise effectively

Contents

Introduction

IELTS Foundation is designed to help you improve your IELTS score and progress towards your goal of studying at an English speaking university. There are 12 topic - based units which cover each of the four IELTS academic modules and all task types, as well as giving carefully guided support and exam focused practice. This book aims to build up your skills and confidence, so earlier units are graded to allow skills development, while reading and listening texts in later units are of a level authentic to IELTS.

What do you need to do to improve your IELTS score?

1 You need to improve your productive language skills

IELTS Foundation gives you step-by-step guidance with each task type in the Writing module. At the back of the book there are model answers for each of the Writing questions with notes to help you improve your own writing techniques.

There are also plenty of questions to prepare you for the Speaking module, as well as Pronunciation sections to give you practice in difficult areas of spoken English, such as sentence stress and intonation. For both Writing and Speaking there are Useful language boxes containing vocabulary and phrases to use in these modules of IELTS.

2 You need to improve your receptive language skills

For the Reading module there are not only a variety of texts and IELTS tasks, but also exercises to help you deal with unknown vocabulary and improve your active reading skills.

As well as the Listening module task types, IELTS Foundation gives you extra exercises to improve your confidence and active listening skills in addition to the complete recording scripts which are used and analysed for language use.

3 You need to improve your language accuracy

Throughout the book, essential grammar exercises have been built into each unit. These have been selected as areas where students at your level most often make mistakes in writing and speaking. The language work is put into a context, to show you how grammar really works in academic English. There are also further practice activities in the back of the book which can be used for study at home.

4 You need to increase your academic vocabulary

Academic vocabulary is very important, particularly in the Reading and Writing modules. There are vocabulary building exercises throughout the book, extra practice exercises at the back, and in addition, a Dictionary focus box at the end of each unit. These boxes contain words that have been carefully selected from the unit to be of maximum use for you in your academic reading and writing. Using these words correctly will help you achieve a better academic style in your writing.

5 You need to learn about the exam

For any exam, learning about the structure and about the task types will help you to succeed, and IELTS is no exception. IELTS Foundation takes you through all parts of the exam, giving strategies to help you answer the task types and useful exam tips.

6 You need to improve your study skills

Succeeding in a test is not just about doing well on the day - improving your English significantly means knowing how best to use your study time. Each unit of the book includes useful and relevant study skills, which will also help you in both IELTS and life at university.

1 Studying abroad

Why study IELTS?

1  01 Listen to Li Cha talking to the Admissions Officer. Complete the form.

Name: Li Cha

Tutor: Stephen Ennis

Age: 1 _____ Class: 2 _____

Start date: 14th February Finish date: 3 _____

Contact number in Australia: 4 _____

Years of study of English: 5 _____

Forming questions

1 Use this information about Li Cha to complete the questions.

Family and friends	I live with my grandmother in Beijing. My brother is called Shao – he's nineteen.
Hobbies	I like playing table tennis.
Reasons for taking IELTS	I want to study IT and Computing at Sydney University in Australia.
Future plans	I'd like to work with computers.

0 Who *do you live with* .... ?
   My grandmother.

1 How .... ?
   He's nineteen.

2 What .... ?
   I like playing table tennis.

3 Why .... ?
   So I can go to the University of Sydney in Australia.

4 What .... ?
   IT and Computing.

5 What .... ?
   I'd really like to work with computers.

Do you can speak Chinese?

2 Correct the mistakes in these questions.

0 Does he lives here? _Does he live here_ ?

1 Do you can speak Chinese? .... ?

2 How often speak you English? .... ?

3 How old you are? .... ?

4 Why you went there? .... ?

5 Who teaching you? .... ?

6 What you are doing? .... ?

7 How to complete this form, please? .... ?

8 Where do he live now? .... ?

9 When you will go home? .... ?

10 What time is it start? .... ?

Speaking skills

Expanding answers

1 Choose the most suitable extra information (**a–h**) for the short answers (**0–5**).

0 My grandmother. ....h....

1 He's nineteen. ....

2 I like playing table tennis. ....

3 So I can go to the University of Sydney in Australia. ....

4 IT and computing. ....

5 I'd really like to work with computers. ....

a In fact, I'm good at most indoor sports. I'm not very interested in watching them on the TV, though.

b He's a year older than me. We've always got on really well and spend a lot of time together.

c I'm a bit nervous about my final exams though!

d I think I could be quite successful. I'm very motivated and I'm not frightened of hard work!

e They do exactly the course I want to do and I think campus life abroad will be fascinating.

f I'm really fascinated by them and can spend hours working on my own PC at home.

g He works for a major software company. He works long hours, and gets very tired. But he likes what he does.

h She's quite old, but full of life. Sometimes she's a bit strict though.

Speaking 1

Exam information

In Part 1 of the Speaking module the examiner will ask you general questions about yourself.

TIP

Give full answers and add extra information about the topic.

1 Imagine you are the examiner. Write down five questions about these subjects.

Their home town
Family and friends
Hobbies
Their studies
Future plans

2 Work in pairs. Take it in turns to be the examiner and candidate.

1 🔊 02 Listen to Professor Gooding talk about her experiences in other countries. Complete the table below as you listen. Write **NO MORE THAN THREE WORDS** for each answer.

Country	Problem
Indonesia	**1** ....
Egypt	**2** ....
3	short days
Japan	**4** couldn't ....
China	**5** couldn't ....

Dependent prepositions

After many adjectives, verbs and nouns we use a preposition.

Example:
I'm **bored with** this film. Let's watch something else.

1 Find five adjectives and their dependent prepositions in the Expanding answers section on page 7.

2 Now complete the following sentences from Listening 2 with the correct preposition.
0 I was interested ......*in*....... learning all about the country.
1 I was particularly fascinated .... the architecture.
2 Life in Indonesia is very different .... life in New Zealand.
3 I'm very keen .... spicy food.
4 I was pretty good .... cross-country skiing.
5 I was a bit nervous .... going to a country where I couldn't read anything.
6 He was really enthusiastic .... his work.

3 🔊 02 Listen to Professor Gooding again and check your answers.

4 Look at sentences 0 and 5 in exercise 2. What happens to the form of the verb after a preposition?

5 Fill in the missing dependent prepositions in the table below.

6 Work in small groups. Roll a dice and look at the sentence with this number. Then talk about it for 30 seconds.

Three countries you are **interested** .... visiting.	**1**
A culture you are **fascinated**	**2**
A country where life is very **different** .... your own.	**3**
A country you wouldn't be **keen** .... visiting.	**4**
A language you'd be **enthusiastic** .... learning.	**5**
A city you'd be **nervous** .... visiting.	**6**

1 Read the <u>first paragraph</u> of the text about culture shock.

What is culture shock?

'Culture shock' describes the impact of moving from a familiar culture to one which is unfamiliar. It is an experience described by people who have travelled abroad to work, live or study; it can be
5 felt to a certain extent even when abroad on holiday. It includes the shock of a new environment, meeting lots of new people and learning the ways of a different country. It also includes the shock of being separated from the
10 important people in your life, maybe family, friends, colleagues, teachers: people you would normally talk to at times of uncertainty, people who give you support and guidance. When familiar sights, sounds, smells or tastes are no longer
15 there you can miss them very much. If you are tired and jet-lagged when you arrive, small things can be upsetting and out of all proportion to their real significance.

2 According to the author there are many different causes of culture shock. <u>Underline</u> any you can find in the text.

3 What do you know about the climate, food, language, dress and rules of behaviour in Britain? How are they different from your country?

4 Now read the rest of the article and compare your ideas with the author's.

Climate

Many students find that the British climate affects
20 them a lot. You may be used to a much warmer climate, or you may just find the greyness and dampness, especially during the winter months, difficult to get used to.

Food

You may find British food strange. It may taste
25 different, or be cooked differently, or it may seem tasteless or heavy compared with what you are used to.

Language

Constantly listening and speaking in a foreign language is tiring. Although you may have learned
30 English very thoroughly, it is possible that the regional accents you discover when you arrive in the UK make the language harder to understand than you thought. People may also speak quickly and you may feel too embarrassed to ask them to
35 repeat what they have said.

Dress

If you come from a warm climate, you may find it uncomfortable to wear heavy winter clothing. Not all students will find the style of dress different, but for others people's dress may seem
40 immodest, unattractive, comical or simply drab.

'Rules' of behaviour

Every culture has unspoken rules which affect the way people treat each other. For example, the British generally have a reputation for punctuality. In business and academic life keeping to time is
45 important. You should always be on time for lectures, classes and meetings with academic and administrative staff. Social life is a little more complicated. Arranging to meet and see a film at 8pm means arriving at 8pm. But if you are invited
50 to visit someone's home for dinner at 8pm you should probably aim to arrive at about 8.10, but not later than 8.20. When going to a student party an invitation for 8pm probably means any time from 9.30pm onwards!

Glossary

dampness – slight wetness in the air
immodest – clothing or behaviour that shocks or embarrasses some people
comical – funny
drab – dull or boring, colourless
reputation – the opinion that other people have about someone
punctuality – not being late

5 Look at the model of culture shock below which shows the first five stages of adjustment marked **1–5**.

A Differences and similarities are accepted. You may feel relaxed and confident and you become more familiar with situations and feel well able to cope with new situations based on your growing experience.

B When you first arrive in a new culture, differences are intriguing and you may feel excited, stimulated and curious. At this stage you are still protected by the close memory of your home culture.

C Differences and similarities are valued and important. You may feel full of potential and able to trust yourself in all kinds of situations. Most situations become enjoyable and you are able to make choices according to your preferences and values.

D A little later, differences create an impact and you may feel confused, isolated or inadequate as you start to notice more and more cultural differences and family and friends are not immediately available for support.

E Next you may reject the differences you encounter. You may feel angry or frustrated, or hostile to the new culture. At this stage you may be conscious mainly of how much you dislike it compared to home. Don't worry as this is quite a healthy reaction. You are reconnecting with what you value about yourself and your own culture.

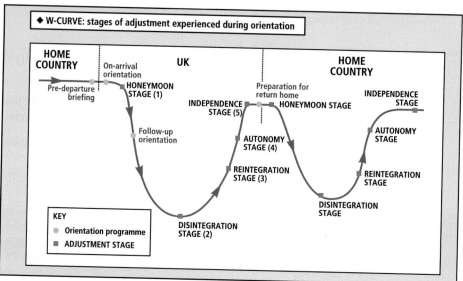

Now match the stages (**1–5**) with paragraphs (**A–E**).

Multiple choice

6 Circle the appropriate letters **A–D**.

1 According to the writer, you may feel positive when you first arrive in a new culture because
   A you have no experience of this culture yet.
   B you still feel in touch with your own culture.
   C your family and friends are not around.
   D you do not notice any differences to your own culture.

2 According to the writer, in the third stage of the transition it is normal to feel
   A negative about the new culture.
   B frightened of asking for help.
   C happy to return home.
   D protected by the recent memory of your home.

3 This text was written
   A to help international students returning home after a period of study.
   B to promote international study to students from around the world.
   C to warn international students of the dangers of living abroad.
   D to aid international students who have just arrived in a new country.

7 Work in pairs. Discuss which country you would like to live or study in. What do you think you might enjoy about living there?

Strategy

Read all the choices carefully and underline key words in the question (see first example).

Eliminate answers which are clearly wrong.

Make sure you can find the answer in the text (not just what you think is true).

Note completion

Complete the gaps with
EITHER the exact words you hear if they fit grammatically
OR different words which have the same meaning

1 🔊 03 You are going to hear an international student adviser giving advice on culture shock. Listen and complete the notes below using **NO MORE THAN THREE WORDS** for each answer.

Ways to minimize the effects of culture shock

Keep **1** .... friends and family at home, through phone calls or email. Make sure you have **2** .... of your friends and family too.

Eat well, especially food from **3** ....

Make new friends – **4** .... will understand what you're feeling. Also make friends with local students if you can.

Use the drop-in centre and other services which can give you **5** ....

Strategy

Use the preparation time well. You can make notes if you like, but remember you only have **1** minute. Think of one or two things to say about each point on the card.

Exam information

In Part 2 of the Speaking module, the examiner will give you a card with some prompts. You have **1** minute to prepare to talk for **1–2** minutes on the topic on the card. The examiner will not interrupt you or ask questions while you are speaking.

In Part 3, the examiner will ask you some more general questions related to the topic in Part 2.

1 Work in pairs.
Student A: Look at Card A.   **Student B:** Look at Card B.
Take **1** minute to prepare. Then take it in turns to talk on your topic for **1–2** minutes. When you have finished, your partner may ask you one or two questions.

A

Describe a leisure activity eg a hobby, sport or game that is popular in your country.

You should say:

What this activity is and what people do
Where they do it
Why people enjoy doing this activity

And also say what you like or dislike about this activity.

B

Describe a typical dish from your country that you would like to give a visitor from another country.

You should say:

What it is made from
When it is eaten (every day or on a special occasion)
Why this dish is popular
And also say whether you like or dislike this dish.

2 Work in pairs.
Student A: Imagine you are the examiner. Ask your partner three of the questions in the box. Afterwards, change roles.
Student B: You are the exam candidate. Answer the questions as fully as possible. Afterwards, change roles.

- Have you ever been to a country where you found the food strange?
  Did you try it, or did you look for food from your own country?

- What do you think is the best way to keep in touch with friends and family when you're away from home? Why?

- Who would you go to for support if you were studying abroad and you had a problem?

- Have you ever been to a country where people behaved differently from people in your country? What happened – or what do you think might happen?

- What do you think are the best ways to find and make new friends when abroad?

- What things do you like most about your own culture?

Writing 1

TIP

The opening statement should contain general information, but don't simply repeat the words in the diagram.

The main part of your answer should contain specific reference to data shown in the diagram.

Understanding key features of data

1 In a Task 1 question, you are asked to describe a chart, diagram, table or graph in at least 150 words. Here is a typical question:

This bar chart illustrates the number of students studying different subjects at university level over a five-year period.

Write a report for a university lecturer describing the information below.

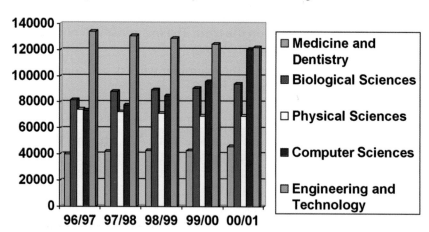

axes   horizontal axis
bar chart   key
line graph
vertical axis

2 Label these diagrams with words from the box.

a ....

b ....

c ....

d ....

e ....   f ....

Ask yourself these questions about <u>any</u> Writing Task 1.

Firstly, make sure you understand what the diagram shows. Then select the main ideas and group the information. Do not simply list every statistic.

3 Look at the bar chart and answer these questions.

1 What information does the horizontal axis show?
2 What information does the vertical axis show?
3 What do the columns represent?
4 Does the bar chart show facts and figures about (a) one time or (b) changes over time?
5 What are the most significant changes?
6 Should you group facts and figures by (a) number of students or (b) subjects?

Writing an introductory statement

4 Look at this introductory paragraph taken from an answer to the example writing task and answer the questions.

The graph shows how many students were studying five different subjects at university level between 1996 and 2001. According to the chart some subjects became more popular over this period, while others dropped in popularity.

1 The first sentence tells us
   A what the graph shows.
   B what the horizontal axis shows.
   C what happened in 1996 and 2001.

2 The second sentence tells us
   A about specific subjects.
   B about the vertical axis.
   C generally what happens in the graph.

3 In an answer, the wording of the introductory paragraph should be the same as the wording of the question. **T/F**

4 The introductory paragraph should cover the main ideas. **T/F**

Describing data which shows changes over time

5 The second and third paragraphs give more specific details. Complete these sentences with the name of the subject area.

Subjects which became more popular
0 There was **a slight increase** in the number of students taking ..*Medicine and Dentistry*....... .
1 .... showed **a steady increase**.
2 There was **a sharp increase** in the number of students studying

....
3 Together with .... , ... was still one of **the two most popular subjects** in 2001.

Subjects which became less popular
4 There was a **slight fall** in the number of students studying ....
5 .... showed **a steady drop** in popularity.
6 .... remained **the least popular subject** of the five.

6 Add some figures from the bar chart to support the statements in exercise **5**. Use figures and/or these phrases.

> just under   nearly   just over   over

Example:
There was a slight increase in the numbers of students taking Medicine and Dentistry, __from just under 40,000 in 1996 to nearly 47,000 in 2001.__

7 Using the sentences from exercises **2–6**, write your answer to the question on page 12.

8 When you have finished your answer, compare it with the model answer on page 160. Your answer does not have to be exactly the same, but can you see anything in the model answer that you could have used in yours?

Language focus 2

Understanding how sentences work

1 Look again at the last part of the model answer on page 160.

...Engineering and Technology showed a sharp drop in popularity, from nearly 140,000 to just over 120,000. However, together with Computer Sciences, Engineering and Technology was still one of the two most popular subjects in 2001.

1   Find an example of each of these parts of speech.

0	a verb in the past tense	*showed*
1	an adjective	....
2	a linking word	....
3	a noun	....
4	an article	....
5	a preposition	....
6	an adverb	....

2   What is the subject of the sentence?

2 Look at these sentences which are taken from the model answer on page 160. Divide each sentence into three parts as in the examples. Write each one in the table.

1   Others dropped in popularity.
2   This remained the least popular subject of the five.
3   Biological Sciences showed a steady increase over the five-year period.
4   There was a sharp increase in the popularity of Computer Sciences.
5   There was a slight fall in the number of students studying Physical Sciences.

TIP

There + verb *to be* is a common pattern in this type of writing.

The pattern of subject, verb, object is nearly always used in written English sentences. This may be different from your language.

Subject	Verb	Object
The chart	shows	how many students were studying five different subjects ...
Some subjects	became	more popular over this period.

3 These sentences are part of a Writing Task 1 answer. Look at the bar charts and put each sentence into the correct order.

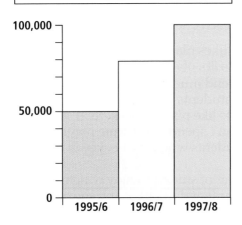

US students studying abroad, 1995–1998

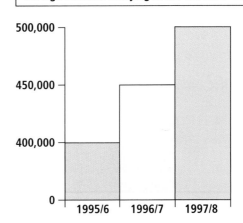

Foreign students studying in the US, 1995–1998

1 More and more college students from the United States/to study/are going abroad
2 college credits abroad/100,000 American students/in 1997 and 1998/earned
3 are coming to study in the US/that while American students/however, recent figures/are leaving/the country to study abroad,/thousands of foreign students/show
4 in 1998 to 1999,/were/there/500,000 foreign students studying at American colleges and universities,/over 10% more than in the previous year

Writing 2

1 Read this question.

This bar chart shows the percentage of Australian graduates in full-time employment four months after graduating, between 1995 and 2001.

Write a report for a university lecturer describing the information.

Write at least 150 words.

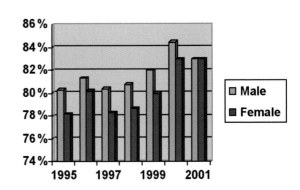

Quantifiers

A class of students conducted a survey into which sports they enjoyed playing and watching. The bar charts show the results.

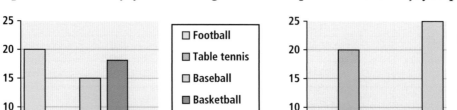

Sports students enjoyed watching   **Sports students enjoyed playing**

1 Look at the sentences describing the bar charts and correct the mistakes with quantifiers in each one.

0   A lot of student likes playing table tennis.
    A lot of students like playing table tennis.
1   The students spend much time watching football.
2   Majority of the students prefer watching football to playing it.
3   Some of students like playing basketball.
4   The students don't spend many time playing basketball.
5   A number of students who play hockey is larger than a number who play football.
6   The large number of students enjoy watching football.
7   Several of the student don't play any sports.
8   The students spend the large amount of time watching sport.

2 <u>Underline</u> the best alternative.

0   *A lot of* is followed by a **singular/plural** noun and verb.
1   *The majority of* or *The number of* is followed by a **singular/plural** noun.
2   *Much* is generally used in **statements/questions/negative sentences** with **countable/uncountable** nouns.
3   *Many* is used with **countable/uncountable** nouns.
4   You can add adjectives to *a number of* and *an amount of* to show how large or small the number or amount is, eg a *large number of* people, a *small amount of* time. *A number of* is used with **countable/uncountable** nouns. *An amount of* is used with **countable/uncountable** nouns.
5   You use *the number of* or *the amount of* when you want to say something about that number or amount, eg *The number of* students who play football is greater than the number who play basketball.
    Most, several and *some* can be used with a noun, eg *some* students, or with of + the + noun, eg *some of the* students. The **first/second** use is more specific in meaning.

3 Write more sentences about the bar charts using these quantifiers.

> Some (of)   most (of)   several (of)   the majority of   a/the number of
> an/the amount of   a lot of   much   many

Note: *Lots (of)* is rather informal, and not suitable for academic writing.

Studying abroad   **1**

Ways of recording vocabulary

Translation is not always the best way to remember the meaning of a word or phrase. Look at these three different suggestions.

1 Use the word or phrase in a sentence that means something to you. Write sentences using these adjectives and prepositions.

Example:
*I'm **keen on** Chinese food and playing basketball.*

1 keen on
2 nervous about
3 good at
4 interested in
5 fascinated by

2 Draw pictures or diagrams to illustrate the following trends.

Example:
A sharp increase

1 a sharp increase
2 a steady increase
3 a slight fall
4 a sharp drop

3 Look up the words in a good English–English dictionary. Match the definitions with the words.

		a	calm and not worried
		b	behaving in a very unfriendly or threatening way
1	relaxed	c	wanting to find out about something
2	confused	d	certain about your abilities and not nervous or frightened
3	confident		
4	excited	e	unable to understand something or think clearly about it
5	frustrated		
6	curious	f	very happy and enthusiastic because something good is going to happen
7	hostile		
		g	feeling annoyed and impatient because you are prevented from achieving something

Look at the words from this unit in the dictionary focus box. Record them using one of the ways suggested in the Study skills section.

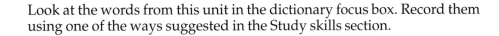

eliminate p.10	reject p.10	illustrate p.12
adjustment p.10	accept p.10	specific p.13
potential p.10	minimize p.11	statistic p.13

2 Earth today

In groups, list some of the problems and benefits of different modes of transport.

Reading 1

Strategy

Making predictions about what you are going to read can help you to understand the text more quickly when you read it. Look at any pictures with the text and at key words in the title or first paragraph (here in **bold**).

Prediction

1 Read the first paragraph of this article.

A **They** are **noisy, smelly and dirty**, and **cost more and more every year. We moan about them** all the time, yet **we are hopelessly addicted**.

2 Answer these questions
1 Who or what do you think **they** are?
2 What type of problems do **they** cause?
3 Why are we **hopelessly addicted** to these things?

3 What do you think the main focus of this article will be? Quickly read the article to check.

B Britons love their cars more than any other Europeans, a major new EU study shows. The number of commuters cycling and walking in this country is declining, while the number of cars and lorries on the road has tripled in the last 30 years.

C The report, The Hour of Choice – the first major transport study by the European Commission for a decade – says congestion costs Europe up to £85 billion a year.

D Road traffic in the EU is forecast to increase by 50 per cent by 2010 and air travel by 70 per cent. 'Europe is being asphyxiated by congestion,' the study says. Transport chiefs will use its findings this week to urge Ministers to do more to reduce road traffic.

E In Britain that means trying to cut the need to travel, said David Begg, chairman of the Commission for Integrated Transport – the Government's advisory body: 'We rely far too much on the car.'

F Begg blamed the increase in traffic on the growth of out-of-town shopping and business parks in the Eighties. 'Bad policies have increased car and truck use which makes people demand more roads, but that only leads to more congestion. It's a bit like a heroin addict always looking for another fix.'

G Brussels wants to cut traffic and pollution with extra taxes on motorists and hauliers. The money would help the rail and bus services.

H While road congestion grows, the study shows, the cost of alternative forms of transport is rising sharply. Britons pay some of the world's most expensive bus and train fares for services that are crumbling through lack of investment.

I In the last 20 years public transport fares have risen by an average of 65 per cent. Only 10 per cent of our fares are subsidized, compared with an average of 40 per cent on the Continent.

J In an attempt to ease overcrowding in the skies, the EU is to consider forcing airlines to pay a tax on aircraft noise and greenhouse gas emissions, which could raise air fares.

K But EU sources say Brussels will avoid recommending large rises in petrol and diesel taxes after the protests in Britain and France last autumn.

L Congestion charging – forcing motorists to pay to drive into city centres – is seen as more effective. The report will encourage other countries to follow Britain in allowing local authorities to adopt such measures.

M Environmental campaigners hope a strong endorsement at the European level will bolster what they see as Britain's weakening resolve to push congestion charging and other green measures.

Guessing meaning from context

4 Find a word in the text that means the same as:

0	person who regularly travels a (long) distance to get to work (paragraph B)	*commuter*
1	abbreviation for the European Union (paragraph B)	....
2	ten years (paragraph C)	....
3	full of traffic (paragraph C)	....
4	unable to breathe (paragraph D)	....
5	given financial aid by the government (paragraph I)	....
6	mainland Europe (paragraph I)	....

Exam information

In the IELTS Reading module there will usually be more headings to choose from than paragraphs. Also, you may not need to find a heading for every paragraph. Remember to read the instructions carefully.

Matching paragraphs to headings

5 Choose the most suitable headings for paragraphs B–H from the list of headings below.

Example:

0 *The cost of public transport in Britain*

H While road congestion grows, the study shows, the cost of alternative forms of transport is rising sharply. Britons pay some of the world's most expensive bus and train fares for services that are crumbling through lack of investment.

1 The cost of congestion
2 Predictions of traffic increases
3 Causes of the traffic congestion in Britain
4 A summary of what the report says about Britain and transport
5 A British suggestion to improve the situation
6 A suggestion from Brussels to improve the situation

Strategy

Decide what you are looking for (a number, a noun, an adjective, a verb etc.).

Do not use more words than you are allowed.

You may omit articles (a/the).

Short answer questions

6 Read the text again and answer these questions. Underline the section where you found the answer. Write **NO MORE THAN THREE WORDS AND/OR A NUMBER** for each answer.

1 How many more cars and lorries are there in Britain now compared with 30 years ago?
2 How much does congestion cost Europe each year?
3 By how much will road traffic in the EU rise by 2010?
4 By what percentage have public transport fares risen in the last 20 years?
5 What percentage of public transport fares are subsidized in *Britain*?
6 What percentage of public transport fares are subsidized in *Europe*?

7 Answer these questions using **NO MORE THAN THREE WORDS** from the passage.

1 What methods of getting to work are now less popular in Britain?
2 Why is the service offered by trains and buses in Britain getting worse?
3 What does Brussels think is likely to be a more effective measure than increasing taxes on fuel?

Choosing the best title

8 Choose the most suitable title for the reading passage.

1 The increase in road accidents in Britain
2 The need for public transport
3 The rise of road traffic in Britain
4 The cost of pollution
5 The solution to road traffic

Subject-verb agreement

1 These sentences are taken from the reading text. <u>Underline</u> the subject and verb in the sentence. Is the verb singular or plural?

0   <u>Road traffic</u> in the EU <u>is</u> forecast to increase by 50 per cent.   <u>singular</u>/plural
1   Bad policies have increased car and truck use.   singular/plural
2   The cost of alternative forms of transport is rising
    sharply.   singular/plural
3   In the last 20 years public transport fares have risen
    by an average of 65 per cent.   singular/plural
4   Only 10 per cent of our fares are subsidized.   singular/plural

2 Look at the subject-verb agreement in each of these sentences. Is it correct or incorrect? Rewrite the incorrect sentences.

0   Nobody seem to enjoy travelling to work by train.   *Nobody seems…*
1   One of my sisters drives a sports car.
2   None of the cars was stopped by the police.
3   Much of my work involves visiting different companies.
4   Most people in my country owns a car.
5   Some of the students in my class cycle to college.
6   Neither of us travels on public transport much.
7   A lot of my time is spent driving to and from work.
8   Car users in Britain pays high motoring taxes.

3 Complete the sentences using these verbs.

drive   travel   cycle
catch   commute
walk   own   ride

0   Children in my country   *walk to school*   .
1   Most people in modern society   ....
2   None of the students in my class   ....
3   Some of today's younger generation   ....
4   Everyone I know   ....

Numbers and figures

Academic courses often involve the interpretation and analysis of different numbers and figures.

$450   80km/h
6,900m   30kg   3.75
13/11/86   59%   ¾
600km^2 4,016km
4:1   54°C

1 Look at the figures in the box. Identify the following:

1   A decimal   5   A weight   9   A speed
2   A date   6   A distance   10   A percentage
3   The size of an area   7   A price   11   A temperature
4   A height   8   A fraction   12   A ratio

2 Work in pairs.

Student A: Say the category.   **Student B:** Read the figure.

Short answers

Exam information

Read the question carefully – usually you have to answer this type of question with a number or up to three words, but you may be asked for something else, eg, no more than **TWO** words.

Your answers will be in note form, not whole sentences, but they need to answer the question grammatically.

The order of the questions always follows the order of the text.

1 04 Listen and answer the questions using **NO MORE THAN THREE WORDS OR A NUMBER**.

1 How much waste, on average, does one person produce each year? ....

2 What proportion of our waste is biodegradable? ....

3 What proportion is glass? ....

4 How much waste is buried? ....

5 Why is some waste burned? ....

6 When will waste have to be reduced? ....

Exam information

Make sure you keep to the word limit, and that your answers make grammatical sense.

Your answers might be words from the text, but you may also have to change them to fit the word limit.

Sentence completion

2 Complete the notes. Write **NO MORE THAN THREE WORDS** for each answer.

Government policy is to **7** .... and **8** .... waste.

Local councils have to **9** ....

Sites have been set up to collect different types of waste separately, for example **10** .... , **11** .... and **12** ....

Some local councils have also provided **13** ....

Switzerland has a tax on **14** .... to reduce waste.

Present simple vs. present continuous

1 Look at this extract from the listening text. <u>Underline</u> examples of the present continuous and the present simple.

J: There are quite a few things that are being done, mostly by local councils. They're responsible for household 'dustbin' collections, or taking away all the rubbish you produce in the home. In recent years many more sites have been set up to collect waste separately for recycling. There are often containers in car
5 parks or outside supermarkets for people to put bottles in: clear, green and brown bottles are separated. Also newspapers and magazines can be recycled as well as tins made of aluminium. One of the problems of this, though, is that most people are not bothering to take their rubbish there. To overcome this, some local councils also provide special containers, often called 'recycling bins',
10 for residents to collect glass and paper in. They put these outside their houses at the same time as their rubbish, and they are collected and recycled.

L: I see. So are you saying that recycling is more important than actually reducing waste?

J: No. Nowadays, many products are increasingly being designed with reuse or
15 recycling in mind and I think, in general, people are far more aware about these issues.

2 Write in your own examples from the text.

The present simple can be used to describe:

1   A regular habitual action

    ....

    ....

2   Something which is generally true

    ....

    ....

The present continuous can be used to describe:

1   Something in progress <u>at this specific moment</u>

    ....

    ....

2   A changing, developing or temporary situation happening around now but <u>not necessarily at this specific moment</u>

    ....

    ....

Sentence stress

1 In English, not every word in a sentence has the same stress. <u>Underline</u> the word or words in these phrases from the listening you think would usually be stressed.

1 … keeping animals in zoos is really cruel …
2 … they cause so much noise and pollution.
3 I'm convinced that more people would recycle if …

2 ⊞ 05 Listen to the people giving their opinions. What kinds of words in a sentence are usually stressed? Which ones are not usually stressed?

3 Usually the important words in a sentence are nouns, verbs and adjectives. Which words are stressed in these phrases to make them sound 'stronger'?

1 If you ask me …
2 I much prefer …
3 I honestly think that …

4 ⊞ 05 Listen to the tape again to check. Now practise saying these phrases with the correct stress and use them next time.

> **TIP**
>
> Using correct stress patterns will make it easier for you to be understood.

Giving and justifying opinions

1 ⊞ 05 Listen to the different people talking about three of these topics and complete the table.

Should cars be banned in city centres?	Should we control urban growth?
Why are rainforests destroyed?	Why recycle?
How can pollution be reduced?	Are zoos cruel or useful?

Topic	Opinion	Main reasons
Zoos	Cruel	

2 Look at the words and phrases in the language box below. Use them to give your opinions on the topics in 1.

> **Useful language**
>
> **Personal**
> In my view/opinion …
> If you ask me …
> I'd rather (+ base form) / I prefer (to + base form or -ing) …
> I (strongly/firmly/personally/ honestly) believe/think/feel that …
> I'm convinced that …
>
> **More impersonal**
> Some people say/argue/think that …
>
> **Backing up opinions with examples**
> For example/instance, …
> In my experience/country …

3 If you live in a city now, would you say it is too crowded? In what situations do you notice this most? Describe to your partner how you feel in these situations.

4 Look at some of the problems caused by overpopulation in cities. Rank these problems, putting numbers next to the categories. (1 the most serious – 6 the least serious).

housing shortages   unemployment   pollution
street crime   traffic congestion   health problems

5 Compare your ranking with your partner and give reasons for your choices.

Writing

Organizing your writing

1 Writing any essay or assignment involves a number of different stages. Decide on a logical order for these stages.

Write the essay.
Note down a rough essay plan organized by paragraph headings.
Analyse the question.
Check for errors.
Read the instructions and question carefully.
Brainstorm ideas.

2 Read this question.

> Present a written argument or case to an educated reader with no specialist knowledge of the following topic.
>
> *There is an excessive number of cars on our roads today and this leads to many problems. Individuals and governments should ensure that public transport plays a more important role in modern life in order to tackle these problems.*
>
> *To what extent do you agree with this statement?*
>
> Time: 40 minutes   Write at least 250 words.

3 Answer these questions.

1 Who are you writing for?
2 What is the main topic in this question?
3 How long do you have to write this essay?
4 What is the minimum number of words you are required to write?

4 Think about what the writing task involves. Underline the key words in the question.

5 Answer these questions.

1 Who are you writing for and how will this change your writing style?
2 Is it possible to start your essay by changing the first sentence of the question?
3 What does the second sentence suggest?
4 What does the actual writing task ask you to do in this essay?

TIP

Look at a previous piece of writing. How many words on average do you write on a line and how many lines would make a 250-word answer? This will give you a good idea about the minimum amount that you need to write in IELTS Writing Task 2.

6 Brainstorm ideas. The first part of the question states that *too many cars on the roads can lead to many problems*.

1 Write down three problems caused by an excessive number of cars and any vocabulary you might want to use.
2 How are individuals and governments responsible for causing some of the problems mentioned above?
3 How can *governments* reduce some of these problems in terms of public transport? Give examples.
4 How can *individuals* reduce some of these problems in terms of public transport? Give examples.

7 From your ideas, outline a rough plan.

Paragraph 1 *Introduction – Increase in traffic in general*
Paragraph 2
Paragraph 3
Paragraph 4
Paragraph 5 *Summary of opinion – Public transport very important*

8 Write the essay.

Strategy

Follow your rough outline and write your essay as quickly as possible.
Use paragraphs.
Express ideas and opinions backed up by examples and evidence.
Pay attention to grammar, vocabulary, spelling and punctuation as you write.

9 Editing. Check grammar, vocabulary and spelling.

Make sure that you leave yourself a few minutes to check your work for any obvious grammar (for example articles, tenses, plurals, 3rd person, subject-verb agreement, etc.), vocabulary or spelling mistakes. You will not have time to change the main content of your essay but you might notice some errors that can be easily corrected.

10 Work in pairs. Read the example of a student's answer to this question. Then discuss the questions.

1 Do you think the candidate has answered the question sufficiently? Give reasons.
2 Do you think the answer has been well organized?
3 Are the mistakes (1–8) grammar, vocabulary or spelling? How would you correct them?
4 What other mistakes can you find?
5 What is your opinion of the essay in general?

These days, as the amounts of **(1)** transports is increasing **(2)** considerablely, people think this is one of the main reason causing the pollution. So, it is a good idea that, the government and individuals should use the public transport more than the private transport in order to tackle the numerous problems.

To begin with, **(3)** the raising of the use of the public transport can help the government to reduce the amount of the private transport. For example, if more and more people go to work and go home by buses, trains, or underground, there will be fewer people **(4)** use their own cars, so that, there will be less transport on the road. In this way, lots of problems will be solved, such as air pollution, traffic jams, road accidents, and so on. Anyways, the idea should be based on the high quality public transport services, which are provided by the government in order to attract more passengers.

Besides, as people's living standards **(5)** is improving, the amount of people who have their own transports is increasing dramatically. This is another reason cause the increasing of the road accidents. **(6)** Because there would be numbers of drivers who have their own transports **(7)** are not qualified, some of them may just driving for fun. So, it is safer to travel by the public transports due to the qualified and experienced drivers, buses are the best example.

To sum up, I strongly support that the **(8)** increasing of using the public transports is an efficient way to tackle the traffic and the environment problems.

Writing: further practice

11   Follow the stages on pages 25 and 26 and write an essay for this question.

Present a written argument or case to an educated reader with no specialist knowledge of the following issue.

Overpopulation of urban areas has led to numerous problems. Identify one or two serious ones and suggest ways that governments and individuals tackle these problems.

Time: 40 minutes   Write at least 250 words.

Quantifiers

Complete the exercises and check your answers in the grammar boxes.

1 Replace the words in *italics* with *few/a few/little/a little*.

0 *Hardly any* people stopped driving altogether.
  Few people stopped driving altogether.
1 There was *not much* change in the number of people driving into the city as a result of the congestion charge.
2 *Some* people try to reduce the number of car journeys they make, but it is still not enough.
3 *Not many* people believe that cars should be banned in city centres.
4 The Government have had *some* success in controlling the number of cars, but not as much as they had hoped.

We use *a few* and *a little* to talk about small quantities in a positive way. We use *few* and *little* in a similar way but the meaning is negative. *A few/few* are used with countable nouns and *a little/little* with uncountable nouns.

2 Underline the best alternative.

0 Nowadays *every people/person* who can afford it *has/have* a car.
1 Everyone *need/needs* clean air.
2 Some people are in favour of a congestion charge, others are against it. *Each/Every* side has some good arguments.
3 Not *every/all/each* car journeys are necessary.
4 It will take some time to rid the world of *every/all/each* congestion.

All is followed by a plural or uncountable noun. *Each* and *every* are followed by a singular or countable noun. Often it does not matter if we use *each* or *every*, but we must use *each* to refer to *two* things.

3 Complete the sentences with *both/either/neither*.

0 ....*Both*.... local people and the council should do more to recycle waste.
1 The council must .... provide more recycling bins or accept that waste will grow.
2 .... option will really do much to help the environment.
3 We should reuse or recycle, but preferably ....
4 .... local people nor the council will accept responsibility.

All these quantifiers are used to refer to *two* people or things. *Both* means this one and that one. It is followed by a plural noun. *Either* means this one or this one. It is followed by a singular noun. *Neither* means *not either*, not this one *nor* this one.

4 Underline the best alternative.

0 The government has come up with *other/another* solution to the problem.
1 The report will be of interest to environmentalists and *other/another* people interested in the debate.
2 There is only *other/another* three months before the next world summit on the environment.
3 The charity reported that *other/another* children would die without more drinking water.
4 The Environmental group said the policy would eventually lead to *other/another* environmental disaster.

Both *other* and *another* can be used to refer to additional people or things of the type already mentioned. *Other* is used with plural countable nouns and *another* before single countable nouns and before numbers.

What makes a good learner?

1 Look at these statements. Tick the ones that are true for you.

1 I keep a record of new vocabulary and can use it again when necessary.

2 After a lesson or unit I always review my work or anything new I've learnt.

3 I own and know how to use a monolingual dictionary.

4 I use English outside the classroom whenever possible.

5 I try to read and listen to English outside the classroom whenever possible.

6 I am aiming to develop an academic writing style.

7 I try to use only English in the classroom.

8 I check my work and make a note of errors I commonly make.

9 I take note of useful academic words especially when reading.

10 I know the most effective ways to prepare for tests and exams.

2 Work in pairs. Discuss how and when you have used the strategies in 1.

3 Now decide which three study skills you do most effectively now and which three you would most like to improve.

Current *Good learner* strengths	Example of what you do now
1	
2	
3	
Future *Good learner* goals	Example of what you will do
1	
2	
3	

Dictionary focus

Find these words in the unit. Then check their meaning in your dictionary and record them.

major p.19	interpretation p.21	evidence p.26
force p.19	analysis p.21	urban p.27
measure p.19	category p.25	individual p.27

3 Out of this world

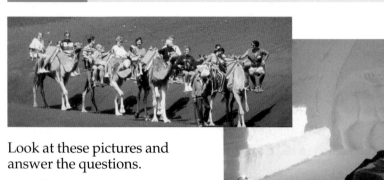

Look at these pictures and answer the questions.

1 Which holiday would you most/least like to go on?
2 What is the appeal of each of these holidays?

Reading skills

Strategy

Look quickly through the article for just the numbers. When you find one, look at the words around it to get the answer.

Skimming and scanning

1 The numbers below all appear in the article. What do they refer to? Find the answers as quickly as possible.

1	60	*Dennis Tito's age*	4	14 ....
2	220	....	5	7 ....
3	8	....	6	25 ....

2 Read the article quickly. Are these statements **True** or **False**?

1 Dennis Tito's space trip cost more than any other holiday. **T/F**
2 Tito went to space with an all - American crew. **T/F**
3 Dennis ate hamburgers in space. **T/F**

Reading 1

True, False or Not Given

1 Do these statements agree with the information in the article?

Write: **TRUE** if the statement is true according to the passage
FALSE if the statement is false according to the passage
NOT GIVEN if the information is not given in the passage

1 The weather on the day of the launch was good.
2 Tito slept in a specially designed Russian sleeping bag.
3 Tito was the first non professional astronaut in space.
4 The rocket was launched at 3am Moscow time.
5 Tito did not enjoy wearing his cosmonaut's suit.

Short answers

2 Answer these questions using **NO MORE THAN THREE WORDS OR A NUMBER**.

1 What did doctors use to wash the crew? ....
2 Who is Suzanne? ....
3 How long did it take to get to the test centre? ....
4 What will liquids be kept in? ....

First space tourist grins down on planet Earth

A It was a giant leap for the tourist industry and the most expensive holiday in history. When Dennis Tito, a 60-year-old Californian, blasted off yesterday he was burning money at the rate of £30,000 a mile. The International Space Station, with which he docks tomorrow, orbits 220 miles above the Earth and the 8 day excursion is costing him £14m.

B A first class return ticket from London to New York in an aircraft or aboard the QE2 costs a mere £1 a mile, measured in a straight line.

C The Soyez rocket with Tito on board ascended from the launchpad of the Baikonur Cosmodrome on the barren steppes of Kazakhstan in central Asia under sunny blue skies. A television monitor showed Tito in a white spacesuit and a plexiglass helmet, grinning broadly.

D A ground controller asked 'How do you feel?' 'Khorosho (good)' Tito replied in Russian.

E American and Russian space officials had argued whether it was safe for Tito to board the space station, with NASA relenting only after he had agreed not to sue if anything went wrong, and to sleep only in Russian sections of the craft.

F He has been allowed only 7kg of luggage, a dictaphone, two pens designed to work in zero gravity, three cameras and nine CDs – among them songs from the Beatles and Andrea Bocelli, the blind Italian tenor.

G As the surge of power took him skyward, Tito must have cared little. Amateurs have flown in space before – among them three congressmen and a Saudi prince – but he was floating into history as the first paying tourist.

H The final countdown began at 3am Moscow time, when Tito and his companions, Talgat Musabayev, the flight commander, and Yuri Baturin, a former politician who became a cosmonaut three years ago, were awoken at their hotel.

I A team of doctors washed the crew with a special alcohol lotion before they dressed in disinfected long johns and ordinary uniforms for breakfast and a final meeting with relatives. About 25 family members, including two sons and a daughter, as well as business partners, friends, and Suzanne, his former wife, travelled to Kazakhstan to bid Tito farewell.

J After a 40 minute ride to the test centre, he was fitted with his cosmonaut suit. In keeping with superstition, the spacemen were not allowed to watch the setting up of the booster rocket. Instead, they performed their own bizarre ritual; a ceremonial urination on the tyres of the minibus that took them to the launchpad – the same one from which Yuri Gagarin became the first man in space.

K In space, Tito will be sustained by Russian soups, juice, tea and coffee, all in toothpaste-like tubes, fruit and ready cooked vegetables as well as canned meats. 'I do miss a good hamburger,' he said.

L He is unlikely to miss the gruelling physical requirements of securing his place in the annals. Zero gravity flights and head spinning sessions in a centrifuge – creating gravitational forces eight times those on Earth – might have been enough to deter lesser citizens. Tito never lost consciousness and was said by trainers to have been an exemplary student.

M 'I'm not a professional astronaut,' he said, 'but I'm as dedicated to the mission as any astronaut would be'.

Guessing meaning from context

3 Guess the definitions of the words from the context.

1 *blasted off* (para.A)
  A exploded
  B landed
  C left Earth for space

2 *docks* (para.A)
  A joins together
  B arrives
  C sees

3 *orbits* (para.A)
  A goes round
  B goes down
  C goes up

4 *ascended* (para.C)
  A moved quickly
  B went up
  C flew

5 *deter* (para.L)
  A make s.o decide not to do something
  B encourage s.o to do something
  C force s.o to do something

6 *exemplary* (para.L)
  A lazy
  B excellent
  C healthy

Language focus

Articles

1 Look at these examples of how articles are used. Match the examples with the rules.

Indefinite articles (a/an)

1 'I do miss **a** good hamburger,' he said.
2 'When Dennis Tito, a 60-year-old Californian, blasted off yesterday he was burning money at the rate of £30,000 **a** mile.'
3 A team of doctors washed the crew with a special alcohol lotion ...

a Use *a/an* with singular, countable nouns the first time they are mentioned.
b Use *a/an* to mean *per* or *every* with distances, times, etc.
c Use *a/an* when the noun referred to is one of many.

Definite article (the)

1 'It was a giant leap for the tourist industry and **the** most expensive holiday in history.'
2 '...and nine CDs – among them songs from the Beatles and Andrea Bocelli, **the** blind Italian tenor.'
3 '...Yuri Gagarin became **the** first man in space.'
4 'A team of doctors washed **the** crew with a special alcohol lotion...'

a Use *the* with singular, countable nouns, after they are first mentioned.
b Use *the* with nouns which are unique.
c Use *the* with superlatives.
d Use *the* with particular sequencing adjectives: the first, the second, the last, the next.

2 Look at these sentences taken from the text and fill in the missing articles. Then check your answers against the text.

1 It was .... giant leap for .... tourist industry ...
2 When Dennis Tito, ... 60 year old Californian ...
3 .... International Space Station, with which he docks tomorrow ...
4 .... first class return ticket from London to New York ...
5 ... costs a mere £1 .... mile ...

6   .... Soyez rocket with Tito on board ascended from .... launchpad …

7   .... television monitor showed Tito in .... white spacesuit …

8   … and to sleep only in Russian sections of .... craft.

9   … he was floating into history as .... first paying tourist …

10   … 'I'm not .... professional astronaut', he said …

Exam information

There are four parts to the Listening module. This Listening is a Part 2 type text. In Part 2 you will hear one person talking in an everyday or social situation.

Listening for gist

1 [▭] 06 You will hear someone talking to a class in a language school about a trip. Listen and answer these questions.

1   Where is the trip to?
2   How long will the trip last?

Multiple choice

2 [▭] 06 Listen to the first part of the recording again and answer questions **1–4**. Circle the appropriate letter.

1   Mary Golding is
    A   a student.
    B   a coordinator.
    C   the student officer.
    D   the French teacher.

2   The trip begins on
    A   Wednesday 4th April.
    B   Saturday 31st March.
    C   Saturday 4th April.
    D   Wednesday 31st March.

3   They will cross the Channel
    A   by coach.
    B   by hovercraft.
    C   by ferry.
    D   by train.

4   They will return home at around
    A   10:00
    B   21:00
    C   22:00
    D   11:00

Exam information

For classification tasks, you will need to match statements to one of three options. You might have to use each option more than once.

Classification

3 [▭] 07 Listen to the next part of the recording and answer questions **5–8**.

Will you have to pay for these activities?

Write   **F**   if it is free
       I   if it is included in the cost of the trip
       P   if you have to pay for it yourself

5   a boat ride   ....
6   a cathedral   ....
7   art galleries   ....
8   train journey   ....

Prediction

1 In groups, brainstorm any negative effects that tourism might have, giving specific examples from your own country if possible.

'Ecotourism is responsible travel to natural areas that conserves the environment and sustains the well being of local people'
(The International Ecotourism Society)

2 What do you think a good ecotourist should/shouldn't do?

Example:
Ecotourists should never leave behind any rubbish.

Reading for gist

3 Quickly read the text *Guidelines for Ecotourists* below. Choose the best answer to this question.

1 When does an ecotourist need to think carefully about their holiday?
   A Before   **C** After
   B During   **D** All of the above

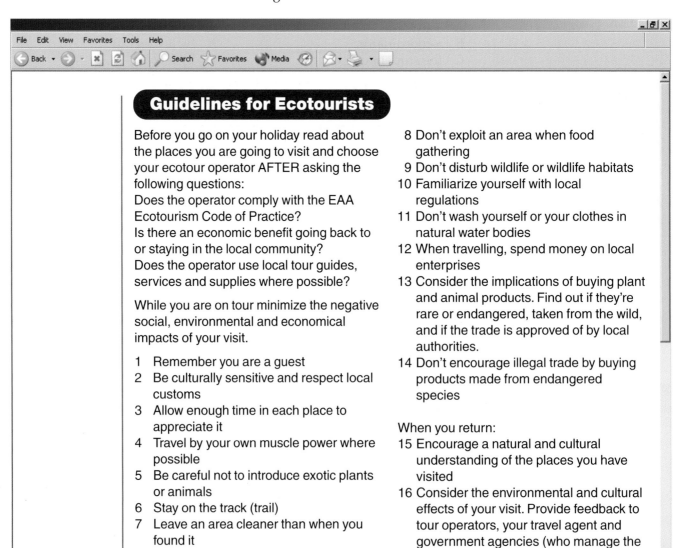

File   Edit   View   Favorites   Tools   Help

Back • ☑ ☒ ☆   Search ☆ Favorites   Media ⊘ ☐ • ☐ • ☐

Guidelines for Ecotourists

Before you go on your holiday read about the places you are going to visit and choose your ecotour operator AFTER asking the following questions:
Does the operator comply with the EAA Ecotourism Code of Practice?
Is there an economic benefit going back to or staying in the local community?
Does the operator use local tour guides, services and supplies where possible?

While you are on tour minimize the negative social, environmental and economical impacts of your visit.

1 Remember you are a guest
2 Be culturally sensitive and respect local customs
3 Allow enough time in each place to appreciate it
4 Travel by your own muscle power where possible
5 Be careful not to introduce exotic plants or animals
6 Stay on the track (trail)
7 Leave an area cleaner than when you found it

8 Don't exploit an area when food gathering
9 Don't disturb wildlife or wildlife habitats
10 Familiarize yourself with local regulations
11 Don't wash yourself or your clothes in natural water bodies
12 When travelling, spend money on local enterprises
13 Consider the implications of buying plant and animal products. Find out if they're rare or endangered, taken from the wild, and if the trade is approved of by local authorities.
14 Don't encourage illegal trade by buying products made from endangered species

When you return:
15 Encourage a natural and cultural understanding of the places you have visited
16 Consider the environmental and cultural effects of your visit. Provide feedback to tour operators, your travel agent and government agencies (who manage the areas visited).

Internet

Guessing meaning from context

4 Look at these verbs from the text. Match them with the dictionary definitions. Use the context of the text to help you.

respect   appreciate   introduce   exploit   ~~disturb~~   familiarize   encourage

0   to frighten animals or birds so they run away.   *disturb*
1   show that you understand the importance of something by not doing anything against it.
2   learn or experience something so that you know about it.
3   to recognize the good or special qualities of a person, place or thing.
4   to use natural resources such as trees, water or oil so you gain as much as possible.
5   to provide conditions that help something to happen.
6   bring something such as a plant or animal into a country or environment for the first time.

Summary completion

5 Look at this summary of *Guidelines for Ecotourists*. Complete it with words from the box.

guests   an ecotour operator   respect   endangered
a holiday package   educate   local   positive   negative   soap
customers   rubbish   dangerous

Strategy

Make sure your answer is grammatically correct and agrees with what is said in the text.

Read the words before and after the gap carefully and then read the whole sentence to check that it makes sense.

According to the EAA ecotourists must choose 1 .... carefully. They must make sure that they follow the code of practice, use 2 .... guides and services, and have a 3 .... economic impact on the community.

Certain guidelines should be followed. For example:

Tourists should not forget they are 4 .... and should 5 .... local habits and laws. When walking they should not leave the track and avoid polluting water with 6 .... They should never buy products made from plants or animals which are 7 ....

Speaking

1 Work in pairs.
Student A: Look at *Guidelines for Ecotourists* 3–6.
Student B: Look at *Guidelines for Ecotourists* 7–10.
Talk for at least one minute about your four guidelines. Paraphrase and add examples to expand on the basic information. Use the expressions from the useful language box.

Useful language: giving advice

It is important/essential/a good idea/necessary to ...

Try (+infinitive) to avoid/use/buy/spend, etc. ...

When travelling/on holiday, ecotourists/people should/shouldn't, ought to/ought not to, must/must not ...

2 Work in pairs. Take it in turns to ask and answer these Part 3 questions.

What are the benefits of visiting different countries?
What are the negative effects of tourism?
What do you need to do before you go abroad on holiday?
What type of problems can people have on holiday?
How should countries encourage tourists to come to their country?
How do you think tourism in your country will change in the future?

Listening 2

Prediction

1 You want to travel by train to Edinburgh and you phone the train enquiry line. Think about the type of information you want and write down the following information.

1 Three questions you might ask, eg *How much does a ticket to London cost*?
2 Three questions the train enquiry person might ask you, eg *What time do you hope to travel?*

Table completion

2 Look at questions **1–6**. Which answers are times? Which is a date?

3 08 Listen to a telephone conversation between a student and a train enquiry assistant. Fill in the information in the spaces in the boxes.

Strategy

Look at the parts of the table that are already complete. These will help you predict the type of answer that is needed.

Date of travel	1	
Single or Return	2	
Standard or First Class	3	

Outward journey	Depart Birmingham	08.05	5
	Arrive Edinburgh	4	14.35
	Change of train?	Direct	Change at Stockport
Return journey	Depart Edinburgh	16.45	18.05
	Arrive Birmingham	20.21	21.57
	Change of train?	Direct	6

TIP

Check if the numbering goes across or down the table.

TIP

Say the table details to yourself, eg Advance purchase.
It will help you to listen for them in the text.

4 〔▭〕09 Listen to the second part of the recording and answer questions **7–10**.

Type of ticket	Apex Super Saver	Apex Peak Saver	9	Off Peak Saver
Advance purchase necessary?	14 days	8	None	None
Travel on Friday possible?	Yes	Yes	Yes	10
Price	7 £	£41.30	£54	£38

Labelling a diagram

Strategy

There are many different types of diagram in the Listening module. There may be a map, a plan, a process or a picture of an object.

Look at the diagram before you listen and think about what it shows. Look for key features and their positions, eg if it is a plan, where is the speaker standing? If it is a process, where does it start and finish?

5 〔▭〕10 The student is at the train station information desk. Listen to the final part of the recording and answer questions **11–14**.

The train station

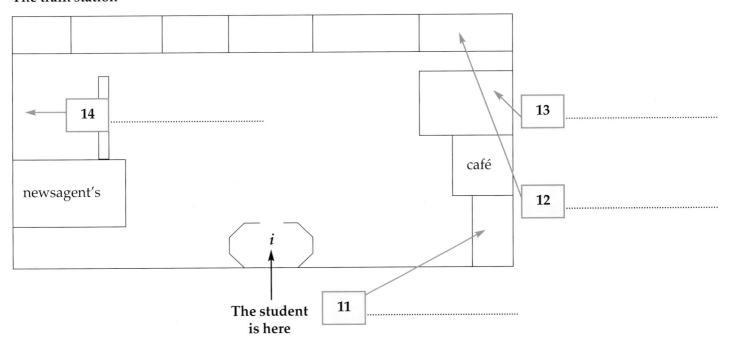

1 Australia is a very popular tourist destination, with plenty of varied sights and things to do. Answer these questions.

1 What reasons can you think of for visiting Australia?
2 Have you ever been to Australia? If not, would you like to go? Why?/Why not?
3 What was your experience like or what do you imagine it would be like?

2 Read this Task 1 question.

The table below shows how many tourists from five countries visited Australia in different years from 1991–1999. Write a report for a university lecturer describing the information below.

Country of Residence	1991	1993	1995	1997	1999
United States	259	267	288	310	393
Canada	51	48	55	61	75
United Kingdom	258	302	335	388	509
Germany	75	102	120	125	140
Other Europe	172	200	259	319	389

Note: The figures are in thousands (000s)

Task 1: Selecting significant information

3 Which of these statements would be the most suitable *general description* for the data above?

1 There was a decrease in the number of visitors to Australia in the 1990s.
2 There was an increase in the number of visitors to Australia in the 1990s.

4 Which three statements from the list below would it be most suitable to include as specific information, and why?

1 There were 102,000 visitors from Germany in 1993.
2 Over the whole period the UK had the most visitors to Australia.
3 The number of visitors from Canada decreased between 1991 and 1993.
4 In this period the biggest increase in tourists was from other countries in Europe.
5 The number of visitors from Germany almost doubled in the 1990s.
6 The number of visitors to Australia from the UK increased by about fifty thousand from 1995 to 1997.

TIP

When describing data you only need to write about the most important information, not all the figures shown in the diagram.

5 Look at this model answer to the question. Quickly read the text and underline one statement about each of the countries.

The table shows the rise in the number of visitors to Australia from a number of other countries worldwide over the 1990s. Looking at the data on the United States, Canada, the United Kingdom, Germany and other countries in Europe, we can see that the number of visitors to Australia from all these countries (1) **increased significantly over the decade**.

(2) **The biggest increase was in** visitors from other countries in Europe, which (3) **more than doubled over the period**.(4) **The largest number of visitors in total came from** the United Kingdom,(5) **which rose from** 258 to 509 thousand. Visitors from the United States also(6) **increased over the decade**.(7)**There were considerably fewer visitors** from Canada, although the figure(8) **rose over the same period from 51,000 to 75,000**, with most of the increase occurring in the second half of the decade.

(9) **There were almost as many visitors from the United Kingdom as from** all of the other European countries, including Germany. However, by 1999 (10) **there were nearly as many tourists from the other European countries as from the United States**.

The table indicates that Australia is increasing in popularity as a tourist destination.

Strategy

Look to see if the data changes over time or is only about one fixed time. If it changes over time, you will need to **describe the general patterns or trends** you can see.

Task 1: Comparing data and describing trends

In Task 1 of the Writing module you will usually be asked to describe a graph, table or chart. This will usually mean **comparing and contrasting different parts of the information or data**.

6 Look at the text again and group the phrases in **bold** into one of these categories. One example for each type is given.

a Description of trends	b Comparing data
(1)...increased significantly over the decade.	(2) The biggest increase was in...

Useful language: describing trends

	rose increased decreased fell	slightly gradually steadily sharply	over the decade/year over the same period in the same time between 1991 and 1994
The figure The number (of...)			from 1990 to 1997
	dropped	significantly dramatically	
	doubled tripled		

7 For each of the examples below, write a sentence describing the trend shown in the data in that section. Use the Useful language box to help you.

0 US

1991	1993
259	267

The number of visitors from the USA increased slightly between 1991 and 1993.

1 UK

1995	1999
335	509

2 Canada

1991	1993
51	48

3 Germany

1991	1993	1995
75	102	120

Useful language: comparing data

Simple comparatives

Australia	is	bigger	than	Germany.
Germany		more expensive		the UK.
Germany	is (not)	as	cold	as	the UK.

Comparative structures to compare figures

There were	significantly considerably far slightly	fewer (C) more less (U)	(noun)	than...
There **were** (not)	nearly	**as**	**many (C)** **much (U)**	(noun)	**as**...
There **were**	almost/more than	twice/three times **as**			

Simple superlatives

Canada	is	the	biggest	country.
Germany			most expensive	

Superlative structures to describe figures

The	biggest	increase	was in ...
	largest	number of ...	was from ...
	smallest		
	most significant		

---

8 Write sentences comparing the data in each section.

0 1993

Canada	Germany
48	102

In 1993 there were more than twice as many visitors from Germany as from Canada.

1 1999

UK	Germany
509	140

2 1991

UK	US
258	259

3 1999

UK	Germany	Canada
509	140	75

Strategy:
Writing Task 1 answers

Read the statements below. Tick the 5 sentences that give good advice.

1 Describe the data and give examples.

2 Write sentences about all the data using similar sentence patterns.

3 Write an introductory sentence saying what the data is describing.

4 Check your spelling and grammar.

5 Give personal opinions.

6 Start with any general statements and move to specific information.

7 Use exactly the same words given in the question.

8 Make all your statements general.

9 Try to explain the data or give reasons.

10 Organize and present the data logically.

Study skills

TIP

At the end of each unit, go back over your work. Check that you understand everything and revise the grammar and vocabulary.

Reflecting on what you have learnt

1 Write down three new things that you have learnt from this unit: a piece of vocabulary, a skills or task strategy, a grammar point, etc. Put them in order of importance for you.

1 ....
2 ....
3 ....

2 Work in pairs. Tell your partner why these things will be useful to you.

3 Look through the unit again and answer these more specific questions.

1 Vocabulary: What does *ascended* mean?
2 Language: (Articles) 'It was _____ giant leap for _____ tourist industry ...', *the* or *a*? Can you explain why?
3 Listening: Write down a strategy to help with a *Table Completion* task.
4 Speaking: Imagine you want to *give advice* to a friend who wants to improve his/her English. Think of two suitable sentences using phrases introduced in this unit.
5 Reading: Write down a strategy to help you in a *Summary Completion* task.
6 Writing: Think of one other way to say *fell sharply* and *increased steadily*. Draw diagrams to show these movements.

4 Is there anything in the unit that you did not understand well? What could you do about it?

5 Is there anything that you want to go back and review to refresh your memory? When will you do this?

Dictionary focus

Find these words in the unit. Then check their meaning in your dictionary and record them.

sustain p.31	conserve p.34	occur p.39
unique p.32	benefit p.34	contrast p.39
implication p.34	basic p.35	trend p.39

1 Imagine you have been given a new machine to use. You have no idea how it works. How would you prefer to learn to use it?

A Read the instruction manual.
B Watch someone else using it.
C Have a go at using it, with some guidance.

2 Compare your answer with others in your class. Do you prefer to learn in different ways?

If you chose:

A You may learn best through words.
B You may learn best through visuals.
C You may learn best by doing.

Is this true for you?

Listening

Summary completion

Strategy

Summary completion is similar to sentence completion, except that the gaps are within a paragraph summarizing the listening.

Read the question carefully – usually you need to use no more than three words, but you might be asked to use a different number.

Read the paragraph before you listen and think about the <u>kind</u> of information that is missing.

Make sure your answers fit grammatically and are spelt correctly.

1 🔲 11 Listen to the first part of the talk. Complete the summary using **NO MORE THAN THREE WORDS** for each answer.

Linguistic intelligence

People with linguistic intelligence are good at communicating with others and they find it easy to **1** .... They like writing and tend to think in words, not pictures.

They have the ability to explain, teach and **2** .... other people to agree with their viewpoint.

Jobs that these people might do include journalists, teachers, **3** .... politicians and writers.

TIP

Read the summary carefully. What kind of information is missing? Underline key words to listen for.

2 🔲 12 Listen to the second part of the talk and complete this summary.

Logical Mathematical intelligence

These people find it easy to see patterns and **4** .... between bits of information.

These people are likely to become involved in science, computer programmming, **5** .... , accounting or mathematics.

Interpersonal intelligence

These people understand how people feel and think and have good **6** .... skills.

They make good counsellors, salespeople, politicians and managers.

Intrapersonal intelligence

Often good researchers or philosophers, these people are good at **7** .... their own abilities and emotions.

Visual-Spatial intelligence

People who like drawing and designing and have a good **8** .... They can use charts and maps too.

Bodily Kinaesthetic intelligence

Being good at dancing or athletics may indicate this is a strength. Gardner argues that skilful control over your body's movement is an intelligence, though others may disagree.

Musical intelligence

These people don't always **9** .... , but they are often good musicians or songwriters.

Multiple choice with more than one option

3 🔲 13 In the last section, the lecturer makes some suggestions about how people with strengths in each intelligence can study more effectively. Circle the **TWO** activities he suggests for each intelligence.

10 and **11** Linguistic intelligence

A Writing
B Group discussions
C Reading
D Giving lectures
E Memorizing facts

12 and **13** Visual-Spatial intelligence

A Using mind maps
B Looking at paintings
C Problem solving
D Watching videos
E Reading

14 and **15** Musical intelligence

A Tapping out rhythms
B Listening to background music
C Playing instruments
D Learning through song lyrics
E Writing music

TIP

Read the question carefully to see how many answers are necessary.

-ing form and infinitive

1 Look at these statements. Which intelligence do you think they represent?

0 I enjoy (make) things with my hands.   *I enjoy making …*
1 I love (visit) art galleries.
2 I dislike (work) alone.
3 I appreciate (spend) time alone.
4 Before I use it, I need (understand) how something works.
5 I like (learn) the words of songs.
6 I would like (speak) several foreign languages.

2 Now complete the sentences with the correct form of the verb in brackets.

3 Some verbs are followed by an infinitive, some by an *-ing* form and some are followed by both. Put the examples into the table.

Followed by *-ing*	Followed by infinitive	Followed by both *-ing* and infinitive
enjoy		

4 In which column would these sentences go? Why?

1 I learn by (do).
2 I am actively interested in (make) the world a better place.
3 I'm keen on (write).

5 Now put the verbs in the box into the same table. Use your dictionary if necessary.

avoid   consider   try
agree   begin   decide
fail   imagine   mind
hope   promise
refuse   practise
stop   want   wish
remember   forget
involve

6 Sometimes it is possible to use both *-ing* and infinitive.

Example: *Lee began to study/began studying.*

However, there is usually a difference in meaning. Look at these examples and answer the questions.

a *I like watching music videos.*
b *I like to learn more about myself.*
1 Which sentence is about enjoying something?
2 Which sentence suggests that something is a worthwhile thing to do?

Note: This distinction is true in British English, but not in American English where both could be used to suggest enjoyment.

c *I tried to open the window.*
d *Try opening the window.*
3 Which sentence suggests effort or difficulty?
4 Which sentence is a suggestion?

e *I stopped to talk to him.*
f *I stopped talking to him.*
5 In which sentence did I stop doing something else *in order* to talk?
6 In which sentence am I now avoiding him?

g *I remembered to tell him.*
h *I remember telling him.*
7 Which sentence is about a memory?
8 Which sentence is about remembering something *before* you do it?

7 Complete this text with the correct form of the verb.

Being a student involves **1** (take) .... responsibility for **2** (organize) .... your own time. Therefore you need **3** (learn) .... about planning your time and workload effectively. You can learn to do this through practice and through stopping **4** (think) .... about what works or doesn't work for you.

Try **5** (set) .... yourself goals and targets, and give yourself small rewards.

Don't try **6** (do) .... too much at once – have regular breaks. If you fail **7** (finish) .... a piece of work as quickly as you expected, don't feel bad, just be more realistic in your planning next time. If you find that you avoid even **8** (start) .... work, stop **9** (make) .... excuses and start today! You will feel much better once you do.

Pronunciation

TIP

Being aware of pronunciation will help your listening skills.

Connected speech

When native speakers speak English, they naturally join words together.

Two things they do are:

1 Miss sounds out, eg *dinner and dancing* /'dɪnə æn dɑːnsɪŋ/

Which sounds are missed out in these examples?
next week
brand new

/t/ and /d/ are usually missed out when they are followed by a consonant sound.

14 Look at Recording 14 on page 168 and see if you can find other examples. Then listen and check your answers.

2 Change sounds, eg *in Bristol* /ɪm brɪstəl/

Which sounds are changed in these examples?
Tin man
Ten pin bowling

/n/ will often change to /m/ if it comes before the sounds /m/ /p/ or /b/.

14 Now look at Recording 14 on page 168 and see if you can find other examples. Then listen and check your answers.

1 In groups, discuss which animals you think are the most/the least intelligent. Give reasons for your views.

Table completion

Strategy

Look at the table and any examples given and check:
what is needed in each column,
if you should take words from the passage or from a box,
how many words you are allowed to use.

2 Read one of the three short passages and complete the table. Choose **NO MORE THAN FOUR WORDS** from the passage for each answer.

	Text 1: Crows	Text 2: Dolphins	Text 3: Orang-utans
Organization that carried out the research	1	1	1 ....
City or place where research took place	2	2	2 ....
Main aim of research	3 Test ability to	3 Discover if	3 Test ability to ....

Betty

This experiment was carried out by the Zoology Department at Oxford University and set out to test the ability of Betty, a New Caledonian crow, to make simple tools.

A male and female crow were given a choice between a straight garden wire and a hook in order to lift a small bucket of food from the bottom of a plastic tube. After the male bird took the hook, Betty the female crow bent the tip of the straight wire to make a replacement. This was an amazing achievement as Betty had been kept in a laboratory for two years by the ecology research group and had never seen garden wire before.

In the next stage the birds were set the same challenge – to retrieve the bucket of food, but this time the researchers only provided straight wires. In nine out of ten trials, Betty bent the wire and pulled up the bucket. To bend the wire she sometimes stuck one end into a sticky piece of tape wrapped around the bottom of the tube or held it in her feet, then pulled the tip with her beak.

This species of crow is very skilful at making tools and often uses sticks and leaves in the wild. However, the fact that this bird had the ability to make the right implement for the job from unfamiliar materials, as this study proved, shows unheard of animal intelligence, say the researchers.

PROJECT DELPHIS

These studies were undertaken by Earthtrust, an international research and educational organisation, in Hawaii as part of Project Delphis. The main objective was to conduct scientific research in order to find evidence that dolphins are extremely self-aware. In addition, Earthtrust aims to raise global awareness about dolphins and to improve conservation efforts worldwide.

Although it has been well-recorded that dolphins are large-brained social creatures, having the capacity for self-awareness is an even more revealing sign of intelligence. In the past only man and a few apes were thought to possess this faculty.

As with previous research carried out in this area on man and apes, self-awareness is measured by marking a subject, then observing the animal's reaction to a mirror-image – touching himself indicates self-awareness, whereas touching the mirror shows social behaviour suggesting the subject is investigating another individual.

Five bottleneck dolphins were 'marked' by putting zinc oxide on their sides and then their behaviour was videotaped through a one-way mirror. Control experiments were also conducted in order to:

A   compare 'marked'/'unmarked' behaviour
B   compare mirror behaviour to behaviour with a real stranger through a barred gate
C   compare dolphins watching themselves on TV and in the mirror

In the project the dolphins looked in the mirror then twisted and turned a lot revealing that they seemed to have seen the zinc oxide mark and therefore suggesting that they are self-aware. If this is the case, then such evidence provides a significant insight into animal intelligence as previously only man and apes had demonstrated the capacity for self-awareness.

Orang-utan Language Project

This research was undertaken as part of the Orang-utan Language Project at the Smithsonian National Zoological Park in New York which has been ongoing since 1995. The main purpose was to test the ability of orang-utans to communicate and the study was carried out by testing whether these creatures could remember abstract symbols and then use this system to accurately label objects. Unusually, the public could actually watch these observations take place at the zoo.

Computers with touch-sensitive screens were placed in the cages of Azy and his little sister Indah. Female orang-utans in particular are known to have good manual skills but the males tend to use their lips more. Objects were passed through the bars and when the creatures touched the screen, a particular symbol based on Arabic numerals would appear. Once a number of objects and their corresponding symbols had been introduced, more symbols were put up on the screen to increase the number of choices. Tests were then conducted on the animals to find out if they could make the correct selection and what their accuracy rate was. If they did choose the right symbol for an object, a bell rang and then rewards were given in the form of food or praise.

The results of the research show that orang-utans achieved 90% accuracy and therefore have the ability to communicate by quickly relating abstract symbols to objects. In fact the animals have now progressed to using symbols to identify actions and they are now also using Arabic numerals to identify quantities.

Note completion

3 Complete these notes about the passage you have read.
Choose **NO MORE THAN THREE WORDS** from the passage for each answer.

Text 1

<u>Method used to conduct tests</u>

Crows chose hook or straight wire in order to

1 .... container. After male crow took hook, the female bird (Betty) **2** .... wire to make another one. Researchers gave Betty more straight wire and in ten tests she managed to make a hook **3** ....

<u>Research findings</u>

Crows able to make an appropriate tool from **4** .... that they had not seen or used much, providing new evidence of animal intelligence.

Text 2

<u>Method used to conduct tests</u>

Zinc oxide was put on sides of bottleneck dolphins and their behaviour was filmed through a **1** ....

After seeing **2** .... the dolphins moved about a lot suggesting they had noticed the **3** ....

<u>Research findings</u>

Dolphins, like **4** .... may be self-aware.

Text 3

<u>Method used to conduct tests</u>

Objects were passed into the orang-utans' cages and as they touched a computer screen a corresponding **1** .... would appear. They then learnt which of these matched which object. If they made the **2** .... choice a bell rang and they received **3** .... , which could be food or praise.

<u>Research findings</u>

Orang-utans showed the **4** .... by making connections between abstract symbols and objects.

Writing

Task 2: Organization and coherence: paragraphing

1 Read this question.

Present a written argument or case to an educated reader with no specialist knowledge of the following topic.

Academic achievement at school or university is the only true measure of a person's intelligence.

To what extent do you agree with this statement?

Time: 40 minutes   Write at least 250 words.

Think of your essay as a sandwich – the introduction and conclusion paragraphs are the bread while the main body (usually 2–4 paragraphs) is the filling. The first and last paragraphs are essential in holding the sandwich together!

Introductions

Paragraph 1

The first paragraph is the introduction to the topic.

2 Look back at the question, then read the three introductions below and decide which is best. Why is it more suitable than the other two?

Introduction 1
Academic achievement at school or university means passing exams such as A levels or getting a Degree or Masters. There is no doubt that you need to be clever to do this.

Introduction 2
Many people believe that academic achievement at school or university is the only true measure of a person's intelligence. However, there are two sides to this statement and other people would disagree with this view.

Introduction 3
There is no doubt that people are often judged in terms of their educational success. People need to pass exams to go to university and study for a degree and the majority of jobs and careers require these types of qualifications. However, this is surely not the only way to measure intelligence.

The main body

There are 3 paragraphs in the main body of this essay.

Paragraph 2

3 Identify the topic sentence and the main idea from the sentences below. Then put them in the correct order (1–4) to form a coherent paragraph.

This is often particularly true of people with practical skills such as carpenters or plumbers. ....

There are also further examples of people who have not achieved academic success in education. ....

Although they may not have passed many exams at school, they have successfully learnt a trade or skill which definitely requires intelligence. ....

There are many people who leave school at the age of 16 yet go on to have successful careers. ....

Now answer these questions:

1 What specific examples are given to support the main idea?
2 Which different type of intelligence is mentioned to support the main idea?
3 How does the writer provide a link with paragraph 3?

Paragraph 3

4 Now do the same task with this paragraph which is the next section in the main body:

Such skills cannot necessarily be learnt on a course or from a book yet could be considered to be more 'natural' forms of intelligence. ....

It cannot be denied that creative or artistic ability is another form of intelligence. ....

Musicians have the skills to perform complex pieces of music while artists can create beautiful pieces of work through painting or sculpture. ....

1 What type of 'intelligence' is the main topic of this paragraph?
2 What specific examples of skills are mentioned to support the main idea?
3 How is 'academic' intelligence different from this type of skill?

Strategy

A good introduction will include clear, relevant information about the topic but should not repeat the question word-for-word. It can also include the view of the writer which will be developed later in the essay.

Paragraph 4

5 Read the last paragraph in the main body and then answer the questions.

A final example of another aspect of intelligence is knowledge, which people often acquire through self-study or experience. They may not have done well at school or university but have become 'educated' by learning about a subject independently or by dealing with a variety of real-life situations and problems. Indeed, there are many highly-qualified, successful people who often lack 'common sense' and who would be less able to cope with such difficulties.

Sentence 1: Which phrase introduces a further type of intelligence (and thus provides a link with the previous paragraphs)?
Sentence 2: Which words refer back to the *people* in sentence 1?
Sentence 2: Which words refer back to *self-study* in sentence 1?
Sentence 2: Which words refer back to *experience* in sentence 1?
Sentence 3: Which words refer back to *problems* in sentence 2?

Conclusions

6 Write a conclusion by reading the Introduction and Main Body and then summarizing the line of argument used in this essay.

7 Read this question.

Present a written argument or case to an educated reader with no specialist knowledge of the following topic.

Parents and family background have more influence than teachers on a young person's learning and academic achievement.

To what extent do you agree with this statement?

The main body of an answer to this question is provided. First, read it quickly. Then underline the main ideas and supporting information in each paragraph.

Paragraph 2

Many people believe that we inherit intelligence from our parents and it is often the case that children of gifted parents go on to repeat their parent's success at school. However, this is not always the case. In fact, it is far more likely that children who have supportive and interested parents often have higher academic achievement than those who do not receive such support.

Paragraph 3

Early childhood is a key stage in a child's development and experiences at this time can have far-reaching consequences in the child's future. It is usually at this time when a parent's input is most influential. At this stage a parent often has sole charge of their child and therefore their influence is very significant.

TIP

Good writers show links *between* paragraphs in an essay and *within* a paragraph. This is shown by **reference** or **lexical links**.

Useful language

<u>Introductions</u>

It is true to say that …
There is no doubt
  that …
In recent years …
Many people
  consider …

<u>Conclusions</u>

In conclusion, …
To conclude, …
To sum up, …
Overall, it is clear
  that …

Paragraph 4

Later in life, as the child starts school, teachers begin to have a greater influence. Often, one or more teachers can have considerable influence over a child's future, inspiring them in a particular subject or helping them to choose a career path. Teachers can have a particularly important role to play if a child lacks support from home due to emotional or financial difficulties which can have a negative effect on their learning. Therefore, it is definitely possible for a child to succeed academically, even without the help of a supportive family.

Conclusion

8 Work in pairs or small groups. Add an appropriate introduction and conclusion.

Listening skills

Listening and writing simultaneously

1 🔲 15 Listen to part of a tutorial discussion between a student and tutor (Dr Williams). As you listen, complete the notes.

Topic: 'Nature versus Nurture'

Is a child **1** ....   Or do parents, teachers, friends **2** ....

Length of assignment **3** ....

Previous studies/research

Comparison between:

Genetic factors   **4** .... factors

Points to remember:

Focus on studies with similar pattern and compare with those that don't

follow same trends then analyse why the **5** ....

Personal opinions – back up statements with clear **6** ....

Using references – Cite source of information
              Include bibliography at end of assignment
              Put in alphabetical order **7** ....

Further questions /points to discuss in **8** ....

TIP

Writers use different words with similar or related meanings to link different parts of the text together. Understanding these links can help you.

Lexical links

1 Look back at the texts on pages 46 and 47.

Replace each word below with another word in the text which has a similar meaning.

Text 1	Text 2	Text 3
tool (n)	animal (n)	undertake (do research) (v)

2 Look at this text. The first sentence of each paragraph is missing. Match the paragraphs and the sentences in the boxes.

Then <u>underline</u> what lexical links helped you to do this task.

.... They can, and do, communicate with humans. There is a linguist chimp called Nim Chimpsky with a vocabulary of 125 signs, all used correctly. Chimps can solve problems, use tools and when they lose their teeth, even improvise a makeshift food blender. Two observers have now claimed to see chimps in the wild leaving each other "notes". Separate groups of chimpanzees have different ways of doing things, and pass these ways on through the generations: that is, chimpanzees have culture, just as humans have culture. In a word, they might be human. Morris Goodman, a geneticist at Wayne State University school of medicine in Detroit, argues that chimpanzees should be included with humans in the same evolutionary grouping.

.... The evidence is in the DNA. Instead of comparing digits, or spinal structure, or the teeth, taxonomists – scientists who deal in evolutionary relationships – have now begun to consider the basic information of life, reproduction and development. Goodman and his colleagues report in their article that they compared 97 genes in six different species: humans, chimpanzees, gorillas, orang-utans, old world monkeys and mice. DNA is common to all life: the closer the DNA match, the closer the evolutionary link. Humans and chimps came out with a similarity of 99.4%. On the strength of this, Goodman says: think again, humans.

.... But at another level, he is raising an argument about human links with the rest of creation. Are humans a breed apart, with dominion over fish, flesh and fowl? Or are humans just gifted apes, lucky enough to have an edge over their nearest relatives? And if the latter, then what responsibilities do humans owe to their fellow creatures?

.... If apes were reclassified as human, would they then be entitled to human rights? And if apes were classified as human, would Homo sapiens be guilty of genocide?

A At one level, he is reviving an argument about classification: what is it that makes animals alike, and different, and how do you logically group them.

B Chimps have language.

C So a small change in classification translates into a big one in moral attitudes.

D The evidence is not in their capacity to stand upright or use computer touch screens.

Using a dictionary

What do you use your dictionary for? Looking up the meaning of words? A good dictionary has so much more useful information than just the meaning and is essential for learning a language.

In order to use a dictionary effectively, you need to understand the abbreviations that are used in it.

1 Match these abbreviations to their meaning.

[C]	uncountable noun – that cannot be used with a/an and have no plural form
adj	somebody
[T]	countable noun – that are used with a/an or a number and have a plural
sb	adverb
[U]	something
adv	adjective
[I]	abbreviation
sth	transitive verb – used with a direct object, eg *I ate my lunch.*
abbrev	intransitive verb – has no direct object, eg *He slept until noon.*

Now look in your dictionary to find an example of each one.

What other abbreviations does your dictionary have?

A good dictionary has a lot of information about each word. Find out how much your dictionary can tell you.

2 Look up:

1 **intelligent** – How many different words are listed with a similar meaning?
2 **should** – What grammatical rules are there about using *should*?
3 **instruction** – Which words are often found together (collocate) with *instruction*?
4 **policy** – Is this word commonly used?
5 **high/tall** – Which word do we use for a shelf which is a long way off the ground?
6 **equipment** – Is it countable?
7 **fortuitous** – Is this a formal or informal word?
8 **sometimes** – What part of speech is this word?
9 **subway** – What is the difference in meaning of this word in England and America?
10 **eye** – Why would you *look somebody in the eye*?

Find these words in the unit. Then check their meaning in your dictionary and record them.

abstract p.47	essential p.48	input p.50
symbol p.47	correspond p.48	lack p.51
insight p.47	influential p.50	capacity p.52

5 | A career or a job?

1 Work in pairs. Take it in turns to practise these exam questions.

> **Part 2**
>
> Describe a job you would like to do in the future.
>
> You should say:
>   what the job is
>   why you would like to do this job
>   what skills are needed to do this job well
> You should also say what you would like most about this job.

Part 3

What is the best way to prepare for a job interview?
Which jobs do you think are the most dangerous?
How can employers keep their staff happy?
Do you think pop and sports stars earn too much money?
How important is appropriate dress at work?
Is it better to stay in one job for a long time or have many different jobs?

Listening

Multiple choice

Sally and John are two university students who are thinking about what they will do when they graduate.

1 🔲 16 For questions **1–6**, circle the correct answer.

1 Where does Sally want to go
   after graduating?
   A Europe
   B South America
   C America
   D Australia

2 Sally wants to be
   A a doctor.
   B a teacher.
   C a singer.
   D a businesswoman.

3 Who is giving the talk?
   A Professor Davis
   B Mr Davidson
   C Professor Donaldson
   D Mr David

Strategy

Look carefully at the pictures and think about what each one shows and the differences between them.

Use the questions to predict the kind of information you will be listening for.

TIP

Important information is often repeated in different ways in the text.

Don't circle the first thing that you hear unless you are sure it's correct.

4 What does the speaker look like?

 A
 B
 C
 D

5 What time do Sally and John arrange to meet?
   A 7.30pm
   B 6.30pm
   C 6.55pm
   D 7.00pm

6 Where do Sally and John arrange to meet?

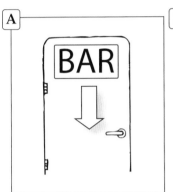 A
 B
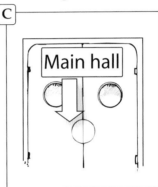 C
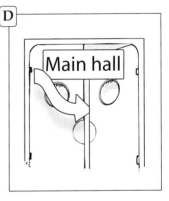 D

Completing a flow chart

2 Work in pairs. Look at the flow chart below. How much can you predict?

3 [🔲] 17 Listen to the talk and fill in the answers using **NO MORE THAN THREE WORDS**.

Exam information

Flow charts usually describe a process, and have notes boxed in a logical order. Check the word limit for the answers. The order of the questions follows the text.

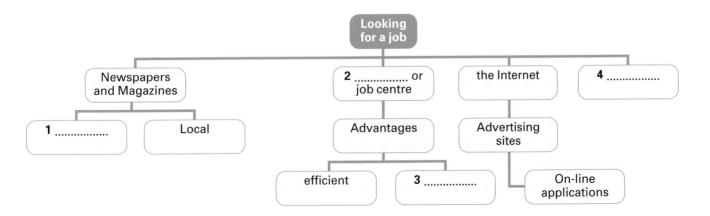

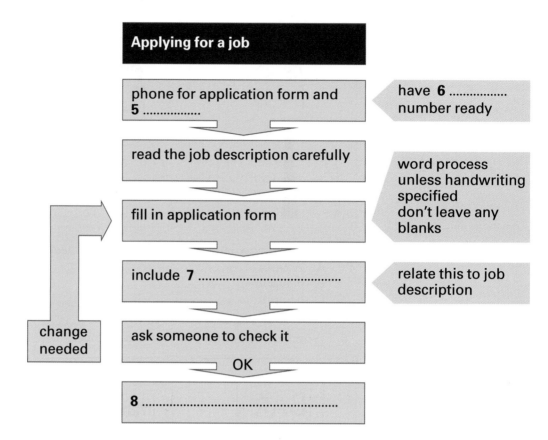

Applying for a job

phone for application form and 5 ....

have 6 .... number ready

read the job description carefully

fill in application form

word process unless handwriting specified
don't leave any blanks

include 7 ....

relate this to job description

change needed

ask someone to check it

OK

8 ....

Language focus 1

Future plans and arrangements

There are several different ways of talking about the future in English. Look at these examples.

> I'll meet   I'm going to meet   I'm meeting   I meet

1 Look at the <u>underlined</u> sentences from the listening below. Find an example of:

1　a future plan/intention made at the time of speaking
2　a future plan/intention made previously
3　a future fact or prediction
4　the present continuous used to talk about a future arrangement
5　the present simple used to talk about a scheduled or timetabled event in the future

J:　So <u>what are you doing on Wednesday?</u> Shall we go to this talk?
S:　Maybe – <u>what's he going to talk about?</u>
J:　Umm, let me see – it says here that <u>the lecture will cover looking for work and writing applications,</u> including tips on how to impress your potential employers. It says that there'll be time for questions as well.
S:　That sounds perfect, actually. <u>What time does it start?</u>
J:　Says 7 o'clock here.
S:　OK, <u>I'll meet you here,</u> …

2 ▭ 16 Choose the best option to complete these extracts from the listening. Listen again to check your answers. <u>Underline</u> the best alternatives.

S: Do you know what you want to do? **0** <u>*Are you going to be*</u> / *Will you be* / *Are you being* a singer in a band all your life?

J: No, I'd like to be, but my dad would kill me ... With a degree in Business, I've got quite a few options, but I think I'd like to go into marketing.

S: That'd be interesting – **1** *you're going to make/you'll make/you're making* good money too, **2** *aren't you/won't you*?

J: I could do, but that's usually after you've worked your way up a bit. What about you – do you know what **3** *you're going to do/you do*?

S: I really want to try and get a job overseas – my sister and her two kids live in Australia, and I'd like to go out there ...

J: Really, that'd be great! **4** *I'm going to come and visit you/I'll come and visit you*!

J: Why don't we make it a bit earlier – say half six, and we can go and have a quick drink in the bar first.

S: Great! Listen, I've got to go, **5** *I'm meeting/I meet/I'll meet* Tariq in ten minutes. **6** *I'm seeing/I'll see/I see* you in the bar at 6.30 on Wednesday, then.

J: OK – see you then.

Scanning

1 Quickly read these three job adverts and find the information.

Which job
1 only requires 6 months' previous experience?
2 is temporary?
3 requires a degree?
4 uses languages other than English?
5 involves delivering letters?

Job A

PA to Marketing Manager
(Fluent in French or Dutch)

Maternity contract for 6 months. Large, Birmingham-based company require a PA with at least 2 years' experience in a busy secretarial role, <u>fluent in French</u> or Dutch to business level, written and spoken. Duties will include <u>WP</u>, general correspondence, producing reports/presentations, client contact and hotel/travel bookings. You should be <u>computer literate</u> in Powerpoint or another presentation package and have a <u>stable CV</u>, and <u>good communication and organizational skills</u>.

Job B

Administration Assistant – Car Credit Sales

Our client is looking for an Administration Assistant to join their young, dynamic team in Car Credit sales. Your role will be inputting and processing new applications and generally assisting the administrators. This post requires <u>a team player</u>, who is <u>flexible</u>, well organized and <u>methodical</u> with a <u>good sense of humour</u> and at least 6 months' previous experience in a similar role. A <u>confident telephone manner</u> is essential. Duties will include arranging overseas travel, receiving visitors, post distribution and maintaining stationery levels as well as word processing. You should be very familiar with Word and Excel.

Job C

Business Graduates

Are you graduating in Business this summer? Are you looking for an opportunity to explore and reach your full potential? Look no further! We are a large, multi-national company looking for graduates to be future leaders through a series of challenging roles and development and training. You must have a <u>2:1 or first</u> in Business or a <u>related discipline</u>, or a relevant <u>post-grad qualification</u>, eg an MBA.

Guessing meaning from context

2 Match the underlined words in the job adverts with their definitions.

0 a similar subject
  related discipline
1 able to talk on the phone easily
2 you have not moved jobs frequently
3 word processing
4 a high pass mark from university
5 someone who works well with other people

6 able to speak French very well
7 able to use a computer
8 able to adapt to changes
9 a second degree (after a Bachelor's)
10 able to speak, write and organize well
11 logical and careful
12 cheerful and able to see the funny side of things

3 Now put the phrases into these categories.
Qualities   Qualifications
Skills   Other

Understanding information in tables

1 The table below shows women's attitudes towards work and family life in the UK, between 1980 and 1999. Work in pairs. Which statements do you agree with? Why?

% agreeing with the statement	1980	1993	1999
A man's job is to earn the money; a woman's job is to look after the home and family.	48	19	18
Women can't combine a career and children.	29	15	14
A job is all right but what most women really want is a home and children.	40	15	13
If her children are well looked after it's good for a woman to work.	75	72	67
If a woman takes several years off to look after her children she should expect her career to suffer.	42	35	33

2 Answer these questions.

1 What do the statistics tell you about how attitudes have changed in Britain?
2 How have things changed in your country over the last 50 years with regard to women working?
3 How do people feel about these issues in your country?

TIP

Make sure you can find the evidence in the text if you answer **Yes** or **No**. If you cannot find the evidence answer **Not Given**.

Yes, No, Not Given

3 Read the text on the changing profile of the labour force in Canada. Do the statements below agree with the information given in the reading passage? Write:

YES if the statement agrees with the information
NO if the statement contradicts the information
NOT GIVEN if there is no information about this in the passage

1 In 1999 more than half of Canadian women were in paid employment.
2 Most women now continue to work when their children are young.
3 In the future, there is unlikely to be a shortage of teachers in the labour force.
4 More workers are likely to be sharing a house with both their children and their parents.
5 Employers will need to employ a wider range of people.
6 Organizations employing people from just one ethnic group will die out.

One of the most remarkable demographic events of the last half century was the dramatic influx of women into the paid labour force. Although women have always worked in their homes and communities on an unpaid basis and a proportion of women have worked for pay outside the home, women's rate of entry in the paid labour force has increased markedly since the early 50s. In 1951, less than one quarter of women in Canada (24%) were in the labour force. By 1999, the proportion had more than doubled to 55%. The most notable increase in women's participation rates has been among women with children. Between 1976 and 1999, the participation rate for women with children under 16 grew from 39% to 71%. Women now maintain a strong labour force attachment, including during their childbearing years, reflecting a commitment both to their family roles and to their paid work.

Concomitant to this shift in the gender distribution of the labour force has been a shift in its age structure. Like the population in general, the labour force is ageing. As the baby-boomers, now concentrated in their mid to late career years, approach retirement age, labour shortages are forecast in a wide range of occupations, including medicine and health, teaching, and public service. Forecasts indicate that the retirement wave will continue until at least 2020. Beyond 2015, the Canadian labour force is projected to grow at a rate of less than half a percent per year, under one third of its current growth rate. It is unlikely that all vacancies can be filled by young people, as the traditional labour force entrant population (youth aged 15–24) itself is shrinking. Labour shortages have already been noted in certain geographic locales and in selected fields such as information technology, skilled trades and health care services.

As the labour force becomes more diverse demographically, it also becomes more diverse in terms of employees' needs, family demands and potential caregiving responsibilities. Individuals with young children may span a wide age range, especially if they have delayed childbearing. Employees may face multiple caregiving demands, with both children and ageing family members to care for. An increasing number are likely to provide care for an immediate or extended family member with a health problem or long term disability, either on a regular basis, or unexpectedly in times of acute need. Many will have family members in distant locales whose needs will be of concern to them.

Projections indicate that 50% of the workforce of 2015 is already in the labour market. The combination of a shrinking labour pool and skills shortages means that in order to meet their resource needs, organizations will need to retain and develop an increasingly diverse workforce, comprising women and men, new immigrants, visible minority groups, people with disabilities, young people and older workers looking for a post retirement career. This workforce will have a wide range of obligations outside of the workplace and will not be well served by 'one size fits all' human resource policies. Employers who provide flexibility, 'balance', and opportunities for continuous learning and development will have a strategic advantage in a tight labour market, and will make an important contribution to the well-being of employees, families and communities.

Matching headings to paragraphs

4 Choose the most suitable headings for paragraphs **A–F**.

1 Women interrupt their careers to care for family
2 Both men and women in the labour force have child care demands
3 Increasing proportion of employees with both child and elder care demands
4 The majority of women still work in 'traditional' female occupations
5 Most mothers in the labour force work full time
6 Mothers less likely to be employed than women without children
7 Number of Canadian women working increases
8 Greatest increase in working women is among those with children

Strategy

Identify key words in the headings.

Look for similar or related words in the paragraphs.

A In 2000, 60% of Canadian women aged 15 and over were in the Canadian labour force, up from 42% in 1976. Between 1976 and 2000, the number of women in the labour force grew from 3.6 million to 7.4 million, an increase of 106%. Over the same period the number of men in the labour force grew by only 40%, from 6.2 million to 8.7 million.

B The largest participation rate increase has been among women with pre-school children. Between 1976 and 1999, the participation rate of women with a youngest child aged 3 to 5 grew from 37% to 66%. The increase was even more dramatic among women with a toddler or infant: the rate for women with a youngest child under 3 more than doubled, from 28% in 1976 to 61% in 1999.

C Work continuity is important to career development, future employability and current and future earnings, but the majority of women experience significant breaks in employment. Nearly two thirds of women (62%) who have ever held paid jobs have experienced a work interruption of six months or more. In contrast, only one quarter of their male counterparts (27%) have had a work interruption lasting six months or more. Marriage, maternity leave and care of children account for 62% of women's work interruptions.

D In spite of the remarkable growth in their participation rate, women with children are still less likely to be in the labour force than those without. In 1999, 76% of women under age 55 without children under 16 at home were in the labour force. This compares to a participation rate of 69% among women with children under 16.

E The vast majority of employed women with children work full time (30 hours or more per week). In 1999, 71% of employed women with at least one child under age 16 at home worked full time, as did 68% of employed women with one or more children under 3 years of age.

F A nationally representative employee survey conducted by the Conference Board of Canada in 1999 indicated that the proportion of employees who both care for elderly family members and have children at home is now 15%, as compared to 9.5% a decade ago.

Strategy

Look at the diagrams carefully and check you understand what they show.

You may be asked to choose labels from a box or from the text. If you choose from a text, check how many words you are allowed to use.

Labelling a diagram

5 Look at Figures 1–3 which are based on the paragraphs on page 60. Choose the most appropriate label (**A–E**) for each figure from the box.

A Percentage of women in the labour force with pre-school children and with children aged 3–5.

B Percentage of women with children who work full time.

C Number of men and women in the labour force.

D Proportion of employees who both care for elderly relatives and children.

E Percentages of men and women who have not taken a break in employment.

Fig. 1

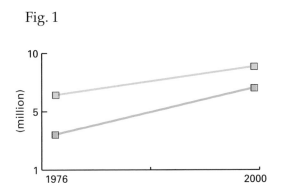

Fig. 2

Fig. 3

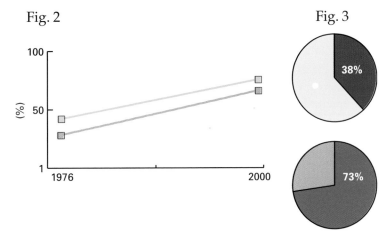

Vocabulary

Suffixes

A suffix is a letter or a group of letters added to the end of a word. Recognizing suffixes can help you to guess the meaning of words you don't know.

Look at these words from the reading texts on pages 59 and 60. These suffixes are all typical NOUN endings.

projec**tion**
flexibil**ity**
attach**ment**

1 Look back at the texts and find further examples of words ending in:

-tion (11)
-ity (5)
-ment (4)

What other words do you know in the same 'family' as the words you have found? Are there any suffixes which tell you what part of speech they are?

eg *organize* (-ize=verb) *disorganized* (-ized=adj)

Use a dictionary to help you.

Task 1: Comparing and contrasting data

1 Unemployment is a problem in many parts of the world. Answer these questions.

1 Do you know what the unemployment rate (%) is in your country?
2 Which age groups/sections of the population are most affected by unemployment in your country?
3 What are the best places to look for a new job?

2 Look at this IELTS Writing Task 1 question and answer these questions.

1 What period of time is shown?
2 What are the key points you would mention?
3 How would you group the data?

The table below shows the unemployment rates in 2000 for men and women in different parts of the world.

Write a report for a university lecturer describing the information below.

Time: 20 minutes   Write at least 150 words.

Country	Unemployment rates (%)		
	Both sexes	**Male**	**Female**
Australia	6.5	6.7	6.5
Belize	12.7	8.9	20.3
Japan	4.7	4.9	4.5
Morocco	22.0	20.3	27.6
Netherlands	3.3	2.6	4.2

3 Now read this sample answer and compare your ideas with the author's.

The chart indicates that unemployment <u>differs widely</u> both between nations and sexes. In the Netherlands, for example, unemployment is remarkably low (only 3.3%), <u>but</u> the rate for women is <u>considerably more than</u> that for men. <u>Conversely</u>, in other developed countries, such as Japan and Australia, there is <u>only a small difference between</u> the male and female rates, and in both cases, <u>unlike</u> the Netherlands, men are slightly more likely to be unemployed. <u>However</u>, the total rate in these countries is slightly higher.

<u>In marked contrast</u>, the figures in less developed countries are much higher, 12.7% in Belize, and an enormous 22% in Morocco on average. <u>Nevertheless</u>, <u>although</u> the difference between men and women in Morocco is large, in Belize women are more than twice as likely not to have paid work. Therefore, <u>despite</u> the much lower general unemployment in Belize, there are as many unemployed women there as there are unemployed men in Morocco.   153 words

Contrast linkers/markers

1 Look at the <u>underlined</u> words in the sample answer. What do they have in common?

2 Although many of these expressions have similar meanings, they often have different forms. Look at this information.

<u>But</u>

Example:
The economies of the Netherlands and Australia are similar <u>but</u> the unemployment rate is much higher in the latter.

Where does it go in a sentence? Between two clauses – it cannot begin a sentence.
What do you notice about its punctuation? Usually, it is not used with commas.
What is it followed by? A subject and a finite verb (… the unemployment rate is …)

Note: A finite verb is one which is marked according to tense, number or person, eg *she plays*, *they have played*, *I play*.

3 Now write example sentences and answer the questions above for these contrast markers.

Although	However/On the other hand
Inspite of/despite	Conversely/On the contrary

4 Study this graph.

The graph below shows the unemployment rates in different areas of the world from 1991–2001.

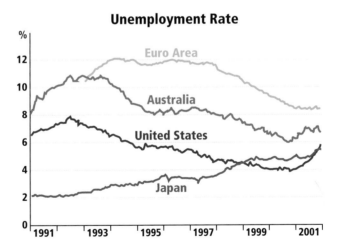

Unemployment Rate

Write a report for a university lecturer describing the information below.

Time: 20 minutes   Write at least 150 words.

Note: The trends shown for the four areas can be compared and contrasted but in this graph changes over time also need to be described.

5 Complete the gaps in the sentences below using a contrast marker or appropriate word or phrase selected from the box. You do not have to use all of them.

> despite   different   higher   rose significantly   however   although
> similar   rise   fall   increased   bigger

1   *In most of the areas shown on the line graph, the unemployment rate .... from 1991 to 1992. .... , from about 1993 the rate began to ....*

2   *..................... Australia and the United States showed .... trends overall, Australia usually had an unemployment rate about 2% .... than the US.*

3   *..................... having the lowest unemployment rate in 1991 at 2%, the number of people unemployed in Japan .... to just under 6% in 2001.*

6 Write two more sentences comparing or contrasting the areas shown in the graph.

TIP

In what order would you do these tasks?

  Brainstorm ideas
  Start writing
  Make an outline/plan
  Understand the question

Exam information

The data in IELTS Writing Task 1 may be shown in more than one diagram – it could be a piechart, a graph or table.

It is important to study all the information carefully and then compare and contrast the key facts.

Writing: further practice

1 Work in pairs. Look at the question below and answer the questions.

1   What do the pie charts tell you about each country?
2   What time period is shown?
3   What comparisons and contrasts are there between the two countries?
4   How will you group the information?

The two pie charts below show how employment is divided in Tanzania and Ireland.

Write a report for a university lecturer describing the information below.

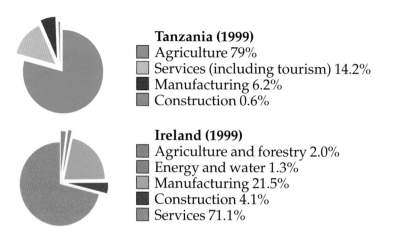

Tanzania (1999)
  Agriculture 79%
  Services (including tourism) 14.2%
  Manufacturing 6.2%
  Construction 0.6%

Ireland (1999)
  Agriculture and forestry 2.0%
  Energy and water 1.3%
  Manufacturing 21.5%
  Construction 4.1%
  Services 71.1%

Time: 20 minutes   Write at least 150 words.

Extensive reading and listening

1 A good way to make faster progress is to use English outside the classroom. Which do you have access to?

Reading
English language:
newspapers
novels
text books
graded readers (stories written in simplified language, written for students)
magazines
the Internet

Listening
English speakers
the radio in English
films in English (with or without subtitles)
TV in English
the Internet
taped stories in English
songs

2 How many do you use regularly?

3 Work in pairs. Discuss these questions.

1 Which of the the activities in 1 do you do? Give examples.
2 Which of the activities do you not do? Why not?

4 Choose four of the activities you have access to and plan to use one a week for the next month. Fill in the table below as you do them.

Week	Activity	Details	Date used	Comment
1	Listening to the radio	News programme	22nd August	Made notes on the headlines – they spoke very quickly, but I understood the main ideas.

Set yourself realistic targets – it would be great to read a whole newspaper every day, but most people don't have that much time!
Read something or listen to something in English every day.
Read and listen to a range of text types that interest you – including ones that contain more formal language.
Expose yourself to authentic written and spoken English as much as possible.

Dictionary focus

Find these words in the unit. Then check their meaning in your dictionary and record them.

issue p.58	retain p.59	contradict p.59
project p.59	diverse p.59	proportion p.60
notable p.59	influx p.59	expose p.65

Vocabulary

1 Read these definitions of six crimes and match them with the crimes in the box.

> shoplifting mugging terrorism robbery vandalism
> burglary kidnapping fraud

1 to illegally take someone away and make them a prisoner, especially in order to make their family or the government give you some money
2 to steal things from a shop
3 to attack someone in a public place and steal their money or possessions
4 to deliberately damage or destroy things, especially public property
5 to take money or property from someone illegally
6 to enter a building illegally in order to steal things

2 What are the definitions of the two extra crimes above?

3 Using monolingual dictionaries, look up these punishments and rank them from the least severe (1) to the most severe (5).

A fine
A caution
Capital punishment
A suspended sentence
Imprisonment

4 Work in pairs. Compare your rankings and discuss which punishment you think would be most suitable for each of the crimes in 1.

1 <u>Underline</u> the main aim of this charity.

2 <u>Underline</u> the specific type of help they offer.

Victim Support is the national charity for people affected by crime. Every year they offer help to around 1.75 million people through a network of local member charities across England, Wales and Northern Ireland. At the time of the Home Office survey in 1998, the organisation had more than 650 employees and over 10,000 trained volunteer visitors working with its branches in the community. They now have over 1,500 staff and around 12,000 volunteers, including 6,000 community-based volunteers. Trained volunteers offer a free and confidential service, whether or not a crime has been reported and regardless of when it happened. They provide emotional support, information and practical help to people who have suffered a range of crimes. Most referrals to Victim Support are made by the police and several major offence categories are automatically referred to Victim Support. The traditional initial contact is made by Victim Support to the victim. Victim Support is committed to the principle of providing services to all victims of crime and, with this in mind, also encourages self-referral with the victim making the initial contact.

Yes, No, Not Given

3 Read this text on burglary. Do the statements below reflect the claims of the writer in the passage below?

Write:
YES if the statement reflects the claims of the writer
NO if the statement contradicts the claims of the writer
NOT GIVEN if it is impossible to say what the writer thinks about this

1   There are more cases of burglary dealt with by Victim Support than any other charity.
2   It is common for victims to want to discuss the effects of a crime.
3   Specially trained volunteers from this charity sometimes visit the victims' houses.
4   People must inform the police about a crime before contacting Victim Support.
5   People who have been burgled will never feel safe and relaxed in their homes again.

Burglary is a serious but very common crime. In 2001, around one in every six crimes recorded in the UK was burglary. Victim Support is a charity that offers support and gets in touch with over a million people affected by crime each year.

Most victims of crime want to talk to someone about what has happened and how they are feeling. Talking to friends and family can be helpful, but Victim Support provides a service which involves talking to a specially trained volunteer. This charity can help, regardless of whether or not you have told the police or anyone else.

People who are victims of burglary can be affected in a wide range of different ways even if none of their property has been stolen. Those whose houses have been burgled may be upset just at the thought that someone has been in their home against their wishes, and this can often make them feel insecure.

As well as offering support, Victim Support can also help victims deal with people who usually need to be contacted after a burglary such as landlords, the police or insurance companies.

Strategy

Try looking at the first line of each section. This is often the **topic sentence**. Then look for similar or related words to those in the summaries.

BUT remember that a summary will cover all or most of the main ideas in the section or paragraph, not just one.

Matching sections and summaries

4 Now read the article on Victim Support. Match the summaries (**1–6**) to the sections (**A–D**).

Note that there are more summaries than section so you will not see them all.

1 Range of crimes which had affected victims.
2 Different kinds of help given to victims.
3 How successful victims felt the Victim Support service was.
4 How successful members of the public felt the Victim Support service was.
5 Which victims were most likely to be contacted by Victim Support.
6 How Victim Support got in touch with victims.

Victim Support: Findings from the 1998 British Crime Survey

A Among those victims contacted, the initial contact made by Victim Support was by letter (and/or leaflet) in most cases (69%). Only 13% of all initial contacts were 'unannounced' visits ie a volunteer calling at the home, but follow-up visits after letters and telephone calls doubled the numbers of victims visited. Among all victims contacted by whatever means, the proportion eventually visited (26%) was similar to earlier findings: 1994 (25%) and 1996 (27%).

Types of contact varied considerably between victims of different offence types. Victims of burglary and assault were more likely than victims of other offences to be visited by Victim Support volunteers. Over 30% of contacted victims in these categories eventually received a visit, compared with only 6% of contacted victims of theft.

B Victim Support appears to be successful in matching support to the types of case in which needs are likely to be greatest. Victims who said that they had wanted help – especially those who said they had wanted 'someone to talk to' – and those who described themselves as 'very much affected', were considerably more likely to have been contacted (and to have been visited) by Victim Support than those who did not express any needs or were less affected.

For example, 23% of those who said they wanted 'someone to talk to' were contacted by Victim Support in comparison with 5% of those who did not express such a need. Victim Support visits were 15 times more likely to those who said they had been 'very much' affected. This may be partly due to the kinds of offence which receive highest priority – burglary and violence – and partly the result of co-ordinators making 'educated guesses' from crime reports to identify victims most likely to need help.

C A high proportion of people Victim Support contacted were helped with at least one problem: 91% when volunteer and victim met face-to-face. 74% of such victims felt they had been given 'moral support'. Even 25% of those receiving a letter from Victim Support said they had been given moral support. The proportions who said they were helped with security advice were 27% for face-to-face contact and 9% for letters.

Numbers were too small to undertake a systematic correlation between the kinds of help given and the needs expressed. However, 50% of those naming 'moral support' as a need said that they had received this kind of help. In contrast, the need for 'information from the police' was rarely met by Victim Support. However, it is probably more appropriate for the police to provide this information direct to the victim.

D Among respondents who recalled some contact with Victim Support, 58% rated the service as 'very' or 'fairly helpful'. The proportion was considerably higher among those who had had visits (80%) or contact by telephone (69%). Even letters/leaflets alone were found helpful by nearly half (46%). Although 58% is a slight drop on previous years (see Figure 1) from 65% in 1996 and 60% in 1994, the 80% rating of face-to-face contact as 'very' or 'fairly helpful' had increased on previous years (76%, 1996 BCS; 70%, 1994).

The quality of Victim Support service appeared to have the strongest effect on 'very' or 'fairly helpful' ratings, particularly for the more personal kinds of contact (face-to-face and telephone); the speed with which Victim Support made contact appeared to be less significant.

Sentence completion

5 Complete each of these statements with words taken from the reading passage on page 68. Write **NO MORE THAN THREE WORDS** for each answer.

> 1 Victims were usually first contacted by ....
>
>   Which two responses given were most likely to generate contact from Victim Support?
>
> 2 Needing someone ....
>
> 3 Being ....
>
> 4 The most effective types of contacts were ....

Identifying text type

6 This text is taken from

A a guide for new workers within Victim Support.
B an official government report.
C a textbook for students studying sociology.
D a newspaper article about a new Victim Support scheme.

Language focus 1

Defining relative clauses

1 Look at these sentences from exercise 2 on page 67. Find and <u>underline</u> the defining relative clauses and circle the relative pronoun.

0 Victim Support is a charity (that) offers support and advice …
1 … but Victim Support provides a service which involves talking to a specially trained volunteer.
2 People who are victims of burglary can be affected in a wide range of different ways …
3 Those whose houses have been burgled may be upset just at the thought …
4 Victim Support can also help victims deal with people who usually need to be contacted after a burglary.

2 Answer these questions.

1 What two relative pronouns can be used for things? People?
2 What is the difference between *who* and *whose*?
3 Are commas needed in defining relative clauses?

3 Look at this sentence.

A high proportion of people who Victim Support contacted were helped with at least one problem.

Victim Support is the subject of the sentence.
A high proportion of people is the object.
What does the relative pronoun refer to – the subject or the object?

Note that a relative pronoun is not necessary if it refers to the object of the sentence.

4 Complete each of the spaces below with an appropriate relative pronoun. Choose from *that/which/who/whose/none needed*. Some will have more than one possibility.

0 The treatment ..*that/which/none needed*.. victims receive from the police varies from area to area.

1 Some people .... are burgled find it no more than an irritating inconvenience.

2 Unfortunately, people .... have been burgled once are statistically more likely to be burgled again.

3 Face to face contact was the method .... most people found helpful.

4 Burglars usually sell the things .... they stole quite quickly.

5 If you make an insurance claim, you will need the crime reference number .... the police give you.

6 All volunteers .... work with victims have been specially selected and trained.

7 Convicted burglars are sometimes asked to apologize personally to the people .... possessions they stole.

8 Volunteers are people .... work free of charge because they think the work is important.

5 Rewrite this passage adding the relative clauses to make it clearer. The first one has been done for you.

> who has already been convicted of burglary   which are reported
> who commit burglary   ~~which people commit~~   who are burgled

Burglary is one of the most common crimes *which people commit*. Some figures show that up to one in six crimes is a burglary. Therefore, many people will be burgled at some point in their life. Some of those will find it devastating, even if none of their possessions are actually taken. People should realize the effect they may have on someone else's life. In my opinion, if someone offends again, they should receive a stiffer sentence.

Task 2: Evaluating and challenging ideas, evidence or an argument

1 Complete this sentence in your own words.

The main aim of sending a person to prison is to ...

2 In Task 2 of the IELTS Writing module you have to 'evaluate and challenge ideas, evidence or an argument'. Read the IELTS Writing Task below and answer the questions.

Present a written argument or case to an educated reader with no specialist knowledge of the following topic.

Future plans to design prisons for learning and working, with bigger cells containing computers that will enable study and communication, have been criticized for trying to turn prisons into 'holiday camps' and for 'wasting taxpayers' money'.

To what extent do you agree or disagree with these views?

Time: 40 minutes   Write at least 250 words.

1   According to the statement, what will prisons be like in the future?
2   According to the statement, what might be wrong with these prisons?
3   Would you say that these new prisons are a good or bad idea? Why?

3 Quickly read this sample answer and decide if the writer is *for* or *against* new style prisons.

1   When discussing the prison system in this country it is important to point out that people have strong views both for and against any changes to the existing system. In this country there has been a lot of negative criticism of new proposals in recent weeks, as many people feel they are a waste of money. However, there is no doubt in my mind that the prison network needs to be reviewed urgently. Therefore, *a* .... with reasons given to support any changes.

2   First of all, prisoners studying and working, *b* .... is a positive measure. I believe that this will not only give prisoners motivation and interest, but also help them live a relatively normal life. In a similar way, I tend to think that improved facilities and living conditions will have a more beneficial effect on the prisoner than the opposite. For these reasons, *c* .... changes need to be made.

3   Some people argue that these new style prisons will turn into 'holiday camps' *d* ....

For example, prisoners would be getting both physical and mental exercise in this scheme and would not be able to laze around and do nothing. Of course there would be some opportunities for leisure time but again this is better than depriving inmates of all enjoyment whatsoever. *e*

4   .... these new developments will make going to prison seem like a holiday. Since this new system would give clear goals for prisoners, I am certain it is a more constructive approach.

5   A further criticism of this new system is that it is a waste of public money. Although such changes will undoubtedly be expensive, I still feel that it would be a good idea to spend money on developing these prisons. If the scheme was successful, it would turn prisoners into better citizens less likely to commit crimes in the future. *f* .... the level of crime might be reduced and we would be able to live in a safer world.

TIP

Produce a clear essay by structuring each paragraph. Use appropriate language to give opinions and back up each view.

4 These phrases have been removed from the essay. Put them in the appropriate category in the box and then place them in the essay.

1 but I am unconvinced that this would be the case
2 in my view,
3 as a result,

4 it is clear that this issue needs to be considered carefully
5 I fully agree that
6 I cannot accept that

Introducing the main topic to evaluate
In order to discuss/examine this issue, it is important to consider ...
Some people say/argue that ...
The issue of X is ...

....

Challenging ideas
I disagree with the view ...
I do not believe that ...

....

....

Agreeing with ideas (to be backed up by reasons)
I strongly agree with this view ...

....

Giving opinions
I feel/believe that ...
In my opinion ...

....

There is no doubt in my mind ... (which also expresses certainty)
I tend to think ... (more tentative)

Consequences/result
Therefore, ...
Consequently, ...

....

If X happens/happened, Y will/might/would result ...

(See Unit 8 for more information on conditional sentences)

5 In order to see how the writer has structured this essay, identify the main idea and supporting information from each paragraph (2–4). Paragraph 1 has been done as an example.

Paragraph 1
Main idea:
People for and against changing prison system but definitely needs reviewing.

Supporting information:
Lot of negative criticism. Topic will be discussed in essay.

Prediction

1 Work in pairs. Discuss these questions.

1 What are acceptable reasons for missing school?
2 What might children do instead of going to school?
3 Did anyone in your school play truant?
4 Do you know what the consequences or punishments are for truancy in your country?

Note completion

2 🔲 18 Listen to the interview on truancy and complete the notes. Write **NO MORE THAN THREE WORDS** for each answer.

> According to David Renshaw, continued absence from school could be harmful to a child's education and also lead to a **1** ....
>
> The government is trying to stop truancy using:
>
> • long term imprisonment
> • **2** .... prison sentences
> • **3** ....
>
> Lorna says reasons for truancy include:
>
> • unhappiness at home
> • peer pressure
> • **4** ....
>
> Lorna thinks the following people should be involved: parents, children, **5** .... , the government and social services.

Exam information

In this type of question, you have a number of answers to match together. It is similar to classification, but you can only use each choice once. There will usually be more choices than you need.

Matching

3 For questions **6–8**,

if Lorna Coates (the charity representative) states this write L.

if David Renshaw (the government official) states this, write D.

if Jennifer Simpson (the mother) states this, write J.

if the presenter states this, write P.

6 Over 12,000 children played truant in the Spring. ....
7 Prison sentences won't help children who are unhappy at school. ....
8 Counselling works well. ....

Reason/result clauses

In the IELTS Writing module (and most academic writing tasks) it is important to be able to link ideas together well so that your argument flows.

1 Look at these examples from the model answer and identify which linking words are used to join the ideas.

In this country there has been a lot of negative criticism of new proposals in recent weeks, as many people feel they are a waste of money.

... there is no doubt in my mind that the prison network needs to be reviewed urgently. Therefore, it is clear that this issue needs to be considered carefully with reasons given to support any changes.

Since this new system would give clear goals for prisoners, I am certain it is a more constructive approach.

If the scheme was successful, it would turn prisoners into better citizens less likely to commit crimes in the future. As a result, the level of crime might be reduced and we would be able to live in a safer world.

2 Which of the linking words above are used to give a reason? Which are used to express a result?

3 Put *so* or *because* in the gaps below.

1   This new system would give clear goals for prisoners, ... it is certainly a more constructive approach.
2   It is certainly a more constructive approach .... this new system would give clear goals for prisoners.

4 After which of the linking words or phrases in this section should you use a comma?

5 Complete the sentences with an appropriate linker showing reason or result. More than one choice may be possible in each case.

> therefore
> consequently
> as   because   so
> since   as a result

1   Allowing prisoners to study is a good idea .... they may get better jobs when they are freed.
2   These days prisoners feel that prisons are more comfortable than life 'outside' and .... they are happy to commit more crime to return there.
3   Providing more opportunities for prisoners to improve their lives would mean fewer criminals returned to prison. .... society would benefit in the long term.

Writing: further practice

6 Look at this sample IELTS Writing Task 2 question.

Present a written argument or case to an educated reader with no specialist knowledge of the following topic.

In recent years, many countries have become extremely concerned about the increase in crimes committed by young people. Tough measures and strict punishments are necessary to stop youths from re-offending.

To what extent do you agree or disagree with this opinion?

Time: 40 minutes   Write at least 250 words.

7 Here is part of a student's answer. Rewrite and improve the answer to include some more linking words.

The number of crimes committed by young people keeps growing each year. The government is not doing enough to cut crime. Every year they promise an improvement. It never happens. They don't take tough enough measures.

I would agree that young criminals are not frightened of the consequences of their actions. They do not seem to mind the punishments they receive. These punishments are too light. They commit more crimes.

Light punishments such as community service do not work. Young people should be punished more severely. This will make them think more carefully about what they do.

8 Compare your version with the rewritten version on page 162. Then write your own answer to the question.

Compare your version with the rewritten version on page 162.

Pronunciation

Word stress

In some languages, all words are stressed in the same place. English has many rules about word stress and they can be confusing. However, some of the common ones are useful to learn.

1 How many syllables do these words have?

punishment   suspension   absentee   prisoner
detention   expulsion

2 Put each word in 1 under its stress pattern.

Ooo	oOo	ooO

3 What do you notice about the words that have the pattern oOo?

4 Look at these words that all end in the sound /ʃən/ and mark the stress pattern above them. What do you notice?

politician   situation   station   examination

5 A good dictionary will tell you where the stress is on a word. Look at this dictionary entry. How is the stress marked?

examination /ɪgˈzæmɪˈneɪʃən/ noun

TIP

When you learn a new word, make sure you note where the stress is otherwise you may be misunderstood.

Speaking

1 You have one minute preparation time. Read the instructions carefully and make notes before speaking to your partner.

Part 2

Describe a subject you enjoyed at school or college.

You should say:
  what the subject was
  how long you studied it
  what kind of topics this subject included

You should also say what you liked most about this subject.

Part 3

2 Work in pairs. Take it in turns to ask and answer these questions.

1 Which subjects at school do you think are the most important?
2 How strict should school teachers be?
3 What are the best ways to deal with young people who break the law?
4 Do you think police officers should have higher salaries?
5 If famous people commit a crime, should they be treated any differently?
6 How can people protect their homes from burglars?

Listening skills

Listening and writing simultaneously

Students taking the IELTS Listening module often find it difficult to write down answers and continue to listen at the same time. Predicting the kind of information you are listening for will help.

1 Work in pairs. Look at this note completion exercise and discuss these questions.

Neighbourhood Watch is a partnership between the Police and

1 ....

In the past, people didn't

2 ....

Nowadays, people frequently move and this has reduced

3 ....

The policeman mentions two crimes

4 .... and

5 ....

If you see something suspicious, you should

6 ....

You could become a committee member, if

7 ....

Being involved in Neighbourhood Watch may also lower the cost of your

8 ....

1 What is the subject of this listening? Do you know anything about it?
2 What kind of information is missing? (eg a location, a date)
3 What kind of word or words will grammatically fit the space? (eg a noun, a verb)

2 📼 19 Listen and fill in the gaps using **NO MORE THAN THREE WORDS**.

Understanding verbs in essay titles

When writing essays or assignments it is important to understand the verbs that tell you what to actually do in the question.

1 Look at the examples below in *italics* and answer the questions. Use a dictionary to check the meaning of any unknown words.

'*Compare and contrast* recycling schemes in different areas of the country.'
'*Discuss* the arguments for and against recycling schemes.'
'*Describe* how a recycling scheme works.'
'*Explain* why recycling schemes have proved to be effective.'
'*Identify* the key advantages of recycling schemes and *justify* your opinion.'
'*Evaluate* the effectiveness of the new recycling scheme.'

1 What is the difference between *compare* and *contrast* and *explain*?
2 What is the difference between *evaluate* and *describe*?
3 What is the difference between *identify* and *discuss*?
4 How should you *justify* an opinion?

2 Look at these essay extracts.

Which is an example of:

1 *Comparing and contrasting*   3 *Evaluating*
2 *Justifying an opinion*   4 *Describing*

A 'I do not believe that capital punishment helps to reduce the number of people murdered. In fact, in America, where many states have the death penalty, there are many more murders each year than in my country.'

B 'On balance, I think that the government's policy of encouraging community work rather than prison sentences has proved quite successful.'

C 'The number of people arrested for petty crimes each year is quite similar in each country. However, the sentences given to these criminals are quite different.'

D 'If a crime is considered less serious, the criminal is tried by a magistrate. A jury of 12 people will only be used in more serious cases, such as assault or murder.'

Find these words in the unit. Then check their meaning in your dictionary and record them.

systematic p.68	challenge p.71	approach p.74
priority p.68	deprive p.71	version p.75
constructive p.71	consequence p.73	scheme p.77

7 Globalization

'The idea that the world is developing a single economy and culture as a result of improved communications and the influence of very large companies.' *Macmillan Essential Dictionary*

Reading

Scanning

1 Work in pairs. List three positive aspects and three negative aspects of globalization.

2 Put the paragraphs in the text under the following headings. Note that you will find one positive statement and one negative statement for each heading.

Global Communications Global Media
Global Travel and Tourism Global Business

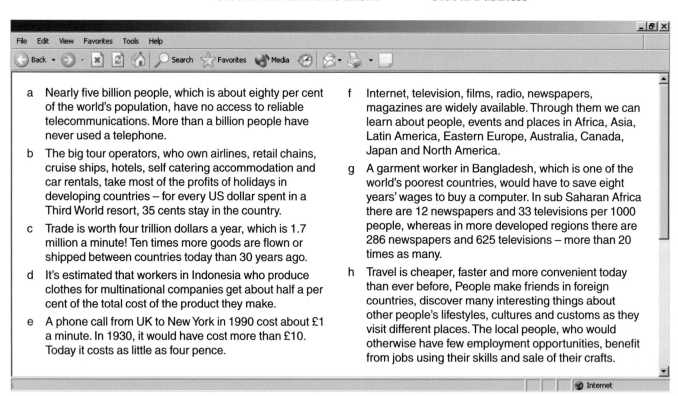

File Edit View Favorites Tools Help

Back · · Search · Favorites · Media

a Nearly five billion people, which is about eighty per cent of the world's population, have no access to reliable telecommunications. More than a billion people have never used a telephone.

b The big tour operators, who own airlines, retail chains, cruise ships, hotels, self catering accommodation and car rentals, take most of the profits of holidays in developing countries – for every US dollar spent in a Third World resort, 35 cents stay in the country.

c Trade is worth four trillion dollars a year, which is 1.7 million a minute! Ten times more goods are flown or shipped between countries today than 30 years ago.

d It's estimated that workers in Indonesia who produce clothes for multinational companies get about half a per cent of the total cost of the product they make.

e A phone call from UK to New York in 1990 cost about £1 a minute. In 1930, it would have cost more than £10. Today it costs as little as four pence.

f Internet, television, films, radio, newspapers, magazines are widely available. Through them we can learn about people, events and places in Africa, Asia, Latin America, Eastern Europe, Australia, Canada, Japan and North America.

g A garment worker in Bangladesh, which is one of the world's poorest countries, would have to save eight years' wages to buy a computer. In sub Saharan Africa there are 12 newspapers and 33 televisions per 1000 people, whereas in more developed regions there are 286 newspapers and 625 televisions – more than 20 times as many.

h Travel is cheaper, faster and more convenient today than ever before, People make friends in foreign countries, discover many interesting things about other people's lifestyles, cultures and customs as they visit different places. The local people, who would otherwise have few employment opportunities, benefit from jobs using their skills and sale of their crafts.

Language focus 1

1 Both of these sentences use relative clauses. Answer the questions.

a *It's estimated that workers in Indonesia who produce clothes for multinational companies get about half a per cent of the total cost of the product they make.*

b *Nearly five billion people, which is about eighty per cent of the world's population, have no access to reliable telecommunications.*

1 Which sentence has a relative clause that identifies which person or thing is being talked about?

2 Which sentence has a relative clause that adds extra information, or a second idea to the main idea?

Non-defining relative clauses

2 Look at these sentences with non-defining relative clauses and identify the main idea and the extra information given.

0 Nearly five billion people, which is about eighty per cent of the world's population, have no access to reliable telecommunications.

Main idea:
Nearly five billion people have no access to reliable telecommunications.

Extra information:
Five billion people is about eighty per cent of the world's population.

1 The big tour operators, who own airlines, retail chains, cruise ships, hotels, self-catering accommodation and car rentals, take most of the profits of holidays in developing countries.

Main idea: ....

Extra information: ....

2 Trade is worth four trillion dollars a year, which is 1.7 million a minute!

Main idea: ....

Extra information: ....

3 A garment worker in Bangladesh, which is one of the world's poorest countries, would have to save eight years' wages to buy a computer.

Main idea: ....

Extra information: ....

4 The local people, who would otherwise have few employment opportunities, benefit from jobs using their skills and sale of their crafts.

Main idea: ....

Extra information: ....

3 Underline the correct alternative in these rules for non-defining relative clauses.

1 The relative clause provides extra information and can/cannot be left out.
2 *Who* or *which* can/cannot be replaced by *that*.
3 The relative pronoun can/cannot be left out.
4 Commas are/are not used.

4 Link the ideas in the two sentences, using commas to form one sentence.

0 Main idea: In 1999 Thailand had more mobile phones than Africa.
Extra information: Thailand is a relatively small country.

In 1999 Thailand, which is a relatively small country, had more mobile phones than Africa.

1 Main idea: Greater cultural contact has been encouraged by tourism.
Extra information: Tourism has doubled over the last 15 years.
2 Main idea: The banana is worth more than £5 billion in world trade.
Extra information: The banana is Britain's most popular fruit.
3 Main idea: Shima earns less than $1.50 for a day's work.
Extra information: Shima lives in Bangladesh.

TIP

Although longer, complex sentences are often better in academic writing, do not include a relative clause in every sentence. Remember, you can also join clauses with linking words.

1 Which of these organizations do you know about? Match them to the descriptions below.

1   The United Nations

2   Trade unions

3   International Monetary Fund

4   World Trade Organization

5   Friends of the Earth

6   International Aid Organizations (such as Oxfam)

a   The international organization that controls trade between countries.

b   Campaigns on environmental issues such as the greenhouse effect.

c   An international organization that works to balance and manage the world's economy and to help countries with weak economies to develop.

d   An international organization that encourages countries to work together in order to solve world problems such as war, disease and poverty.

e   Charities that raise money for famine and disaster relief.

f   Organizations of workers that aim to improve pay and conditions of work.

Exam information

In the IELTS Listening module you will have about half a minute to look through the questions before you listen to the tape. Read as many as you can and underline key words to listen for.

2 Predict which of these organizations are pro-globalization or anti-globalization.

3 You are going to listen to a lecture in three sections. Before each section spend half a minute reading the questions and underlining key words.

20 Look at questions **1–6** and listen to the first section.

Questions **1** and **2**

Which of the following areas does the lecturer say she will cover? **CIRCLE TWO ANSWERS**.

A   Global inequalities
B   Poverty in the developing world
C   The history of globalization
D   The key arguments for and against globalization
E   Trade and economics
F   The World Trade Organization

Questions **3–5**

Complete the following sentences using **NO MORE THAN TWO WORDS OR A NUMBER**.

3   Many people feel globalization is about the economy or ....
4   An example is the export of Japanese ....
5   Globalization began approximately .... ago.

Question 6

Which of these is NOT mentioned as important to the development of globalization?

A the telephone   C the postal service
B the fax   D air travel

4 🔲 21 Look at questions **7–9** and listen to the second section.

Questions 7–9

Complete the following notes using **NO MORE THAN TWO WORDS**.

Anti-globalization groups – eg Greenpeace and Friends of the Earth. These are **7** .... organizations. They feel globalization causes global warming, and depletion of oil, gas, **8** .... and sea life.
Many businesses in developed nations are against globalization because of competition from **9** ....

5 🔲 22 Look at questions **10–12** and listen to the final section.

Questions 10–12

Complete this table using **ONE OR TWO WORDS OR A NUMBER**.

Organization	Established	No. of member states	Role
WTO	**10**	123	Prevents members favouring home industries
IMF	1946	**11**	Provides temporary financial help
UN	1946	╱	Promotes shared values between UN and the **12** ....

6 Throughout the lecture, the lecturer uses certain words and phrases to signal, or signpost, key stages in the lecture. Recognizing these can help you to understand and follow her argument. Look at these 'signposts' and divide them into these categories.

Introduction	**Sequencing**	**Changing topic**	**Concluding/Summarizing**

1 Turning now to …
2 Now let us look a little at …
3 Lastly, …
4 In the first part of today's lecture …
5 I would like to …
6 Having looked at … let's now consider …
7 I will start by considering …
8 So, we've seen that …
9 I'd now like to move on to …
10 Secondly, I will explain …
11 So, let's begin with …
12 Finally, I intend to …

7 🔲 20–22 Listen to the lecture again and number the signposts in the order in which you hear them.

Skimming

1 Write the numbers in the box next to the sentence you think it refers to. Then check your predictions by quickly skimming the text.

150   10 million   43   8,000 million   25 million   80

	The value of all the coffee produced worldwide each year.
	The number of people who earn their living from coffee.
	The number of countries which produce coffee.
	The age of the farmer this article is about.
	The number of farmers that earn their living from coffee.
	The number of times that coffee beans can be sold between leaving the farmer and arriving in the supermarket.

Strategy

Read the questions or T/F/NG statements through first, and guess the meaning of any words you do not understand.

True, False, Not Given

Read the text produced by the Fairtrade Foundation about one family of coffee growers in Colombia.

2 Do the statements agree with the information in the reading passage? Write:

TRUE if the statement is true according to the passage
FALSE if the statement is false according to the passage
NOT GIVEN if the information is not given in the passage

1   The Menzas have tried growing coca leaf instead of coffee.
2   In trade, only oil is more important than coffee.
3   The Menzas receive 50% of the supermarket price for their coffee.
4   The production of cocoa is less exploitative than coffee.
5   In 1989 both world and supermarket prices dropped.
6   Setting up a co-operative is always an effective solution for these farmers.
7   The farmers have less and less money to spend on their families.

A   Vitelio Menza has been dependent on coffee in Colombia all his life. Now at 43 he is still unable to finish building his house due to lack of funds and is struggling to keep his family together. The fortunes of Vitelio, his wife Maria Enith and their four children have fluctuated dramatically along with the price of coffee.

B   Over the years the family has suffered illness brought on by malnutrition. In other parts of the   5
same area, some families have turned to growing drugs in order to survive; higher prices are paid for coca leaf (the raw material for cocaine). The Menzas have stayed loyal to the coffee crop but not without great personal sacrifices.

C   Coffee is grown in 80 countries in a band around the equator and provides a living for nearly 10 million farmers. Altogether, more than 25 million people worldwide depend on growing,   10 processing, trading and retailing coffee for their livelihood.

D   Coffee is the second most valuable commodity after oil. Not surprisingly, it is the most valuable agricultural commodity in world trade. Its total value – $8,000 million per year – is twice the value of exports of tea and cocoa put together. But the journey from the Menzas' farm in Colombia to the supermarket shelf is a long and tortuous one with a succession of people   15 taking their cut along the way.

E From tree to supermarket shelf it has been estimated the Menzas' coffee beans can change hands as many as 150 times, whilst the Menzas, like millions of other coffee growers, retain only a tiny share of the price consumers pay for the crop.

F Between 1989 and 1993 there was a 50% reduction in the world market price of coffee. An examination of the price paid to a farmer like Menza and the cost to a shopper in the supermarket reveals that both have lost out while many of the players in between have still managed to make gains. 20

G When the world price fell by 50% during 1989, farmers suffered an immediate fall in their incomes yet there was no noticeable reduction in the supermarket price of coffee. Retail prices remained stable for four more years before there was a fall of 20% in 1993. Yet when the market picked up in 1994 and the market price of coffee rose by 50%, the retail price rose immediately and sustained its price even when the market fell again the following year. 25

H For the farmers, this meant that the price of coffee had dropped below the cost of producing it for several years in a row. This had a devastating impact on their already precarious existence, forcing some farmers to abandon their land and go in search of work in the cities. Apart from the consequences for already overcrowded cities, this created a vicious circle in which the lack of labour for crop maintenance reduced the quality and value of the coffee, further reducing the price. 30

I But for small farmers the world price is only one of the factors undermining their ability to make a decent living. Indeed, if they were able to get a reasonable share of this price, they would be pleased. Without the means to process or transport their crop to market, limited knowledge of the frequently changing world price and a debt-driven necessity to sell their coffee the moment it is ripe (when prices are lowest), small independent farmers find themselves in a weak negotiating position. They are prey to local dealers who buy the coffee and sell it on to international markets. With only one major harvest a year, farmers are desperate for cash by the time their crop is ripe and are keen to sell at whatever price they can get. Not surprisingly, local dealers are quick to exploit this. 35 40

J The farmers' need for a quick sale is a symptom of their inability to get loans at a fair rate from banks, pushing them into the arms of loan sharks to pay for fertilizers, harvest labour and basic living costs prior to harvest. Many farmers have got together to set up co-operative marketing ventures which enable them to by-pass the middlemen. All too often, however, even the co-op cannot get finance to buy the crop, and members still sell to local traders for cash, rather than wait for a better price. Evidence of low and declining living standards is clear. The Fairtrade Foundation's research shows reduced spending on housing, children's education, health and food. 45 50

TIP

Read the instructions. This question asks for **ONE OR TWO** words.

Sentence completion

3 Choose **ONE OR TWO WORDS** from the reading passage for each answer.

1 The Menzas have made .... to continue growing coffee.

2 Coffee is worth .... as much as tea and cocoa.

3 Coffee farmers only keep a .... of the final retail value.

4 Any fall in the world price of coffee in 1989 was not .... in the supermarkets.

5 As there is only one coffee crop each year, farmers have very little .... by the time it is ready to harvest.

6 It is impossible for farmers to borrow money at a ....

Strategy

Think about the target audience. Students? Members of the public? Is the style formal or informal?

Identifying the writer's purpose

4 What is the purpose of the passage on Fairtrade?

A   To advise readers against buying non Fairtrade coffee.
B   To explain to readers how coffee farmers like the Menzas are exploited by international markets.
C   To advise coffee farmers like the Menzas how to make a good living.
D   To encourage readers to protest about the current situation.

Guessing meaning from context

5 Read the text again and try to find words which mean the same as:

1   changed frequently (para A)
2   selling to the public (para C)
3   maintained or kept (para G)
4   not safe or secure (para H)
5   weaken, make less likely to succeed (para I)
6   getting worse (para J)

Vocabulary

1 There are many words in the text connected with money and buying and selling. Match the words and definitions.

When you have finished, check your answers in a dictionary.

1	funds	how much something costs to buy in a shop
2	commodity	available money
3	retail price	how much something costs to buy in large quantities
4	market price	money that someone gets from working
5	income	something that can be bought and sold
6	middleman	someone who lends money to people at a very high rate of interest
7	loan shark	a person or company that buys from producers and sells to customers at a profit
8	trader/dealer	someone who buys something or uses services
9	consumer	a person or organization that influences a situation, especially in business or politics
10	player	someone who buys and sells things

2 Divide these phrases from the text into three categories: expressions which describe prices going up/going down/staying the same.

1   world price fell by 50%
2   reduction in the supermarket price of coffee
3   prices remained stable
4   a fall of 20%
5   the market picked up
6   market price of coffee rose by 50%
7   sustained its price

The passive

1 Read these facts about coffee and <u>underline</u> the passive verbs.

How is the passive formed?

Did you know ...? The word *coffee* is derived from the Arabic word *ogahwao*, which means wine or excitement. Coffee was known in Europe as 'Arabian wine'.

At one time coffee was used as a medicine. The coffee berries were fermented in water to make a strong tasting liquid.

Coffee is grown between the Tropic of Cancer and the Tropic of Capricorn.

One quarter to one third of the world's coffee is produced by Brazil.

Decaffeination is the natural or chemical process by which caffeine is removed from the green (unroasted) coffee beans. 97% of the caffeine is removed in the process.

2 Complete the table with the correct passive form for each tense.

Present Simple	… is grown …
Present Continuous	… is being grown …
Past Simple	
Past Continuous	
Present Perfect Simple	

3 Read the text again.

1 Which sentence includes an 'agent'?
2 List three reasons why an agent is not always needed. Check your answers on page 152.

....

....

....

4 Look at these two sentences and answer the questions. Both are grammatically correct.

a *One quarter to one third of the world's coffee is produced by Brazil.*
b *Brazil produces one quarter to one third of the world's coffee.*

1 Which sentence focuses more attention on the agent?
2 Which sentence focuses more attention on the person or thing affected by the action?

5 Complete the text with passive verbs in the present tense.

Chocolate **1** .... (make) from up to 12 different types of cocoa beans. First the beans **2** .... (sort) by hand before being roasted. Each type of bean **3** .... (roast) separately, which is time consuming but important.

Next, the beans **4** .... (load) into a machine called a 'winnower', which removes the hard outer shells of the beans. After this the beans **5** .... (mash) into a thick paste and sugar and vanilla **6** .... (add). This paste **7** .... (call) the 'chocolate liquor'.

Then the chocolate liquor **8** .... (heat) for up to 72 hours to make sure the liquid **9** .... (blend) evenly. Following this, the liquor **10** .... (temper) for several hours – repeatedly heated and then cooled.

Finally, the chocolate **11** .... (allow) to cool and harden before being packaged.

Writing

Task 1: Describing a process

In IELTS Writing Task 1 you may be asked to describe a process using information taken from pictures or a diagram.

The diagram below shows the process of milk production.

Write a report for a university lecturer describing the information shown below.

Time: 20 minutes

Write at least 150 words.

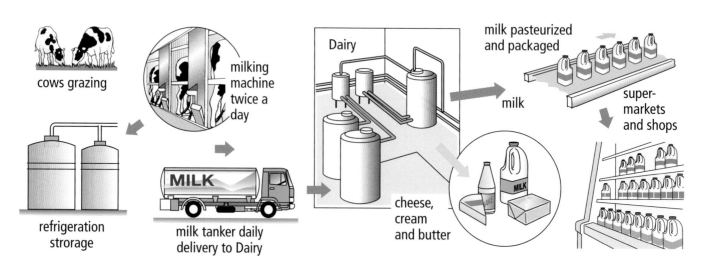

cows grazing

milking machine twice a day

refrigeration strorage

milk tanker daily delivery to Dairy

Dairy

milk pasteurized and packaged

milk

cheese, cream and butter

super-markets and shops

1 To write a good answer to this type of question you need to join the stages of the process together using sequencers. Find six sequencers in this extract from an information leaflet.

Milk is produced on farms from cows that are usually largely fed on grass. First, the cows are milked. This usually happens twice a day, using a milking machine. Then, the milk is cooled and
5 stored in large, refrigerated containers. Refrigerated tankers collect the milk on a daily basis from many small farms and deliver it to the dairy. Next, at the dairy, milk is made into various products including cheese, cream, butter and
10 liquid milk for drinking. Liquid milk is usually pasteurized in order to kill any bacteria. This is done by heating it to 72 degrees for a very short time, usually about 16 seconds. After this, the milk is again cooled and then homogenized,
15 which results in a product that does not separate into milk and cream. Following this, the milk is packaged in plastic containers, which could be of various sizes from 0.5 litres to 2 litres. Finally, these are delivered to supermarkets and shops.

2 There are also two connectors which give the purpose for doing something.

in order to kill any bacteria
which results in a product that does not separate into milk and cream

1 Which of these linkers is followed by a verb phrase?
2 Which of these linkers is followed by a noun phrase?

3 <u>Underline</u> the connectors in these sentences. Then add them to the text above in the appropriate places to give extra information.

1 *as this produces more milk overall than once a day*
2 *because it stays fresher longer at around 4 degrees C*
3 *and therefore ensure that it is safe for consumption*
4 *so that they can be sold*

Writing: further practice

4 Work in pairs. The diagram below shows how sugar is produced from sugar beets. Use the verbs in the box to describe the process verbally to your partner.

spin   cut up
unload   shake
wash   heat   filter
remove   add
extract

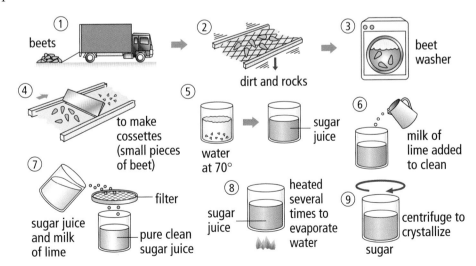

5 *Write a report for a university lecturer describing the information in the diagram about sugar.*

Time: 20 minutes

Write at least 150 words.

1 [23] Listen to this example of a Part 2 answer. Complete the missing details by identifying the topic question and the key points the speaker had to include.

Talk about
....

You should say:

● ....

● ....

● ....

And also say ....

Part 2

2 Practise talking about the points on this card to your partner for 1–2 minutes.

Part 3

3 In Part 3 of the IELTS Speaking module the examiner will ask you some questions related to the topic you were talking about in Part 2. Here are some examples of questions the examiner may then ask.

Nowadays there is more contact between countries on a global level so the world is often described as a 'global village'.

1 How can developed countries help less-developed countries?
2 Do you prefer to buy well-known international products or locally-produced goods?
3 What are the main roles of international organizations such as the United Nations?
4 How has global communication changed in the last 50 years?
5 Are cheap holidays and increased global tourism necessarily a good thing?

TIP

Do not give short answers in Part 3. Give a considered opinion and at least two reasons to support it.

Balancing the argument

1 [24] Listen to a possible answer to one of the Part 3 questions above and decide which question is being answered.

2 Listen again and answer these questions.

1 What two reasons in favour of this point does the student give?
2 What two reasons against this point does the student give?

3 Look at the tapescript on page 172 and answer these questions.

1 What phrase does the speaker use to indicate that there are arguments on both sides?
2 What phrase does he use to give his opinion?
3 What other phrases do you know to give opinions?

4 Part 3 can be quite challenging because you do not have an opportunity to prepare your answers first. Here are some phrases that may help you.

Useful language

If you think you understand the question, but you're not sure.
I'm not exactly sure what you mean, but …
That's a rather difficult question, but perhaps …

If you need a second to think about it.
That's an interesting question.
Let me see.

Revising and recycling vocabulary

Flash cards

These are cards with the word on one side and a translation, drawing or explanation on the other.

domestic

relating to people's homes and family life

1 Work in pairs. Discuss these questions.

1 How could you use them?
2 When could you look at them?

Grouping and categorizing words

fluctuate   negotiate
stable   commodity
sustain   vicious circle

2 Grouping vocabulary will help you to remember individual words. For example, if you had these words you could put them into categories as follows:

describing trends	related to business	collocations I like and want to use
fluctuate, stable, sustain	*negotiate, commodity*	*vicious circle*

victim   clear goals
truancy   constructive
detention   review

Look at these words from the previous unit. Put them into your own categories.

Other ways of remembering vocabulary

3 Here are some other ideas for learning vocabulary. Which of them have you tried?

1 I like keeping a vocabulary diary of words that I learn every day.

2 I try to use new words as soon as possible after I learn them.

3 I stick up a list of new words every week next to the bathroom mirror so that I can look at them while I am cleaning my teeth!

4 I write down each new word I learn ten times – it helps me to remember the spelling, too!

Find these words in the unit. Then check their meaning in your dictionary and record them.

key p.80	prior p.83	reveal p.83
symptom p.83	decline p.83	maintain p.84
impact p.83	suffer p.83	support p.88

What's the alternative?

> **alternative medicine** /ɔːlˈtɜːnətɪv medɪsɪn/ noun [uncount]
> medical treatment using methods that are different from the
> usual Western scientific methods.   *Macmillan Essential Dictionary*

1 What is the difference between conventional and alternative medicine?

2 Look at the statements below.

Put (C) next to those which you think are conventional medicine and (A) next to those which you think are alternative therapies. Then compare your answers with your partner.

1   having an injection
2   having a head massage
3   having an operation in a hospital
4   taking an aspirin/paracetamol for a headache
5   smelling oils
6   taking a herbal drink

3 If you have an illness, which of the following people would you consult? Why?/Why not?

1   a family member
2   a doctor
3   a chemist
4   an expert on alternative therapies

Classification

4 You are going to read a text about four different types of alternative medicine. Quickly read the text and classify the descriptions according to which of the following they refer to. Note that you may use the letters more than once.

Acupuncture (A)
Reflexology (R)
Iridology (I)
Chiropractic Manipulation (C)

1   invented 200 years ago
2   invented more than 2,000 years ago
3   has been successfully used as a painkiller
4   involves applying pressure to neck, elbows, knees and so on
5   can tell the practitioner every illness the patient has had
6   focuses on the hands and feet

Strategy

There may be many examples of each category or none.

Look for words and phrases in the text which are not exactly the same as the descriptions but have a similar meaning.

What's the alternative?

Are complementary and alternative therapies worth the billions of pounds that we spend on them? And do they have the same effects as conventional medicine? The scientific community is split over whether they work.

Acupuncture

What is it? Acupuncture is one of the oldest and most commonly used alternative therapies, originating in China more than 2,000 years ago.

What is involved? Therapists stimulate pressure points throughout the body, using needles. There are 2,000 pressure points which connect to 12 main and eight secondary pathways, which are called meridians.

What is the theory? Acupuncture is believed to regulate our spiritual, emotional, mental and physical balance, which is influenced by the opposing forces of yin and yang. When yin and yang are unbalanced, our qi (pronounced 'chee'), a form of energy, becomes blocked. Western scientists have been unable to explain acupuncture, since meridians do not correspond to either blood circulation or nerve pathways. No one understands fully how acupuncture works, but there is some evidence that stimulation of pressure points increases the flow of electromagnetic signals, which may trigger the release of the body's natural painkillers such as endorphins, or immune cells.

What is the evidence? Researchers at the University of Maryland, Baltimore, discovered that patients treated with acupuncture after dental surgery had less intense pain than patients who received a placebo. The same team has also shown that acupuncture can reduce the pain of osteoarthritis when used with conventional drugs to a greater degree than when these drugs are used on their own. Professor Ernst says: 'There is good clinical evidence that acupuncture works for osteoarthritis, migraine, dental and back pain. But there is good evidence that it does not work for some treatments, such as weight loss and smoking.'

Reflexology

What is it? Reflexology is the therapeutic manipulation of the hands or feet, which, according to practitioners, have areas that correspond to parts of the body.

What is involved? As well as manual manipulation by a qualified practitioner, it is now possible to buy reflexology guides and foot massagers for do-it-yourself reflexology.

What is the theory? The practitioner can diagnose the abnormalities by feeling the hands or feet; by massaging or pressing these areas, he stimulates the flow of energy, blood, nutrients and nerve impulses to the corresponding body zone and thereby relieves ailments in that area.

What is the evidence? A study published in Respiratory Medicine last year described 40 asthma patients who were given ten weeks of simulated reflexology and ten weeks of real reflexology. The researchers, using both subjective tests and objective lung-function tests, could find no evidence that the reflexology helped the patients' asthma.

Practitioners claim that reflexology can cleanse the body of toxins, increase circulation, assist in weight loss and improve the health of organs. Dr Barrett, vice-president of the National Council against Health Fraud in the US says: 'There is no scientific support for these assertions.'

Professor Ernst says: 'Practitioners use reflexology as a diagnostic tool and it does not work. It can be relaxing though.'

Iridology

What is it? According to iridologists, the eye contains a complete map of every body part. This therapy was invented in the early nineteenth century by a Hungarian physician, Ignatz von Peczely, who, during his childhood, accidentally broke the leg of an owl and noticed a black stripe appear in the lower part of the owl's eye.

What is involved? The practitioner looks into the patient's eye and checks the pupil's pigmentation against iridology diagrams. Several dozen configurations exist. Herbs are then prescribed to help the patient with their diagnosed illness.

What is the theory? Iridologists believe that a person's health can be diagnosed from the colour, texture and location of pigment flecks in the eye. Some claim that the eye markings can reveal a complete history of past illnesses.

What is the evidence? According to Dr Barrett, 'there is no known mechanism by which body organs can be represented or transmit their health status to specific locations in the iris'.

Professor Ernst recently published a review of the scientific literature on iridology, but he could find only four studies that had been carried out according to correct scientific procedure. These studies suggest that iridology is not a valid diagnostic tool.

Professor Ernst says firmly: 'Patients and therapists should be discouraged from using this method'.

Chiropractic Manipulation

What is it? Chiropractors diagnose and treat conditions that are due to mechanical faults in the joints, especially the spine.

What does it involve? A chiropractor manipulates joints using the hands to improve mobility and relieve pain.

What is the theory? If the spine is not functioning properly, it can cause irritation of the nerves that control posture and movement. This irritation can lead to 'referred' pain, which is felt in another part of the body. By manipulating joints, chiropractors stimulate the joint's movement receptors, which are sensors that provide feedback to the brain on where the joint is.

What is the evidence? Going to a chiropractor is now mainstream. The British Chiropractic Association reports 90,000 patient visits a week. It is one of the most regulated of the alternative therapies and yet, of those discussed here, it is potentially the most dangerous. Manipulation of the neck can tear the fragile tissue of the vertebral artery and, in the worse cases, result in a stroke.

In January this year the UCLA Medical School published a report on 681 patients who were given chiropractic help when they had lower back pain. After 6 months, 96 per cent of them still had lower back pain, leading the researchers to conclude that chiropractic manipulation had been ineffective. Professor Ernst says: The bottom line is that it works for a very limited number of spinal conditions, and mainly in the short term'.

Glossary

placebo: a substance that is not medicine, but the person taking it believes it is medicine, and so they get better

osteoarthritis: a serious medical condition that affects joints, eg the knees, making it difficult for you to move

ailments: an illness, usually not a serious one

Multiple choice

5 Choose the most suitable answer for questions **1–5**.

1 According to Professor Ernst, acupuncture is not effective if you
   A suffer from back pain.
   B have problems with your teeth.
   C get bad headaches.
   D want to lose weight.

2 Dr Barrett claims that reflexology
   A can help with weight loss.
   B cannot be proved to work.
   C could help solve asthma problems.
   D can be relaxing.

3 According to Professor Ernst, which therapy can sometimes help in the short term?
   A acupuncture
   B iridology
   C reflexology
   D chiropractic manipulation

4 According to Professor Ernst, which therapy should patients definitely avoid?
   A acupuncture
   B iridology
   C reflexology
   D chiropractic manipulation

5 Which of the following statements best sums up the overall content of this article?
   A Alternative therapies will be more common in the future.
   B There is scientific proof that all alternative therapies are effective.
   C There is no scientific proof that alternative therapies are effective.
   D Some alternative therapies can be effective but there are limitations.

6 In groups, discuss which of these alternative methods you would be most willing to try (or have tried already). Give reasons for your choice.

7 Do you know or have you experienced any other alternative medical techniques, eg aromatherapy.

Vocabulary

1 The parts of the body in the box appear in the reading text. Use them to label the diagrams.

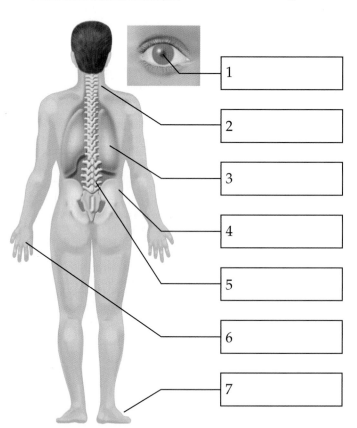

spine hands feet pupil lungs neck back

2 Match these verbs with their definitions.

1 to find out what physical or mental problem someone has by examining them
2 to use your hands to move or press against part of someone's body as part of a medical treatment
3 to press, rub and squeeze someone's body in order to reduce pain or help them relax
4 to make pain less unpleasant
5 to encourage a part of someone's body to work faster or better

a massage
b manipulate
c stimulate
d relieve
e diagnose

Real conditionals

A real conditional is used to talk about a possible situation and its likely results.

Possible situation	Result
(*If* clause)	(Main clause)
If I feel really ill	*I go to the doctor*

1 Read this short text on the common cold.

A cold is a contagious viral disease which infects the soft lining of the nose. If you have a cold, the most characteristic symptom is a runny nose.

Usually it is a mild condition and unless you are unlucky, recovery takes place within about a week.

It is most common during the cold winter months and affects children and adults of all ages. Most people will catch a cold two to four times a year.

If you have caught a cold you will be contagious from the day before the illness breaks out until one to three days after you feel better. When you cough or sneeze the infection will be spread by airborne droplets. It may also be spread by hand if someone has the virus on their hands and then puts them close to their eyes or hands. This is possibly the most common way of catching a cold.

Provided it clears up within one to two weeks, there is no need to see a doctor.

2 Look at the underlined sentences, which are all examples of real conditionals, and answer the questions.
1   What tenses or verb forms are used in the *if* clause?
2   What verb forms can be used in the *main* clause?
3   What other words can be used instead of *if*? Do these have the same meaning?
4   Is it possible to change the order of the clauses? What happens to the comma?

3 Look at these possible situations and use them to write real conditional sentences. Write two or three sentences for each situation.

0   Your temperature drops.

If your temperature drops, you'll be able to go back to work.
If your temperature drops, you may be able to go back to work.
You won't be able to go back to work unless your temperature drops.
Provided your temperature drops, you'll be able to go back to work.

1   You live in a big city.
2   You eat healthy food.
3   You wash your hands.
4   You feel really ill.

Intonation

1 Intonation is the way your voice rises or falls when you speak. Look at these sentences and answer the questions.

1 If your temperature remains high, you won't be able to go back to work.
2 If you stay at home, you'll get better quickly.

   Should the speaker's voice rise in the first clause or the second clause?
   Should the speaker's voice fall in the first clause or the second clause?

2 Work in pairs. What is the intonation in these sentences? Mark them, and say them to each other.

1 Unless you wash your hands, you'll probably catch a cold.
2 When you call the surgery, they make you an appointment.
3 Speak to a pharmacist if you need some advice.
4 If you take this medicine, you'll feel better.

3 25 Now listen and check your answers.

4 Look at the words with boxes above them. Does the speaker's voice rise or fall on each of them? Why?

☐ ☐
Popular alternative therapies include reflexology, acupuncture,

☐ ☐
herbal medicine and massage.

5 26 Listen to a conversation between a student and a lecturer. What do you notice about the student's intonation? How does the lecturer feel?

6 27 Listen to the same conversation again. What difference do you notice? Mark arrows on the tapescript on page 172 to show where the intonation rises and falls.

Part 2

Talk about an activity you have done to keep fit or healthy, eg, some kind of physical exercise, a diet, stopping smoking, etc.

You should say:

What the activity was
What you did exactly
How long you did this activity for

Also say whether the activity was successful or not.

Part 3

What are the best ways to keep healthy?
What type of food and drink should be avoided in a healthy diet?
Do you think healthcare facilities such as hospitals need to be improved?
How important is alternative medicine in today's society?
What sort of person does a doctor need to be?
What will medical treatment be like in 50 years' time?

Writing

Exam information

Task 2 of the Writing module examines your ability to express an opinion logically and clearly. It is usual in academic writing to express your opinions in a more impersonal way than when speaking.

Expressing your opinion

1 Read the extracts below and decide which of the categories each of the opinions belongs to. Write **A**, **B** or **C** next to sentences **1–6**.

A Formal – appropriate for academic writing or more formal speaking.

B Semi-formal – acceptable in some academic writing including IELTS and everyday speech.

C Informal – acceptable in more informal speech but not appropriate in academic writing.

0 Private healthcare is growing in popularity, but it is important to consider those who are unable to afford it. $\boxed{A}$

1 It's really terrible that people have to wait so long to get a hospital bed – don't you think so? $\square$

2 The majority of people accept that modern drugs are the most effective way to cure an illness. $\square$

3 I firmly believe that nurses should earn more money. $\square$

4 It could be argued that people should be offered more choice in the type of medical treatment they receive. $\square$

5 I totally disagree with the view that people should pay for their healthcare. $\square$

6 Modern drugs – the best way to cure an illness? What a load of rubbish! $\square$

Useful language

It is often said/thought that …
It is difficult to understand why …
Many people refuse to accept this …
It is (im)possible that …
It is (un)likely that …
It is (in)conceivable that …

TIP

In academic writing do not use contractions, eg *It's, there's, they're,* etc. or questions and question tags, eg *'Is that fair?', 'doesn't it?,'* etc.

When writing, aim to use more impersonal phrases. However, it is usually acceptable to use *'I'* or *'me'* occasionally in an IELTS essay.

Giving reasons to support your opinions

2 Match the opinions in the left column with the appropriate reasons on the right.

1 The majority of people accept that modern drugs are the most effective way to cure an illness.

2 I firmly believe that nurses should earn more money.

3 It could be argued that people should be offered more choice in the type of medical treatment they receive.

4 I totally disagree with the view that people should pay for their healthcare.

a They work long hours and have very stressful jobs.

b Some people might want to combine aspects of conventional medicine and elements from alternative therapies.

c The state should provide this for everyone from taxpayers' money.

d In many cases they provide the quickest cures.

3 Read these statements and use an appropriate phrase to give your opinion using a different example each time. Then add a reason to each of your opinions.

0   Modern drugs are always the best way to cure an illness.
I totally disagree with this view because in many cases the side effects are worse than the illness itself.

1   Doctors are overpaid.
2   Alternative therapists should get conventional medical training first.
3   A hospital is the best place to recover from an illness.
4   People should get medical advice before visiting other countries.

Using adverbs

apparently
naturally
fortunately
surprisingly
unfortunately
clearly   obviously

4 To show a reader what you think, you may use an adverb. Look at the words in the box and answer the questions.

1   Which one is used to say what seems to be true, when all the facts are not known?
2   Which one expresses a negative opinion?
3   Which one expresses a positive opinion?
4   Which one refers to something that is different from what you might expect?
5   Which three refer to an opinion that is what you might expect?

5 Put appropriate adverbs in these sentences. More than one may be possible as the answer will depend on your opinion.

1   .... , if you have a broken leg, the hospital is the best place to go.

2   .... , many people are suspicious of alternative medicine.

3   .... , some alternative therapies can be dangerous to your health.

4   .... , when doctors make mistakes, there are often serious consequences.

5   .... , 60% of people worldwide rely on non-conventional medicine.

6   .... , large drug companies take a significant interest in herbal medicine.

6 Answer this question.

'Currently there is a trend towards the use of alternative forms of medicine. However, at best these methods are ineffective, and at worst they may be dangerous.' To what extent do you agree with this statement?

Time: 40 minutes   Write at least 250 words.

Matching headings and note taking

Read one of two short texts about medical ethical questions.

1 Work with a partner.

Student A: Read *Genetically modified animals*. Match the paragraphs with the headings.

Student B: Read *Human cloning*. Match the paragraphs with the headings.

Genetically modified animals

Headings

Is this safe for humans?
What else could GM animals be used for?
What about the animals?
What are GM animals?

A ....

They are animals that have had genes from another species inserted into their DNA to give them new characteristics. For example, goats have been genetically engineered to produce spiders' silk in their milk.

B ....

1 To help with medical research – mice have been engineered with human genes to help scientists find out how to cure human diseases such as cancer.

2 To produce organs for transplantation into humans – animals have been genetically engineered with human genes so that human bodies will not reject their organs when transplanted.

3 To make more food – for example, fast growing giant salmon.

4 To change the nature of some animals – for example genetically engineering pet cats so that they don't have a hunting instinct.

C ....

No-one really knows what the effects may be. Some scientists are concerned that eating GM animals may be poisonous because new genes in animals may produce new proteins that the human body is not used to.

There is also a concern that GM animals will escape into the wild, where they will spread their modified genes. Wild fish could be displaced by the new super salmon, for example.

D ....

A lot of animals need to be killed to produce an animal with new genes – up to a hundred for each one. Genetic engineering also tends to produce ill or damaged animals – Dolly the sheep, the first cloned sheep, now has arthritis at a very early age.

Human cloning

Headings

Is it legal?
Why might people want to clone humans?
Why ban cloning?
How is it done?
What exactly is cloning?

A ....

Cloning is the creation of a cell or organism which is genetically identical to another. There are two main issues in talking about human cloning: the creation of a new person with the same genes as someone who is alive or has lived (reproductive cloning) and the creation of embryos in order to make new organs or cells for medical or research purposes (therapeutic cloning)

B ....

Dolly the sheep was cloned by transferring the nucleus of a body cell into an egg which had already had its nucleus removed. Human cloning would probably be done the same way.

C ....

It has been banned in the US and in Britain, Alan Milburn, the health secretary, announced recently that the UK will ban any attempt at human cloning.

D ....

1 To grow a new organ for transplantation.

2 For infertile parents, as a way to have a child.

3 To recreate a loved person who has died.

4 To try to live for ever by cloning yourself.

E ....

There may be a large number of miscarriages and deformities before a human is successfully cloned – it took 272 attempts to create Dolly the sheep, the world's first cloned sheep. It could also have a negative psychological impact on the person cloned because they would not be unique, and there would be confusion in families about relationships – a baby cloned from a man would be more like his twin brother than his son. Many religious groups also object because they see it as 'playing God'.

TIP

Note taking is an important skill. Pick out the main ideas and write them in short, simple sentences.

2 Read your text again and make notes under these headings.

Topic	
Explain what this topic means.	
Why some people are in favour of this.	
Why some people are against this.	
Your opinion on this topic.	

3 Work in pairs. Tell each other about your topic.

Listening

1 28 You are going to hear part of a seminar in which students are discussing human cloning. Listen and answer the questions.

Multiple choice

1 Cloning that is used for disease treatment is called
  A ethical cloning.
  B therapeutic cloning.
  C reproductive cloning.
  D human cloning.

2 According to Ron, clones
  A are non-thinking machines.
  B are robots.
  C would not behave alike.
  D could be used in wars.

3 According to Ron, reproductive cloning would have greatest advantages for
  A identical twins.
  B scientists.
  C governments.
  D infertile couples.

4 Which of these organs does Alice mention could be 'grown'?
  A a kidney
  B an eye
  C a liver
  D an intestine

5 According to Barry, therapeutic cloning is easier for people to accept, because
  A it couldn't really happen.
  B complete humans aren't being made.
  C it isn't 'playing God'.
  D everyone would benefit.

Avoiding repetition

A cough is a reflex action which happens when nerves are stimulated in the lining of the respiratory passages by something which should not be <u>there</u>. <u>This</u> may be dust, a piece of food, or phlegm caused by an infection. The lungs are normally a sterile environment, so if dirt or dust get into <u>them</u> <u>this</u> could cause <u>them</u> to become a breeding ground for bacteria and infection. Coughing clears the lungs. If <u>it</u> is painful you may try not to cough and <u>this</u> can be dangerous because <u>it</u> can lead to a chest infection and even pneumonia.

1 Look at the <u>underlined</u> words in the passage above. Pronouns (*they, them, etc.*) and other reference links such as *then*, *there*, *this*, *that*, *these*, *those* and *one* are used to help avoid repeating the same words and improve the *cohesion* of the text.

In the first sentence of the paragraph, *there* refers to 'the lining of the respiratory passages' earlier in the sentence. What do the other underlined words refer to? (This could be a single word or a whole phrase.)

2 Use reference links to replace the <u>underlined</u> sections.

0   Hay fever is an allergic reaction to dust and pollen. ~~Hay fever~~ *It* is the most common allergy in the world.
1   The nose, sinus, throat and eyes are most affected. <u>The nose, sinus, throat and eyes</u> become irritated and swell up.
2   People usually first start to get hay fever in childhood. <u>People</u> often find that the symptoms improve by the time <u>people</u> are thirty or forty.
3   About 5% of people worldwide have hay fever. <u>The percentage of people who have hay fever</u> is higher in industrialized countries, where about 15% of the population suffer from <u>hay fever</u>.
4   If you have hay fever, don't mow the lawn if you have <u>a lawn</u>, and try to keep your doors and windows shut, as <u>keeping your doors and windows shut</u> will help to keep out the pollen.
5   People sometimes think that hay fever happens in late summer, yet <u>hay fever</u> does not only happen <u>in late summer</u> but throughout the spring and summer.
6   Some of the symptoms of hay fever are red and itchy eyes, sneezing, coughing and a runny nose. <u>The symptoms of hay fever such as red and itchy eyes, sneezing, coughing and a runny nose</u> can be very unpleasant and seriously affect your quality of life.

3 Look at a paragraph you have written recently. Can you improve its cohesion and avoid repetition using appropriate reference links?

Unreal conditionals

An unreal conditional is used to talk about an unlikely or imaginary situation and its result.

unlikely or imaginary situation	result	
(*if* clause)	(main clause)	
If a child were cloned from his father	*he would be* *he might be* *he could be*	*more like his brother than his son.*

1 Look at the example above and answer these questions.

What tense or verb form is used in the *if* clause?
Is the speaker talking about the past?
What verb forms can be used in the second clause?
Is it possible to change the order of the clauses?

Note that in the *if* clause it is considered more correct to use *were* than *was*, although native speakers will often use *was*, especially in less formal situations.

2 Make unreal conditionals from these prompts. Use *would*, *might* or *could* depending on how sure you are about the result of these situations. Remember that the *if* clause can be first or second.

0   you/be/a human clone/you/be affected psychologically.
     If you were a human clone you would/could/might be affected psychologically.

1   human cloning/be legalized/people/live forever.
2   infertile parents/have children/human cloning/be legalized.
3   a human/be cloned/they/not be unique.
4   GM animals/escape into the wild/they/spread their genes.
5   we/make food/from GM animals/it/be poisonous.
6   GM animals/displace wild animals/they/escape into the wild.

3 Write your own sentences using unreal conditionals about:

1   Human cloning
2   GM animals

Editing 1

Learning to correct your own mistakes will help you improve your accuracy and get a better mark in IELTS, as well as being very useful for your future studies.

1 Look at the following extract from a student's piece of writing. One example of each type of error has been identified. Can you identify the other underlined errors?

Spelling	1	Word not needed	5
Punctuation	2	Wrong form	6
Wrong word order	3	Wrong word	7
Word missing	4	Wrong tense	8

*I am an international student **1** studing Business in **2** plymouth University.*

*I have been here for **3** eight months nearly. I belive I am **4** suited business*

*management because I worked in my father's company **5** the last year and*

I was learning practical business knowledge from my father. I am

***6** interesting **7** on many things. I enjoy listen music both classic and pop.*

*I like very much reading foreign novels because **8** it has provided an*

opportunity of learning the English.

2 Correct the errors the student has made.

3 Now find and correct seven more errors in the next paragraph. What type of error are they?

If I will get a good degree, I am going work in my father's company again. This is a best way for me to learning the business. I will work very hardly, that will please my father, and I hope I will soon promoted!

4 Find and correct errors in your own work. Make a note of errors that you often make and look for these first.

Find these words in the unit. Then check their meaning in your dictionary and record them.

involve p.90	subjective p.91	aspect p.95
represent p.91	overall p.92	ban p.97
claim p.91	appropriate p.95	opportunity p.101

9 Gadgets and gizmos

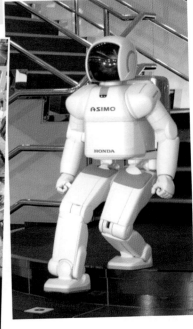

1 [cassette] 29 You are going to listen to a short lecture on the history of robots. First, listen to the lecture and try to put the names of the robots in the order they were built.

> Shakey   Joseph Jacquard's textile machine   the Analytic Engine
> Universal Automaton   Asimo   Talos

2 [cassette] 29 Look at questions **1–5** below and listen to the first part of the lecture again to complete them.

Questions **1–5**
Complete the notes below. Write **NO MORE THAN TWO WORDS OR A NUMBER** for each answer.

In 1774, two brothers from **1** .... created a boy robot that could draw and **2** .... About the same time
3 .... created a mechanical duck.
In **4** .... the Textile Machine was invented, and in 1834, the Analytic Engine, which was one of the first **5** ....

3 [cassette] 30 Look at questions **6** and **7** and listen to the second section.

Questions **6** and **7**
Which two facts are mentioned about robots in the twentieth century?
Circle **TWO** letters A–F.

A In 1970 a robot was developed that showed intelligence.
B The word robot was invented by a Czech playwright.
C The author Isaac Asimov first used the term 'robotics'.
D George Devol designed the first programmable robot in 1954.
E By the 1980s, General Motors was the single largest user of robots in the world.
F Two electric robots were demonstrated at the World's Fair in New York in 1940.

4 [📼] 31 Look at questions **8–12** and listen to the final section.

Questions **8** and **9**
Which two medical uses for robots are mentioned? Circle **TWO** letters A–F.

A providing artificial limbs
B acting as guides for the blind
C conducting surgical operations
D cleaning wounds
E writing prescriptions for medicine
F carrying out nursing duties

Questions **10–12**
Complete the notes below. Write **NO MORE THAN THREE WORDS FOR EACH ANSWER**.

In 1967, **10** .... was 10 years behind in robot technology.
Asimo looks human because he has **11** ....
He is designed to work in the home as 'a partner for people'.
He was the **12** .... to open the New York Stock Exchange.

Language focus 1

Present perfect vs. past simple

1 Look at these phrases from the listening text and divide them into three categories.

A Events and situations which occurred in the past.
B Events and situations which are occurring in the present.
C Events and situations which occurred/are occurring in a period of time which includes the past and the present.

1 … the god Vulcan made two female robots out of gold …
2 Since then, hundreds of robots have been designed and developed for a variety of uses …
3 This also used programs on punched cards …
4 Japan is now a world leader in robotics.
5 Now Honda have created Asimo, who has been made two-legged, in order to look more human.

2 Which two phrases show ideas of both the past and the present? Which tense is used in these two phrases?

Useful language

The present perfect links past events and situations with the present.

It is used to describe:

something that started in the past and continues into the present
Robots have been used for years in Japan. (They are still being used.)
an event which happened recently but the exact time is not important
An operation has been successfully completed by a robot.

---

1 Match the date of invention with the product.

		a	Pager
		b	Cellular phone
1	1926	c	Pop-up toaster
2	1979	d	Transistor radio
3	1955	e	Computer mouse
4	1964	f	Television
		g	Tape recorder

2 Now rank them in order of usefulness to society.

3 Work in pairs. Justify your ranking.

Skimming and scanning

4 Look at these questions about the gadgets and answer them using the descriptions in the text.

Which gadget

0   was used by nearly three quarters of Japanese homes in the mid-fifties?
    Transistor radio
1   may have later been used to keep goldfish in by some people?
2   didn't become popular in Europe until the 1950s?
3   was half the size of earlier models?
4   was used by hospitals as soon as it was introduced?
5   was developed after research carried out during World War Two?
6   has developed many new and different functions since first invented?

True, False and Not Given

5 Read the text in more detail. Do the statements agree with the information in the reading passage?

Write:
TRUE if the statement is true according to the passage
FALSE if the statement is false according to the passage
NOT GIVEN if the information is not given in the passage

1   Galvin changed its name to Motorola to encourage people to recognize their brand-name.
2   Bush TV became popular after the Second World War.
3   Cellular phones were first used in the UK in 1979.
4   Philips was the only company working on cassette recorders in the 1960s.
5   Many Americans had pop-up toasters before the 1950s.
6   A radar screen inspired an idea which eventually became the computer mouse.
7   The first televisions were 12 or 22 inches wide.
8   Transistor radios became immediately successful in Europe.

Cellular Phone

The cellular or portable phone was first developed in 1979 and, although exactly who invented it remains unclear, collective credit is usually attributed to Swedish giant Ericsson. (The first mobile phone network also opened in Japan the same year.)

While these initially bulky devices became reasonably commonplace during the 1980s, it wasn't until the mid-Nineties that massive developments in telephony technology brought the power of instant communication to everybody. The breeze block-size cellular phone of yore is now no bigger than a Swan matchbox, and functions not only as a phone but also as a fax, calculator, games console and most recently, a mini-PC.

Bush TV

The outbreak of the Second World War saw an explosion in the use of radio, not least because the various warring governments realised its potential as a powerful propaganda tool. After the war, the television – which has had probably the greatest impact on domestic lives, more than any other 20th-century invention – began its ascent. Like radios and record players, early televisions were housed in cabinets taking up half the living room, and cost as much as a car. When the cathode-ray tube appeared (capable of receiving high-definition broadcasts), the TV set began to downsize. In 1949, Britain's favourite model was the Bush set with a 12in or 22in screen and dark brown Bakelite casing. With the advent of 625-line tubes in 1964 (replacing 405-line), the Bush TV was phased out. Legend has it that many of these obsolete TVs were shipped out to Japan and turned into fish tanks.

Transistor radio

Seventy-four per cent of Japanese homes had a radio in the mid-Fifties but with typical prescience the Sony bosses reasoned "the figure is 74 per cent of households … if we look at the market in per capita terms, there are plenty of opportunities". The US forces had introduced much-coveted portable battery-powered vacuum-tube sets – of which there were many imitations – but even so, the personal radio market remained small. Sony's TR-55 radio was ahead of its time in that it used specially developed transistors, a printed circuit-board and was manufactured entirely in Japan (Regency was the first on the market, but it used unreliable imported transistors). After its launch, Sony still had to convince the public, so it sold transistors to other companies. If trannies appeared simultaneously under the Matsushita and Sanyo companies, then the reputation of the TR-55 would soon spread. Which of course, it did.

The Pop-up toaster

The first toaster with an inbuilt thermostat that ejected the toast before it had charred to a crisp was invented by American mechanic Charles Strite. McGraw Electric of Minnesota introduced his model to the market in 1926, but it wasn't until the 1930s that the toaster became a regular feature in American kitchens. The Sunbeam model T-9 was patented as an 'ornamental' toaster by George Scharfenberg in 1937. With its smooth, rounded chrome casing, Bakelite base and handles, it served both as an appliance and a status symbol. Typically, toasters didn't really catch on in Europe until the 1950s.

Pager

The Motorola trademark was so widely recognized in 1947 that the company changed its name from Galvin Manufacturing Corporation to Motorola Inc, but it wasn't until 1955 that it introduced the familiar 'batwing' M. A year later, it introduced a new radio communications product – a small radio receiver called a pager. It delivered a radio message to whoever was carrying the device and hospitals immediately adopted it.

Tape recorder

Dutch giants Philips developed the compact audio cassette in 1963. Measuring a mere 4in (10cm), it played back both mono and stereo recordings. The following year, the company introduced the first cassette recorder – the EL 3300. Meanwhile, in Japan, although Sony had begun developing cassette tapes, it hadn't yet penetrated the market. Both Philips and Grundig proposed the co-development of the new format and, because its cassette was smaller, Sony chose to go with Philips. Rather generously, Philips waived royalties (but did not give Sony exclusive rights) and made its technology free of charge to manufacturers worldwide. In 1966, Sony launched the TC-100 'Magazine-matic' cassette recorder. Weighing in at only 1.75kg, the TC-100 was less than half the weight of the lightest reel-to-reel and took half the space.

Computer mouse

The computer mouse was born of research that Douglas C Englebert conducted during World War Two. While staring at a radar screen, he figured it was possible to convert the markings on the screen to 'figural-visual' graphics, around which he could 'glide'. At the Augmented Human Intellect Center, which he set up in the Sixties, Englebert invented the multi-window display, hypertext, the mouse and groupware – the capabilities of which were demonstrated at a conference in 1968. Englebert applied for a patent for the mouse in 1967, which was granted in 1970 as 'the X-Y Position Indicator for a Display System'. This was for the mechanical design only and has long since expired. Xerox's advanced research arm, PARC, developed the GUI (Graphical User Interface) and, in 1984, Apple Macintosh introduced the now ubiquitous mouse – which had been refined by Hartmut Esslinger and his design team.

1 You will hear somebody describing trends in world music sales from the late sixties to the present day. What do you think are the most significant changes that have taken place in terms of buying and selling music in this period?

2 [cassette] 32 As you listen to the first part complete Fig. 1 from the information you hear. Note that the first part has been drawn for you.

3 [cassette] 33 As you listen to the second part fill in the missing information from Fig. 2.

Fig. 1

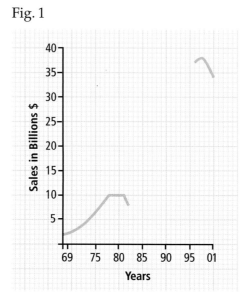

Fig. 2

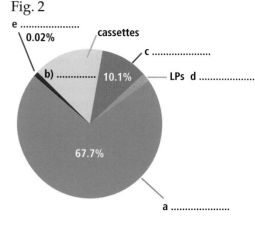

4 [cassette] 34 Now listen to the talk on Internet and mobile phone usage up to the year 2000 and complete the missing information on Fig. 3 and Fig. 4.

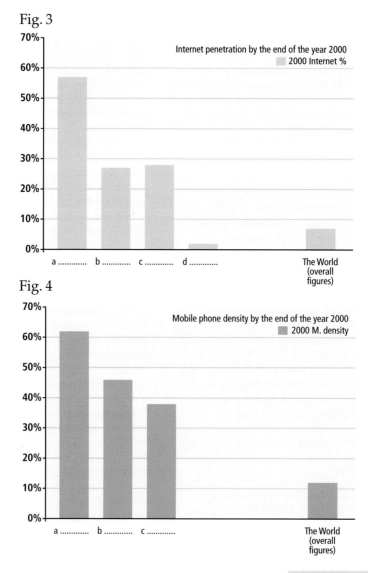

Fig. 3

Internet penetration by the end of the year 2000
2000 Internet %

a .... b .... c .... d ....   The World (overall figures)

Fig. 4

Mobile phone density by the end of the year 2000
2000 M. density

a .... b .... c ....   The World (overall figures)

Exemplification

It is always important to support your statements and opinions by providing examples.

1 Look at these sentences taken from the listening texts. The words in **bold** show ways of giving examples or referring to data.

1 Today I'm going to briefly outline the trends in world music sales from the late sixties to the present day **as shown** on this graph.
2 This increase was caused by new developments **such as** the introduction of stereo LPs and later audio cassettes.
3 America, **in particular**, experienced a tremendous growth in sales, but other European countries, **for example**, Britain and Germany also sold millions of CDs.
4 It may also be connected to the increased availability of hardware to copy music, **for instance**, CD burners.
5 Now if you could look at the following data: this pie chart **shows** that in the year 2000 CDs dominated the market and accounted for 67.7% of sales.
6 The bar chart **illustrates** the percentage of Internet and mobile phone users in different regions of the world by the end of the year 2000.

2 Use the different words or phrases in the box to fill in the gaps in the sentences.

shows   example   for example   such as   as shown
in the case of   like

1 This bar chart .... the percentage of households in the UK which had a DVD player in 2002.
2 .... in the graph, there has been a dramatic increase in DVD ownership in most countries in Western Europe.
3 Certain countries .... Germany have a large proportion of households owning DVD players, while in others, ... , Portugal, the figure is much lower.
4 In many countries the number of households possessing a DVD player doubled over a short period of time. A clear .... of this is the UK. While in a few countries the figure tripled, as .... Sweden.

> **Useful language**
>
> *For example / for instance* can go at the beginning, middle or end of a sentence (note the use of commas).
> *For example, Portugal's figures are much lower…*
> *while in other countries, for example, Portugal, the figure is much lower.*
> *Portugal's figures are much lower, for example.*

Drawing conclusions

It is important to summarize or highlight the main points that have been mentioned previously in a written text or presentation. Use these phrases to help you.

In conclusion/To sum up/Overall, ...
It can be concluded that ...
It is clear/evident that ...
The evidence suggests that ...

TIP

Essays do not have to have five paragraphs. However, as time is limited in the IELTS Writing Task 2 **4–6** paragraphs is likely to be appropriate.

3 Look at the data you completed in Listening 2. Complete the sentences.

Strategy

The concluding paragraph will sum up the main idea(s) discussed in the essay or give the writer's opinion but should not introduce any new topics.

0 *It is evident from the pie chart that minidiscs have not yet had a significant effect on world music sales.*

1 From the information shown on the graph, it can be concluded that ...
2 From the data shown on this pie chart, it is clear that ...
3 The evidence from the first bar chart suggests that ...

Speaking

1 Work in pairs. Take it in turns to answer these exam questions.

Part 2

Describe a machine that has made a big impact on your life.
You should say:
  What this machine is and what you use it for
  Why you bought this particular machine
  How often you use it
And also say what difference it has made to your life.

Part 3

1 What do you think are the most important inventions of the last 50 years?
2 How have mobile phones made communication easier?
3 Which household appliances do you think people need most?
4 What are the disadvantages of modern technology?
5 Do you think we rely too much on modern technology?
6 What technological developments might happen in the future in transport, education or health?

1 Look at the examples and complete the table.

Countable	**Uncountable**
A car	petrol
the car	the petrol
three cars	(three litres of) petrol
some cars	some petrol
How many cars?	How much petrol?

	Countable	Uncountable
Can use *a/an*	Yes	No
Can use *the*		
Can make the noun plural		
Need to use a quantifier to specify how much (such as a piece of)		
Can use *some*		
Can use *much*		
Can use *many*		

advice   advance
fact   pollution
money   toxin
transport
knowledge   news
progress   machinery
information   research
travel   dollar   journey
vehicle   politics
report   equipment
machine

2 Look at the nouns in the box (left). These are all words that you are quite likely to use in IELTS. Are they countable or uncountable in English?

3 Look at this extract from a student's essay. Find and correct five countable/uncountable errors.

Modern technology enables people to travel further and faster, for less money. This can only be a good thing.

To what extent do you agree with this statement?

Every year we make new progresses in technology and we think that this makes our lives easier. However, sometimes such advances only make our lives more difficult as we are expected to do more and more in the time available.

Now that transports are faster, we may visit another country and return all within a couple of days, which is very tiring. Travel is no longer something to be enjoyed.

Certainly, travelling long distances doesn't cost as many money as it did in the past. However, this encourages people to travel more frequently, which causes more pollution.

On the other hand, a travel does help people to gain more knowledge of other places and cultures. We can get a lot of informations from books, for example, but it will never have the same impact as actually seeing something for ourselves.

Writing 2

Task 1: Describing how something works

1 Work in pairs. Discuss these questions.

1 Would you like to go up in a hot air balloon? Why?/Why not?
2 How do you think they work?

2 The diagrams below show how a hot air balloon flies. Use a dictionary for any unknown vocabulary.

3 Draw lines between the labels and the relevant part of the diagram.

How a hot air balloon works

1
Hot air balloon used for sport
Rip-proof nylon – light and strong
Steel ropes
Basket

3
Propane gas burner
Powerful jets of flame heat air

2
Quick release rope attached to vehicle
Balloon inflated by fans (cold air)
Crown rope attached to balloon

4
Wind slightly different at different altitudes
Height maintained/ changed using the blast valve
Direction/ speed determined by wind – not much control
Safety harness

5
Blast valve – controls flow of gas to the burner

Infinitives of purpose

4 Look at these extracts from the model answer and answer the questions.

The balloon itself is made of rip proof nylon, <u>so as to</u> be light and very strong. A crown rope is also attached so as not to launch the balloon before the pilot is ready. A propane gas heater sends powerful jets of flame upwards into the balloon. This heats the air inside the balloon in order to lift it. When the air is hot, the balloon rises.

1   Look at the <u>underlined</u> phrase. Does it describe how something is used, or why it is used?
2   What verb form follows the underlined expression?
3   Which other expression in the example does the same thing as *so as to*?
4   What are the negative forms of these expressions?

5 Use the two expressions from the above exercise to improve these sentences.

0   Pilots wear safety harnesses because they don't want to fall out of the basket.
    Pilots wear safety harnesses so as not to fall out of the basket.
1   Balloons are usually bright colours because they should be easily visible.
2   Many people use mobile phones because they want to stay in close contact with their friends and colleagues.
3   People use computers because they want to get information quickly.
4   The public must use their cars as little as possible because it's important that they don't cause unnecessary pollution and congestion.

6 Look at the diagram of *How a hot air balloon works* and complete the model answer using **NO MORE THAN FOUR WORDS**.

A sports hot air balloon consists of a large bag attached by
1 .... to a 2 .... , in which usually up to
four people stand. The balloon itself is made of rip proof nylon, so as to
be light and very strong. A quick release rope 3 .... to a
vehicle and the balloon 4 .... by fans blowing cold air. A
crown rope is also attached so as not to launch the balloon before the pilot
is ready. A propane gas heater sends powerful jets of flame upwards into
the balloon. This heats the air inside the balloon in order to lift it. When
the air is hot, the balloon rises.

When the balloon is flying, its speed and direction 5 ....
by the wind which varies at different altitudes. However, the pilot, who
needs to wear 6 .... , can maintain or change the height by
7 .... This controls the flow of gas to 8 ....

7 Answer this question.

This is a diagram of a fire extinguisher. Using the diagram and the notes given, write a description of how this fire extinguisher works.

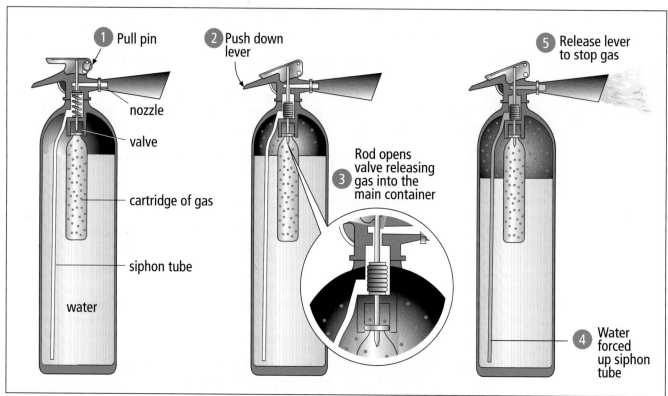

① Pull pin

② Push down lever

⑤ Release lever to stop gas

nozzle

valve

③ Rod opens valve releasing gas into the main container

cartridge of gas

siphon tube

④ Water forced up siphon tube

water

TIP

Don't write down everything you hear, just note down the key information.

Listening and writing simultaneously

1 📼 35 Listen and write down the titles and authors of the set books you need for a course in Economics.

	Title	Author(s)
1		
2		
3		

2 📼 36 Listen to Steven's telephone messages and complete the table below with the information he needs to return the calls.

Name of person who called	Why they called	Contact
1	Hopes to meet for lunch today to discuss contract.	....
2 Joe Fuller	Ring about	....
3	....	01923 4567622.
4	Now too late for lunch, could you .... ?	....

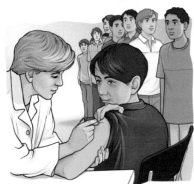

Editing 2

What have been the three most significant technological developments of the past century?

1 Work in pairs. Brainstorm what you think have been the three most significant technological developments.

2 Read this answer to the question. Did the writer mention the same three developments as you?

The past hundred years <u>see</u> enormous developments in technology. These are often labour saving and have made our lives much easier in many ways. <u>Morover</u>, they have also driven many dramatic changes in our society.

<u>It could be argue</u> that one of the most important advances is one which we now all take for granted, the telephone. It is now difficult to imagine a life where contacting someone involved seeing them face to face or writing them <u>letter</u>, which <u>would be take</u> days, or possibly weeks to reach them. Furthermore, in these days of mobile phones, the <u>equipments</u> needed to call someone has become so small and portable, that it seems to be only a step away from telepathic.

The second technological development that has had far-reaching consequences, is the computer, and the information technology revolution. The majority people in the developed world can use the Internet and email to easily access a news, any informations, or get an advice on everything from medical to financial problems.

Another development that has been of great social significance the washing machine. Prior to this, washing clothes was a major household chore, and was one reason why women were trapped in the home and unlikely to be able to have a career. With the advent of such labour saving devices, women had more freedom to choose to have a career as well as a family. They often say that this has had a very destabilizing effect on families, but it has also enabled many women to have satisfing careers, and I feel on balance, has been a very positive force in society.

Although many other advances could say to be significance, in my opinion these three are the ones which have changed society the most.

---

3 Answer these questions.

1 Look at the first two paragraphs. There are six mistakes <u>underlined</u>. Correct them and say why they are wrong.
2 Look at the rest of the text. There are eight more mistakes. Find them and correct them.
3 Compare your answers with your partner's.

Find these words in the unit. Then check their meaning in your dictionary and record them.

rank p.104	launch p.105	enable p.109
convince p.105	simultaneously p.105	significance p.113
attribute p.105	credit p.105	access p.113

Reading

Prediction

1 Work in pairs. Discuss the first paragraph of this text.

Do you think this is a good idea? Why?/ Why not?

Would you want to buy this software? Why?/Why not?

> A Engineers are working on software to load every photo you take, every letter you write – in fact your every memory and experience – into a surrogate brain that never forgets anything.

2 Read the rest of the text and answer the questions.

Software aims to put your life on a disk

B It is part of a curious venture dubbed the MyLifeBits project, in which engineers at Microsoft's Media Presence lab in San Francisco are aiming to build multimedia databases that chronicle people's life events and make them searchable. 'Imagine being able to run a Google-like search on your life,' says Gordon Bell, one of the developers.

C The motivation? Microsoft argues that our memories often deceive us: experiences get exaggerated, we muddle the timing of events and simply forget stuff. Much better, says the firm, to junk such unreliable interpretations and instead build a faithful memory on that most reliable of entities, the PC.

D Bell and his colleagues developed MyLifeBits as a surrogate brain to solve what they call the 'giant shoebox problem'. 'In a giant shoebox full of photos, it's hard to find what you are looking for,' says Microsoft's Jim Gemmell. Add to this the reels of home movies, videotapes, bundles of letters and documents we file away, and remembering what we have, let alone finding it, becomes a major headache.

E Before he speaks at December's Association for Computing Machinery Multimedia conference in Juan Les Pins, France, Bell is going to log everything he possibly can onto his MyLifeBits database.

F Apart from official documents like his passport, he is hoping to post everything from letters and photos, to home videos and work documents. All his email is automatically saved on the system, as is anything he reads or buys online. He has also started recording phone conversations and meetings to store as audio files. The privacy and corporate security risks are clear.

G Of course the system takes up a huge amount of memory. But Bell calculates that within five years, a 1000-gigabyte hard drive will cost less than $300 – and that is enough to store four hours of video every day for a year. Each media file saved in MyLifeBits can be tagged with a written or spoken commentary and linked to other files. Spoken annotations are also converted into text, so the speech is searchable, too.

H To recall a period in his past, Bell just types in the dates he is interested in. MyLifeBits then calls up a timeline of phone and email conversations, things he has read on the Web and any images he recorded.

I The system can also be used to build narratives involving other people, events or places. Searching for a friend's name would bring together a chronological set of files describing when you both did things together, for instance.

J Although MyLifeBits is essentially a large database, it may gradually become a repository for many of our experiences. Now that many mobile devices contain photomessaging cameras, you could save everyday events onto the system. 'Users will eventually be able to keep every document they read, every picture they view, all the audio they hear and a good portion of what they see,' says Gemmell. Bell believes that for some people, especially those with memory problems, MyLifeBits will become a surrogate memory that is able to recall past experiences in a way not possible with the familiar but disparate records like photo albums and scrapbooks. 'You'll begin to rely on it more and more,' he believes.

K A really accurate, searchable store of events could also help us preserve our experiences more vividly for posterity. Doug de Groot, who works on computer generated human beings called avatars and other types of digital 'life' at Leiden University in the Netherlands, says Bell's system could eventually form the basis for 'meet the ancestor' style educational tools, where people will quiz their ancestors on what happened in their lifetimes.

L A system like MyLifeBits was first suggested in 1945, when presidential technology adviser Vannevar Bush hatched the then farsighted idea of an infinite personal archive based on the emerging digital computer. His ideas also inspired the internet archive website.

Glossary

Surrogate – a replacement
Dubbed – called, or given the name of
Repository – a place where large quantities of things are stored
Disparate – belonging to very different groups
Posterity – the people who will live in the future after you are dead
Muddle – to put things in the wrong order

Multiple choice

Questions 1–3

3 According to the text, which **THREE** of the following are problems with conventional ways of storing our memories?

A We forget when things happened.
B It can be difficult to find a suitable shoebox to keep things in.
C It can be difficult to find where we have stored our photos, letters, etc.
D We forget what records of our past we have.
E We accidentally throw away important documents.
F We tend to keep too much stuff.

Questions **4** and **5**

According to the text, which **TWO** of the following are possible disadvantages of the MyLifeBits project?

A It can be unreliable.
B It may not be very secure.
C It can be very time consuming.
D It requires a very large amount of computer memory.
E It is very complicated to use.

Note completion

4 Complete these notes using **NO MORE THAN THREE WORDS** from the reading passage.

Bell is saving **1** .... onto his MyLifeBits database: letters, photos, home videos, work documents, emails and his online shopping or whatever he **2** .... online and on audio he is saving **3** .... and meetings.

Bell can remember what happened at a particular time in his life by keying in the **4** ....

Or he could look for **5** .... and find all the files that tell him what they did together.

Classification

Strategy

In this classification task you have to identify which people the statement refers to.

Scan through the text to find the names and read backwards and forwards around them.

Remember that the answer could be in direct speech: 'It's interesting' or reported speech: He said it was interesting.

Check your answers carefully as sometimes two people's opinions are very close to each other in the text.

5 Classify the following opinions as expressed by:

A Doug de Groot
B Gordon Bell
C Jim Gemmell
D Vannevar Bush

Note: You may use any answer more than once.

1 In the future we will be able to save most of what we see and hear.
2 MyLifeBits will be especially helpful for people whose memories are not very good.
3 Conventional ways of keeping photos and so on are not as good because the memories aren't all kept in one place.
4 Our descendants will be able to learn about our lives through systems like MyLifeBits.
5 The price of storing information will go down in the near future.

Expressing the future: predictions and intentions

1 Look at some ways of talking about the future taken from the text on pages 114 and 115.

1   … <u>engineers</u> at Microsoft's Media Presence lab in San Francisco <u>are aiming to build</u> multimedia databases …
2   … Before he speaks at December's Association for Computing Machinery Multimedia conference in Juan Les Pins, France, <u>Bell is going to</u> log everything he possibly can onto his MyLifeBits database.
3   … <u>he is hoping to post</u> everything from letters and photos to home videos and work documents.
4   But Bell calculates that within five years, <u>a 1000-gigabyte hard drive will cost</u> less than $300 …
5   Although MyLifeBits is essentially a large database, <u>it may gradually become</u> a repository for many of our experiences.
6   Bell believes that for some people, especially those with memory problems, <u>MyLifeBits will become</u> a surrogate memory …
7   Doug de Groot … says Bell's <u>system could eventually form</u> the basis for 'meet the ancestor' style educational tools …

2 Classify each of the statements as
A   a prediction or future possibility (in someone's opinion).
B   an intention or plan.

3 What grammatical similarities can you see between the verbs in A and the verbs in B?

4 Look at the timeline below. Complete the sentences using some of the language from the text on page 114.

This evening	Next weekend	Your next holiday	Next year	In 10 years

0   This evening I … *aim to get my essay finished before I go out.*
1   This evening I …
2   Next weekend I …
3   On my next holiday I …
4   Next year …
5   In 10 years' time …

5 Now find out information about your partner's future and report back to the class.

TIP

You may be asked questions about your future plans in Part 1 of the Speaking module.

TIP

Understanding the meaning of prefixes can help you guess the meaning of new words.

Prefixes

1 How do you know that all these words are negative?

impossible   unlikely   inconceivable

2 Look at the table below. Write the prefixes next to their meanings and add an example for each.

il-   re-   mis-   dis-   micro-   trans-   anti-   pre-

	not or to reverse an action	
	again or back	
	across	
	against	
	wrong or badly	
	not (with some words beginning with l)	*illegal*
	before	
	small	

3 These prefixes indicate a number. Write them in the correct box.

dec-   tri-   uni-   ~~mono~~   qua-   bi-

1	2	3	4	10
mono				

4 Guess the meanings of these words. Then check your answers in a dictionary.

1   unicycle   4   monorail
2   mismanage   5   prepackaged
3   microbiology   6   transnational

1 Work in pairs. Discuss these questions.

Think about a school that you have been to.

How many pupils were there?
What were the teachers like?
Was there one you particularly liked or hated? Why?
Who was your best friend?
Were you happy there?
How many of your old school friends have you kept in touch with?
Do you know what they are doing?
Would you like to know?

Describe it in as much detail as you can to your partner.

1 [📼] 37 You are going to hear a discussion about a web site called 'FriendsReunited', which helps people to contact old school friends. Look at questions 1–6 below and listen to the first part of the discussion to complete them.

Questions **1–3**

Complete the table using **NO MORE THAN TWO WORDS** for each answer.

Julie McDonald	1	Has been looking at the site.
Dr 2 .... Jones	Psychologist	Has done several studies into 3 ....

Questions **4–6**

2 Complete the flow chart using **NO MORE THAN THREE WORDS** or **A NUMBER** for each answer.

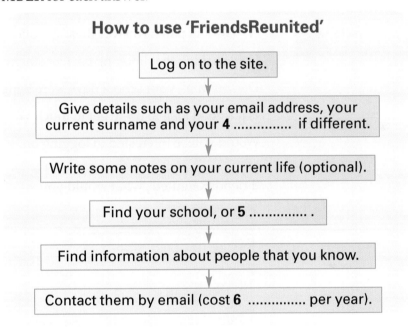

How to use 'FriendsReunited'

Log on to the site.

⬇

Give details such as your email address, your current surname and your **4** .... if different.

⬇

Write some notes on your current life (optional).

⬇

Find your school, or **5** ....

⬇

Find information about people that you know.

⬇

Contact them by email (cost **6** .... per year).

Exam information

Spelling is important in the IELTS Listening module – your answers MUST be spelt correctly, and they MUST make grammatical sense.

3 [📼] 38 Look at questions **7–12** and listen to the second part.

Questions **7–12**

Circle the correct answer.

7 Dr Jones compares the website to
   A a soap opera.
   B a comedy.
   C history.
   D a family reunion.

8 Dr Jones thinks .... shouldn't become too important to us.
   A our own success
   B money
   C other people's opinions
   D material goods

9 The biggest problem of this site is for people who have
   A been in love.
   B been successful.
   C remained childless.
   D been unsuccessful.

10 Another problem that the site might cause is if someone
  A has too many bills.
  B is ill.
  C doesn't like their job.
  D is in an unhappy partnership.

11 Dr Jones thinks that 'FriendsReunited' is .... for most people.
  A harmless
  B damaging
  C useful
  D funny

12 Which one of the following does Dr Jones say is a problem?
  A Curiosity
  B Addiction
  C Insecurity
  D Voyeurism

Speaking 2

1 Work in pairs. Answer these questions.

Do you think that 'looking back nostalgically' is a bad thing?

Do you think your school days were better than your life now, or not? Why?

Is it a good idea to try to get in touch with old friends and acquaintances?

Would you be interested in logging on to such a site in your country?

If you had to describe yourself and your life in 20 words for a website like 'FriendsReunited', what would you write?

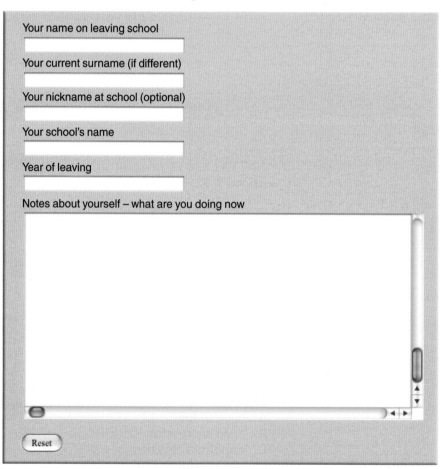

Your name on leaving school

Your current surname (if different)

Your nickname at school (optional)

Your school's name

Year of leaving

Notes about yourself – what are you doing now

Reset

TIP

When you learn a new word, mark the stress. Check that you know the stress patterns in the other words in the same family, too.

Stress patterns

Usually, words in the same family have related and predictable stress patterns.

nostalgia   nostalgic   nostalgically

However, in some word families, the stress patterns depend on the form of the word.

1 Look at the dictionary entry for this word family. Which of the three forms has a different stress pattern?

qualify /ˈkwɒlɪˌfaɪ/   **qualified** /ˈkwɒlɪˌfaɪd/   **qualification** /ˌkwɒlɪfɪˈkeɪʃn/

2 Now look at the word families below. Use a dictionary to find out which three have a shifting stress pattern.

(adj)	(n)
secure	security
responsible	responsibility
compulsive	compulsion
curious	curiosity
addictive	addict
annoying	annoyance

1 Work in pairs. Take it in turns to practise these exam questions.

Part 2

Talk about the emails or letters you write to a particular person

You should say:
  Who the person is you email or write to
  What you usually say in your emails or letters
  How often you communicate
And say why you send emails or letters to this person.

Part 3

What other uses will computers have in the future (eg in education, health, leisure, etc.)?
Do you think children will benefit more from using computers?
Do you think the Internet will change shopping patterns in the future?
How do you think the Internet might affect the way people work?
Are there likely to be more negative effects from the Internet in the future?

Use the language in the box to talk about your predictions. Remember to give reasons for your opinions.

	will probably will definitely	become more popular. change the way people work. help children to learn.
The Internet	could might may	

Task 2: Analysing the question

1 Look at this IELTS Writing Part 2 question and <u>underline</u> the key words.

Present a written argument or case to an educated reader with no specialist knowledge of the following topic.

In the last 20 years there have been significant developments in the field of information technology (IT), for example the World Wide Web and communication by email. However, future developments in IT are likely to have more negative effects than positive.

To what extent do you agree with this view?

Is the main topic Computers in general or Information Technology?
Will you write about the past, the present or the future?
Do you need to give detailed factual information or your own ideas and opinions?

TIP

Even if you have strong feelings about the topic, consider both sides of the argument.

Brainstorming ideas

First, think carefully about the topic in the question. Under the two headings below, write three more positive and negative future developments.

Positive
Lot of information on Internet
Communication quicker/easier

Negative
Difficult to navigate Internet
Reduces face-to-face contact

Balancing your argument

It is important to consider both sides of an argument and this can be done at sentence level and/or in the essay as a whole.

2 Sentence level

Positive
The World Wide Web provides useful information

Negative
The World Wide Web is difficult to navigate

1 Which of the sentences below is more positive about using the World Wide Web?
  a While the World Wide Web can provide useful information, it is often difficult to locate exactly what you are looking for.
  b The World Wide Web can be difficult to navigate. However, it does provide a lot of very useful information.

2 Now read this sentence and answer the questions.
While email communication is quick and easy, it often reduces face-to-face contact.

There are two points:

Point 1
Email communication quick and easy

Point 2
Reduces face-to-face contact

  1 Which point does the writer agree with most?
  2 Does the point that the writer wants to emphasize come first or second?
  3 In the second clause, which word replaces 'email communication'.
  4 What other contrasting linking words could be used instead of 'while'?

3 Look at the positive and negative points you brainstormed about future IT developments. Write sentences showing balanced arguments by following these stages:

Decide which point you want to emphasize.
Change the noun of the second sentence to a pronoun if necessary.
Add a suitable contrasting linker.

Example:
While there are likely to be new types of computer entertainment for children in the future, it is important that they do other activities too.

3 Balancing the essay as a whole

With a 'To what extent....' type of question, you need to decide how far you agree or disagree with the statement and why.

Work in pairs. Read the question again and briefly tell your partner what you think, giving clear reasons why.

Strategy

The main section of an essay contains the main ideas, opinions and supporting information organized into clear paragraphs which progress logically from the introduction to the conclusion.

In coherent essays each paragraph has a main idea and information or examples to support this main idea. The sentence that contains the main idea is known as the **Topic Sentence** and is usually, but not always, the first sentence in a paragraph.

4 Read the sample answer and answer these questions.

Does the writer agree or disagree with the statement?
Does the writer think future IT developments will be more positive or more negative?

Sample answer

In recent years the developments in information technology have been dramatic. For example the World Wide Web and email communication have significantly affected modern life. Although many more advances are likely to take place in the future, it is quite possible that not all the changes will be beneficial.

On the one hand, the Internet, one of the most significant developments in IT, will continue to have a very powerful influence and there is no doubt it has many positive aspects. Global communication has become much quicker and cheaper as there is now easier access to more information. The World Wide Web and email communication have also been used for educational purposes.

On the other hand, there are likely to be serious negative effects in our lives. I believe that the Internet will be used even more for illegal activities such as pornography or information theft. In addition, I think more computer viruses will be created and this might cause large networks to crash.

In addition, more and more people will be able to access the World Wide Web all over the world and this may cause many people to become addicted to surfing, email or chat lines. As a result, face-to-face communication and social contact will be reduced which I think could have negative effects on human relationships in general.

In conclusion it is clear that developments in IT will undoubtedly continue at a rapid pace but there will be many negative effects. What people need to do is carefully consider and aim to minimize the drawbacks so as not to let our lives be totally dominated by information technology.

5 Now look back at the essay in more detail. Summarize the main points in each paragraph to see how the writer balances their argument by giving clear reasons and examples.

Recording vocabulary

1 Look at these two methods of recording vocabulary. Which do you prefer and why?

A list

floppy disk
hard drive
hardware
Internet
keyboard
monitor
mouse
program
screen
software
virus

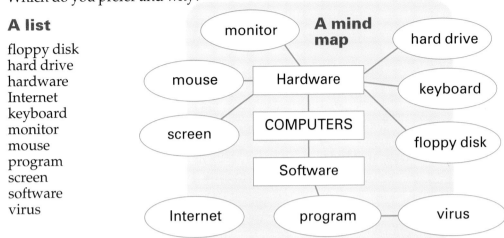

A mind map can be a useful way of recording and revising vocabulary. They are usually topic based. You can draw one as you study a particular subject and then continue to add words to it as you learn them later on.

Check you know all the words in this mind map by looking in a dictionary.

2 In the box below are some more words associated with computers and the Internet.

> memory   an email address   a chatroom   spam   click
> a CD ROM   surf   post   drag   a website   scroll down
> crash   search   save

Work in groups. Add the words in the box to the mind map above. To do this you will need to organize or categorize them.

1 Divide the words into those you think are specifically connected with the Internet and those simply connected with computers.
2 Now divide each group into nouns and verbs (some may be both).
3 Now you may wish to divide your groups again into words with similar or related meanings.
4 Now draw your mind map.

There is no one correct answer. Organize the words in the way that is best for you.

Find these words in the unit. Then check their meaning in your dictionary and record them.

link p.114	conventional p.115	classify p.116
secure p.115	generate p.115	emphasize p.123
chronological p.115	express p.116	locate p.123

1 Look at these advertisements.

What is the product being advertised in each one?
Who are the adverts aimed at?

2 Each one of these adverts would break the code set up by the New Zealand Advertising Standards Association (ASA) and similar codes around the world. In pairs, decide what you think the specific problem is with each advert.

Now look at the statements taken from the ASA code below and match each advertisement (**A–D**) with the correct section from the code (**1–8**).

Note: There are more extracts than advertisements.

1 Advertisements must not portray violence, undue aggression, or menacing or horrific elements likely to disturb children.

2 Advertisements should not encourage anti-social behaviour or depict children behaving in an anti-social manner, eg vindictiveness and bullying, unless the purpose of the advertisement is to discourage such behaviour.

3 Children should not be urged in advertisements to ask their parents to buy particular products for them.

4 Advertisements must be clearly recognisable as such by children and separated from editorials or programmes. If there is any likelihood of advertisements being confused with editorial or programme content, they should be clearly labelled 'advertisement' or identified in an equally clear manner.

5 Advertisements should not suggest to children any feeling of inferiority or lack of social acceptance for not having the advertised product.

6 Advertisements should take into account the level of knowledge, sophistication and maturity of the intended audience. In particular special care should be taken when communicating with younger children who may have a lack of ability to comprehend the purpose of advertising and differentiate between it and non-advertising messages.

7 Advertisements should not depict toy weapons which are realistic (in size, shape and colour) and can be confused with real weapons.

8 Advertisements, except safety messages, should not show products being used in an unsafe or dangerous manner, or which would be unsafe if used by children without proper supervision.

Were you surprised by any of these rules?
Do you know the rules about advertising to children in your country?
Do you think advertising could be harmful for children?
Do you think advertising to children should be banned?

Identification of beliefs or arguments

1 Match the beliefs or arguments in the statements (**1–5**) with the people or organizations mentioned in the text (**A–F**) on pages 128 and 129.

Note: You may use any answer (**A–F**) more than once.

1 Children as young as seven or eight understand what advertisements are trying to do.
2 Poor families see too many advertisements showing products they cannot afford.
3 Children do not understand the difference between adverts and television programmes.
4 Children are more easily influenced than adults.
5 Television companies need the money from advertising to make good children's programmes.

Strategy

To help you with this type of task, first underline the people or organizations in the text to help you locate the answer more quickly

A Dr Brian Young
B Nigel Walmsley
C Independent Television Commission (ITC)
D Stephen Colegrave
E Lars Maren
F The Children's Society

Multiple choice

2 Read the two texts on pages 128 and 129, which argue for and against a ban on advertising to children.

Rupert Howell believes that the current rules on children's advertising in the UK are

A effective in protecting children.
B not tough enough.
C better than the rules in other countries.
D likely to encourage pester power.

3 According to Rupert Howell's article, the results of banning children's advertising could include

Choose **THREE** answers.

A an increase in the number of imported children's programmes.
B an increase in the cost of imported children's programmes.
C an increase in the cost of producing children's television programmes.
D a reduction in the quality of children's programmes.
E a reduction in the quantity of children's programmes.
F a reduction in competition between children's programme makers.

4 According to Helen Seaford, the British advertising industry is worried by Sweden's proposals because

A advertising allows people to make choices.
B Sweden is not the only European country to ban children's advertising.
C British children watch more adverts than in any other European country.
D even four year olds can recognize well known brands.

5 The cost of advertising toys and games

A is less than the cost of advertising chocolate and snacks.
B has increased dramatically in recent years.
C is more in the UK than elsewhere in Europe.
D has an impact on their price to the consumer.

It is the thorniest issue facing advertising – should children be influenced by the hard sell? As Sweden pushes to introduce a Europe-wide ban, a major conference will battle over the arguments. Here, two experts kick off the debate.

NO says Rupert Howell

A In 1991, Sweden introduced legislation to ban television advertisements that 'purposefully' attract the attention of children under the age of 12. Why? Because the Swedish government accepted research stating that most children could not recognise the difference between advertisements and programmes until they were 10. Lars Maren, deputy director of the Swedish ministry of culture, says that television advertising leaves children 'vulnerable to abuse and deception by adults' and 'they do not understand what advertising is'.

B It is widely expected that it will use its presidency of the European Union to push for the introduction of such a ban Europe-wide. The UK government has indicated that it will resist this suggestion from Sweden. That resistance should be supported by the UK media and advertising industry. Let me explain why.

C Let's take research first. The UK has done its own. Dr Brian Young of Exeter University found clear evidence that children's advertising literacy develops from the age of four and that by the age of seven or eight they have developed a good understanding of the purpose and intent of advertising. Last year, the Independent Television Commission scrutinised the rules governing toy advertising and concluded that 'as a result of exposure to media technology of all kinds, the children were quick to assimilate and interpret what they were shown'.

D In 1996, the Ministry of Agriculture, Fisheries and Food commissioned research into the role of advertising in children's choice of food. It found that 'there is no serious evidence to suggest that advertising is the principal influence on children's eating habits.'

E I am convinced that children have an undoubted ability to view and assess advertising competently and with discernment. Kids are not gullible. They're smart. I also have faith in the advertising industry's regulations, which pay special regard to the child audience and contain provisions to ensure that children are not exposed to inappropriate commercial messages or influence.

F Advertising in the UK – and that includes all advertising, not just children's – is conducted responsibly. The ITC's regulations are taken seriously and constantly revised. The number of complaints from viewers is minuscule.

G But there's another aspect to television advertising: a ban on children's advertising would have a catastrophic effect on the funding of independent children's television programming. Nigel Walmsley, Carlton TV's chairman, has made the point that ITV last year invested £35m in original programme commissions for children's television. He says that if ITV did not have the advertising revenue of around £40m that it earns from children's advertising, then 'quite simply, it could not make original children's programmes'. The alternatives would be to remove children's programming from the ITV schedules, or broadcast low-cost programmes brought in from the US and elsewhere, or turn children's television into subscription-only channels. Quality would suffer, and the range of programmes would fall away.

H Advertising is fun. It's educational, too. Advertising helps children to discriminate and to grow up. And, just like adults, they know, or they soon learn, that they can't automatically have what they see advertised. A ban on television advertising would be an infringement of the freedom of commercial speech. If it's legal to sell, it's not only acceptable to advertise it, but essential. Advertising encourages new product development and it fosters competition, which always benefits consumers – including children.

Rupert Howell is chair of HHCL & Partners and president of the Institute of Practitioners in Advertising

YES says Helen Seaford

I Children watch a lot of television. Advertisers know this. And they know that advertising influences children. It gets children and their parents to buy more of what they're selling. The number of advertisements watched by British children tops European league tables. On average British children watch 18,000 adverts per year and those in low-income families see most.

J It's not surprising with statistics like this that the advertising industry is worried by the prospect of Sweden seeking to extend to the EU the controls they and three other European countries have put in place with considerable success.

K A great deal of research has been done – using a variety of different methods – and the conclusion is that children's understanding of advertising develops in line with their own psychological, emotional and intellectual development. So it is not until the age of 12 that their understanding of advertising can be said to be comparable to that of adults. For example, four-year-olds are already 'brand conscious' and nine-year-olds will respond immediately when asked about product preferences.

L At the Children's Society, we see some of the poorest families struggling to keep their heads above water while being bombarded with images of consumption they can ill afford – in a country where one child in five needs free school meals because they live in a low-income family. £50m a year is spent on advertising chocolate and snacks to children, whereas advertisements for healthy foods during children's television time are unheard of.

M And finally there is the issue of pester power. Most parents want to bring their children up well, with decent moral standards and a balanced outlook on life. It is deeply insidious for advertisers constantly to undermine them in what is anyway a difficult task.

N Listen to Stephen Colegrave of Saatchi and Saatchi (an advertising company): 'Children are much easier to reach with advertising. They pick up on it fast and quite often we can exploit that relationship and get them pestering their parents.'

O It is against this highly resourced barrage of aggressive marketing that our current rules must be judged. In the past six years, spending on advertising toys and games during children's television has risen from £26m to £150m.

P The Swedish initiative to extend their ban on advertising during children's television is welcome. Children do not need to practise watching advertisements as a preparation for adult life. and good-quality children's television could be financed by subscription or by reserving a section of the licence fee.

Q As we struggle with the question of how to ensure that children see high-quality television, it is the interests of the child which should be at the centre of our attention.

Helen Seaford is Head of Planning at The Children's Society, a children's charity.

Modals of obligation and prohibition

1 Look at these sentences, taken from the reading texts. They all contain modal verbs.

0 Advertisements **must not** portray violence, undue aggression, or menacing or horrific elements likely to disturb children.
1 Children **should not** be urged in advertisements to ask their parents to buy particular products for them.
2 Advertisements **must** be clearly recognisable as such by children and separated from editorials or programmes.
3 Advertisements **should** take into account the level of knowledge, sophistication and maturity of the intended audience.
4 Children **do not need to** practise watching advertisements as a preparation for adult life.

Put the modals from the sentences above into these categories.

Obligation			Prohibition	
strong	weak	lack of obligation	strong	weak
			must not	

2 Now do the same for the modals in these sentences.

1 Advertisers **have to** follow certain rules about advertising to children.
2 Advertisers **ought not to** encourage children to eat too many snacks.
3 Parents **ought to** monitor the advertising that their children see on TV.
4 Parents **don't have to** respond to 'pester power'.

3 Look back at the texts. What form of the verb follows modals?

Now look at the other sentences from exercises 1 and 2. Some of the verbs are followed by a different form of the verb. Which ones?

4 Work in pairs. How are these modals expressed in the past? Fill in the table.

Present time	Past time
ought to	*ought to have + past participle*
should	
have to	
must	
don't need to	
don't have to	
shouldn't	

5 Here are some other lexical expressions to express prohibition and obligation.

Prohibition

Advertising toys **is banned** …
Advertising toys **is forbidden** …
Advertising toys **is not allowed** …
There is a ban on advertising toys …

Obligation (weak)

Parents **are expected to** monitor …
Parents **are supposed to** monitor …
It is the parents' responsibility to monitor …
Parents **are responsible for** monitoring …

6 Write about five rules in your country.

Example:
You should carry your driving licence with you, but you don't have to.
There is a ban on smoking in public places.

7 🔊 39 Listen to a tutor giving feedback on a student's work. Write down any examples you hear of language to talk about obligation/lack or obligation or prohibition.

Reading 2

1 You should spend about 20 minutes on questions **1–13** which are based on the text below.

The Global Product –
the world as a single market?

A For businesses, the world is becoming a smaller place. Travel and transportation are becoming quicker and easier, communications can be instantaneous to any part of the world and trade barriers are breaking down. Consequently, there are tremendous opportunities for businesses to broaden their markets into foreign countries. The challenge facing those promoting products globally is to determine whether marketing methods should be the same across the world or if they should be adapted to different markets based on specific cultural factors.

B Many theorists argue that, with the 'shrinking' of the world, global standardisation is inevitable. Over time, and as economies develop, it has been suggested that consumer buying patterns will blend into one another and national differences may disappear. Kellogg, the American breakfast cereal producer, has been very influential in challenging consumption patterns in countries outside the United States. In France, for example, breakfast cereals were almost unheard of, and market research suggested that the market was closed to companies like Kellogg. However, today, there is growing demand for breakfast cereals across France. Nevertheless, the standardisation of products for worldwide consumption in this way is rarely the most effective strategy as is evident from an analysis of the following key aspects of global marketing.

C First of all, it is considered better business practice by many large, established companies to change their products from one country to the next. Take the example of Coca Cola. The recipe for this drink is changed to suit local tastes – the brand in the US is much sweeter than in the UK, whilst in India the product's herbs and flavourings are given more emphasis. In terms of the car industry, it would be too expensive for manufacturers to develop and build completely different vehicles for different markets yet a single, global model is likely to appeal to no-one. In response to varying needs, Nissan, for example, sells in 75 different markets, but has eight different chassis designs. The Ford Mondeo was designed with key features from different markets in mind in an effort to make its appeal as broad as possible. The best policy, as far as most multi-national companies are concerned, is to adapt their product to a particular market.

D Secondly, it is also important to consider whether a product should be launched simultaneously in all countries (known as a 'sprinkler launch') or sequentially in one market after another (a 'waterfall launch'). In practice, most companies producing consumer goods tend to launch a new product in one or two markets at a time rather than attempt to launch a product across a range of countries at a single time. Many high-tech products such as DVD players reached the market in Japan before reaching the UK. Hollywood films are often seen in the United States weeks or months before they arrive in other countries. For example, Star Wars Episode One was launched in the US in May 1999, in the UK in July 1999 and in Spain in August 1999.

E The advantage for firms is that it is easier to launch in one market at a time. Effort and concentration can be focussed to ensure the best possible entry into the market. Moreover, for technical products especially, any initial problems become apparent in a single market and can be corrected prior to launch elsewhere. Even though this method can be time-consuming, it is usually a safer approach than a simultaneous launch. Despite this, in certain highly competitive markets such as computer chips, companies such as Intel tend to launch their new products internationally at the same time to keep the product ahead of its competitors.

F The final consideration when planning to enter a global market, rather than assuming the product will suit all markets, is to take cultural differences into account. Prices have to be converted to a different currency and any literature has to be translated into a different language. There are also less tangible differences. It is quite possible that common practices in one country can cause offence and have grave consequences for business success in another. In one situation in China, a Western businessman caused offence to a group of local delegates because he started to fill out the paperwork immediately after shaking hands on a deal. Completing the legal documents so soon after the negotiations was regarded as undermining the hosts' trust. Knowledge about such cultural differences is absolutely vital.

G Therefore, if a company is attempting to broaden its operations globally, it must take the time to find out about local customs and methods of business operation. Equally important is to ensure that such information is available to all necessary workers in the organisation. For example, in order to attempt to avoid causing offence to passengers from abroad, British Airways aims to raise awareness of cultural differences amongst all its cabin crew.

H It can be concluded that global standardisation of products to 'fit' all markets is unlikely to be the most viable option. Marketing methods employed will depend on many factors, such as the type of product, the degree of competition, the reputation of the firm and/or the brand, the state of the economy into which the product is to be launched and how and when to launch. In short, the key to marketing success on a global level is to have sufficient information on how cultural differences are likely to affect the marketing of a product and then allow the appropriate decisions to be made.

Matching headings to paragraphs

Questions 1–7

2 Choose the most suitable headings for paragraphs **B–H** from the list of headings below. Write the appropriate numbers (**I–X**) after each question.

N.B. There are more headings than paragraphs so you will not use all of them.

> **List of Headings**
>
> i   Launching a new soft drink product
> ii   The main benefits of the single market launch
> iii   Researching cultural differences and providing information
> iv   The lack of cultural differences in the world today
> v   Examples of launching a product in one market at a time
> vi   The emergence of global marketing and its challenges
> vii   The world as a single market: a successful case
> viii   Specific cultural differences to consider
> ix   Different markets, adapted products
> x   Success in the global market – key factors

0   Paragraph A   *VI*

1   Paragraph B
2   Paragraph C
3   Paragraph D
4   Paragraph E

5   Paragraph F
6   Paragraph G
7   Paragraph H

Note completion

Questions 8–11

3 Using the information in the passage complete the notes using **NO MORE THAN THREE WORDS**:

Global marketing

World getting smaller – chance for businesses to

8 .... globally.

Companies treating world as single market with standardised product not always appropriate.

Therefore, factors to take into account:

<u>A. Adapt the product to specific markets</u>
eg Coca Cola **9** .... Ford (Mondeo)

<u>B. Compare different ways to launch the product</u>

10 .... launch   or   'Waterfall' launch

All countries at same time   One or two countries after another

Example: Intel   **Example: DVD players**

                                     and **11** .... movies.

<u>C. Consider cultural differences</u>
Acquire knowledge and raise awareness about common business practices and local customs

Multiple choice

Questions **12** and **13**

4 Choose the appropriate letters **A–D**.

12 According to the writer

A all types of company adapt their products to different markets.
B having the same product for different markets can never be successful.
C car manufacturers are unlikely to develop totally different models for different parts of the world.
D it is better to launch a product in different markets at the same time.

13 The writer concludes that

A marketing strategies depend mainly on the product type.
B successful promotion of a product depends on being informed about cultural differences.
C the launch of a product is not particularly significant.
D companies can gain global success by setting up offices all over the world.

Review of useful language

Work in pairs. Talk about products that are advertised in your country. Are they advertised using different methods? Why?
What aspects of advertising are unethical or unacceptable?

1 Look at this IELTS Writing Task 2 question:

Present a written argument or case to an educated reader with no specialist knowledge of the following topic.

Some of the methods used in advertising are unethical and unacceptable in today's society.

To what extent do you agree with this view?

Time: 40 minutes   Write at least 250 words.

Strategy

Check you understand the question
Brainstorm ideas
How many paragraphs do you need?
Express your opinions with supporting evidence
Present a balanced argument
Remember to include an introduction and a conclusion
Use linking words to help make your essay easy to understand

TIP

When writing an IELTS essay, do not use contractions.

2 Place the phrases on page 135 under the correct heading in the Useful language box.

Useful language

Introducing an essay
In the 21st Century, many people.........   Possible results

Sequencing points   Giving examples

Expressing opinions: agreeing with a point   Adding a point

Expressing opinions: challenging/disagreeing with a point   Drawing conclusions

---

Phrases

Taking X as an example …
In recent years there have been many developments in …
This might lead to …
After examining the issues it is evident that …
Firstly, it is important to consider …
I would accept the view that …
There is no evidence to suggest that …
Overall, it is clear that …
The final point to consider is …
It is certainly true to say that …
It is not only … but …
I am unconvinced that …
This would have an effect on …
To illustrate this point …
And there is the issue of …

TIP

Remember in IELTS Writing Task 2 you have 40 minutes and need to write a minimum of 250 words.

3 Write an answer to the question.

Speaking

1 Work in pairs. Discuss these questions.

Think of an advert you have seen recently.

Where did you see it? (TV, radio, billboard?)
What was the brand name?
What was the target market?
Was there a slogan?
What was memorable about it?

2 Advertising companies use many different methods to persuade you to buy their products. Work in pairs. Match these methods (**a–h**) with their definitions (**1–8**).

a Giving information about a product
b Based on scientific evidence
c Endorsement by a famous person

d Anti-advertising
e Special offers
f Positive images
g Repetition
h Comparison

1 The name of the brand is used so often that people begin to associate it with the product, eg Hoover for vacuum cleaners.
2 Simply explaining what the product is. Usually used for new products.
3 This method focuses on why the product is better or cheaper than other similar products.
4 A pop star or an actor says that they like/use the product.
5 An advert says the product has been 'scientifically tested' or 'proven to be better in tests' – often used for cleaning products, eg washing powder.
6 Price – a clear direct method – it's only £9.99!
7 This is a modern method, which is designed to be amusing. It makes fun of other methods of advertising.
8 The product is advertised using attractive visual images, eg healthy, young, beautiful people, beautiful scenery, cute children or animals, etc.

Which of these methods do you think is the most effective? Why?

Classification

Questions **1–5**

1 ⌷⌷ 40 You are going to hear three radio adverts. Write

A if the statement refers to the first advert.
B if the statement refers to the second advert.
C if the statement refers to the third advert.

1 This advert uses the 'special offer' method.
2 This company has a web site.
3 This advert uses the 'anti-advertising' method.
4 This advertises a product that you don't have to pay for immediately.
5 This company claims to be cheaper than its rivals.

Multiple choice

Questions **6** and **7**

2 ⌷⌷ 41 You are now going to hear some Marketing students discussing the same three adverts in a seminar. Listen and answer these questions.

6 The first advert is for

A a commercial organization.
B a shop.
C a government organization.
D a non-government organization.

7 Which of these statements is true for the first advert?

A It is advertising a product, not a service.
B The methods it uses are unique.
C It is expensive.
D It advertises something that other companies probably don't offer.

Questions **8** and **9**

3 Circle which **TWO** adverts use repetition 1st 2nd 3rd

Questions **10–14**

4 Complete the notes below using **NO MORE THAN THREE WORDS**
10 The main method used in the second advert is the ....
11 The offers in the second advert end ....
12 The woman in advert 3 feels .... about the language of advertising.
13 Anti-advertising is often effective because it is ....
14 According to one of the students, people believe what they are told, even if it is ....

Which advert do you think is the most effective and why?

Finding useful language in reading texts

One of the best ways of improving your writing is to notice and use useful language in the texts you read.

1 Look back at the text on pages 128 and 129 and find the following:

Paragraph B
A way of saying many people think something will happen.

Paragraph D
A way of saying that something cannot be proved.

Paragraph E
A way of saying that you really believe something.

Paragraph G
A way of introducing a new argument.

2 Look at these examples of making two points. Which sounds stronger?

If it's legal to sell, it is acceptable and essential to advertise it.
If it's legal to sell, it is not only acceptable to advertise it, but essential.

3 What dependent prepositions are used with the following phrases?

Paragraph D
Have an influence ....

Paragraph E
Be exposed ....

Paragraph G
Have a (catastrophic) effect ....

Paragraph K
Be comparable ....

Write your own example sentences to help you remember these words and phrases.

Advertising to children is **not only** *acceptable,* **but** *a positively good thing, as it allows them to learn that they cannot have everything they want.*

Children should not **be exposed** *to too much advertising.*

Find these words in the unit. Then check their meaning in your dictionary and record them.

differentiate p.126	ensure p.129	broaden p.131
legislation p.128	constantly p.129	feature p.131
discriminate p.129	original p.129	unethical p.134

Listening

1 Work in pairs. List three reasons why students go abroad to study.

How do you think an education in another country can help you be successful in your future career?

2 You are going to listen to someone talking about how his British education has contributed to his success.

[cassette icon] 42 Read the questions below and <u>underline</u> any important words.

3 Answer the questions using **NO MORE THAN THREE WORDS**.

1 Why are the audience visiting the university?
2 What are the speaker's best memories of university about?
3 Where is the speaker from?
4 The speaker says that in his country a degree from a British university helps to get ....
5 What subject did the speaker graduate in?
6 After graduating, which organization did the speaker work for in his own country?
7 Having a British degree shows employers that the student is ....
8 When did he finish his post-graduate course?

⭐ **Top tips for the IELTS Listening module** ⭐

4 What is important to remember when you are doing the Listening module? Look at the hints below and predict what the missing words might be.

5 [cassette icon] 43 Listen to a teacher giving some hints to students about the Listening module. Complete the notes below using **NO MORE THAN THREE WORDS**.

1 .... carefully so you know exactly what type of answer is required, eg multiple choice, no more than 3 words, etc.
2 From the information given, try to predict the context for the task. Who will be speaking, why and on what topic?
3 Read the .... in order to identify the type of information required, eg name, location, date, etc.
4 As you listen write your answers down as quickly as possible but try to keep concentrating.
5 If you are not sure of the answer, make a note of .... to include later.
6 In the extra time section transfer your answers carefully then quickly ....

Collocations

6 Match the words in list A with those in list B. If necessary, use your dictionary to find out what they mean. They were all included in recording 42.

List A		List B	
a field	academic	factor	competition
a strong	a major	of study	sector
the public	fierce	excellence	reputation

7 Check your answers in the listening script on page 175.

Check your answers in the listening script on page 175.

Pronunciation

Schwa in unstressed syllables

1 Look at these words. Which syllable is stressed in each?

What is the sound of the vowels which are underlined?

preparation   technical   presentation   support
university   professional   considered

Remember

Many unstressed syllables, whatever the vowel is, have the schwa /ə/ sound. Make a note of /ə/ as well as the stress pattern when you learn a new word.

2 Use a good dictionary to mark the stress and the /ə/ (there may be more than one) in these words.

organizing   tertiary   politician   inspiration   audience

Reading 1

1 Everybody sometimes worries about exams. Look at these statements. Tick the ones that apply to you.

My future will be ruined if I fail/don't get the grades I want.
I am not lucky with exams.
I'm just no good at exams. Some people are, I'm not.
Exams get more difficult as you work your way up.
I haven't covered the syllabus, so I won't pass.
The exams will expose me as a phoney, or stupid.

Work in pairs. Discuss your answers.

Yes, No, Not Given

2 Do these statements reflect the views of the writer in the reading text on page 140.

Do these statements reflect the views of the writer in the reading text on page 140.

Write:
YES if the statement reflects the views of the writer
NO if the statement contradicts the views of the writer
NOT GIVEN if it is impossible to know what the writer thinks about this

1   If you fail an exam, it may be impossible to get the job that you want.
2   Many people who have not passed exams have had satisfying careers.
3   Practice is not as important as luck.
4   A large percentage of people who fail an exam, fail again when they re-take it.
5   It is unhelpful to compare yourself with others.
6   Exams become more difficult at higher levels because of the greater technical skill or knowledge required.
7   Examiners expect you to have thoroughly studied the syllabus.
8   Time management is an important factor in exam success.

Dispelling irrational beliefs about exams

Here are six common beliefs that are held about exams and their outcome, all of which have some elements of false assumption or irrationality about them.

My future will be ruined if I fail/don't get the grades I want.

Examinations are an important way in which professional groups in our society select their membership. Success in them does open doors to particular jobs and careers. Lack of success will mean certain jobs and careers are not immediately open to you, at least at the level of entry you originally intended. Some may be closed altogether.

However, happiness, wealth, peace of mind, a rich experience of life, meaningful status in the eyes of others, a worthwhile career, a useful job and a sense of purpose and self-belief as a human being do not depend upon examination results. The world is teeming with people who have found that to be the case whether they have passed examinations or not.

I am not lucky with exams.

Some people do appear luckier than others at games of chance, with acquiring money, in making relationships, or in achievements. There is certainly an aspect of chance involved in which questions appear on the examination paper, compared to those you have chosen to revise.

However, examination technique can be learned very effectively by anybody, and the element of luck reduced to a minimum. Practising what you have to do in the examination room is the key, as Arnold Palmer, one of the most successful golfers of all time is quoted as saying: 'The more I practise, the luckier I get.'

I'm just no good at exams. Some people are, I'm not.

There are two elements in this view. One is that your past performance will determine any future attempts. The other is that in comparing yourself with others, you find your performance inadequate. The answer to the first element is that the past frequently *is* escapable. By buying this book and reading this page, you have set out to become 'good at exams'. Other people are largely irrelevant. They do not depend for their success upon your lack of success or vice versa.

Exams get more difficult as you work your way up.

Difficulty is a relative word. What is difficult at one age is not at another; what is difficult when you are inexperienced in an activity is not when you are experienced; what is difficult to one person is not for another; what is difficult on one day is not on another.

Certainly, examinations demand more specialist knowledge, understanding and expertise, as you move through their different levels. They may become more technical, involve more abstract ideas and concepts, involve you in greater specialization and more specialist jargon. This does not mean they become more difficult.

I haven't covered the syllabus, so I won't pass.

It isn't irrational to fear that you haven't revised or understood enough of the subject you have studied to pass a course. It may be true that if you have studied and revised little of the course you have left yourself at risk of failing to accumulate sufficient marks to pass it. It may be that you will need some luck in the choice of questions that appear in the exam paper.

However, it is irrational to believe that if you haven't covered the syllabus you are inevitably going to fail the course. Few courses, teachers or students 'cover the syllabus' in the sense of paying full and equal attention to all parts of it. Examiners do not expect you to have done so. They accept that there are bound to be areas where you are under-prepared, unclear or uninformed. They want to see you demonstrate what you do understand and what you have prepared.

Even when you are struggling to find enough questions to answer, you will find that many have some kind of link or association with your course content. You will normally find some links which you can build up into an answer.

The exams will expose me as a phoney, or stupid.

You may experience the common fear in many students that the exams will expose them as inadequate, lacking in even basic know-how or understanding. There is a further underlying fear – that the exams will expose your lack of ability to be tackling that level of study, whether it be GCSE or post-graduate qualifications. The fear can be further intensified by fantasies of the judgement by examiners, tutors, family and friends. Examiners can be seen as poised with red pens to expose your ignorance and misunderstanding. You may feel that family and friends see you as stupid, or that tutors will reject you, as they feel let down or fooled.

The focus on ability is largely irrelevant. The vast majority of people who set off on a course of study are quite capable of successfully completing it. It is practical life circumstances, false beliefs and negative attitudes, which, coupled with poor study techniques, may cause problems – not lack of ability.

Summary completion

3 Complete the summary using words from the box.

> effective   increase   ineffective   ability   reveal
> disappointed in   satisfied with   decrease   change
> experience   developing   furious with

Many students are worried that exams will **1**........................ their lack of intelligence, or inability to be studying at a particular level. They can also imagine that examiners will deliberately judge them harshly or that teachers, friends and family will be **2**........................ them.

In fact, **3**........................ is not usually the problem. Most people who start a course are able to complete it successfully. More often, problems are caused by the student's negative attitude, **4**........................ learning strategies or simply the circumstances of their life at the time.

⭐ Top tips for the IELTS Reading module ⭐

4 Complete each of the tips (**1–6**) below with a sentence (**A–H**) from the box.

0   Make sure you understand the questions.   ....*C*....
1   To improve your reading speed and comprehension you   ....
    should read in English as much as possible.
2   Don't use your dictionary to check the meaning of every   ....
    new word.
3   Read the title and the first paragraph carefully.   ....
    Reading the first line of each paragraph (the topic sentence) is
    also a quick way of getting a good general idea of the content.
4   You won't have time in the exam to read all of the text very   ....
    thoroughly.
5   Remember that the questions usually follow the same order   ....
    as the text.

A   These techniques will help you to understand what the text is about.
B   Try to guess the meaning from context if you can.
C   Underline key words to help you know what to look for before you start
    reading the text.
D   Remember that your answers must be spelt correctly.
E   As well as books, try newspapers, websites, magazines, even
    advertisements.
F   Answer the questions in order, but if you find one is very difficult, don't
    waste time – leave it until the end.
G   Read the text quickly to locate which section contains an answer and
    read that section carefully to find it.
H   Write your answers in pencil.

Which two sentences are not used? Do they also give good advice?

Vocabulary

Collocations – *make* and *do*

1 Decide if the words or phrases in the box are preceded by either *make* or *do* and then put them in the appropriate column.

> a course   money   a list   an arrangement
> a decision   progress   a choice   an experiment
> an exercise   a speech   some work   an appointment
> research   a noise   a loss   the washing up
> a degree   a mistake   housework   up your mind

make	*do*

2 Decide which of the collocations above could be put into one of these categories.

Relating to study	Domestic tasks	Relating to money
Do homework	Do shopping	Make a profit

3 Now put the remaining words into suitable categories. Be prepared to give reasons.

4 Fill in the gaps in the sentences with *make* or *do* in the appropriate form.

0   What plans have you ....*made*........ for your next holiday?
1   Have you ever .... a speech in public?
2   How good are you at .... decisions?
3   How often do you .... the housework?
4   What do you think is the best way of .... a lot of money quickly?
5   When do you usually .... your homework?
6   How do you feel about .... mistakes when you speak English?

5 Work in pairs. Discuss the questions.

⭐ **Top tips for recording, remembering and using new vocabulary** ⭐

6 Underline the correct verb to complete the sentences.

1 *Set/identify/achieve* yourself a goal of learning 10 new words every week. Choose the words you learn carefully.
2 *Invent/experiment/make* with different ways to record new vocabulary, eg mind maps, pictures, etc. (See Unit 1)
3 *Invest/buy/look* a good learner's dictionary.

4 As well as writing down what a new word means *do/get/make* a note of pronunciation, collocations, an example sentence, part of speech, etc.
5 Try to *use/experiment/create* the new vocabulary in suitable contexts.
6 Try to *revise/view/watch* vocabulary as often as possible. Just ten minutes a day can really make a difference.

IELTS speaking

You are now going to carry out a whole IELTS Speaking module. You will also be assessing your partner's performance in this section.

1 Part 1

In Part 1 of the Speaking module you will be asked to talk about familiar topics.

1 Write down possible questions that the examiner might ask you on the following topics.

Where .... ? (Country/City/Town)
What .... ? (Family)
What .... ? (Study/work)
Where/Who .... ? (Live now)
How/What .... ? (Free time/interests)
What .... ? (Plans for the future)

2 Read the information in the box and underline the most suitable answer.

Part 1 tips

Be *relaxed and friendly/formal and serious.*

Give *one word answers/longer answers* to the questions.

Answer the questions *clearly giving details/quickly without details.*

It is possible/not possible to prepare for this section.

3 Work in pairs. Take it in turns to ask your partner the questions. Then give your feedback.

2 Part 2

1 Read the information in the box below and <u>underline</u> the most suitable answer

> **Part 2 tips**
>
> You have to talk about one *topic/more than one topic* which *should be easy to talk about/you may not know anything about.*
>
> *Start talking immediately/Make some notes or think before you start speaking.*
>
> *Organize your reply as it is on the card/speak freely without worrying about organizing your reply.*
>
> You *don't need to/should* mention all the points on the card.
>
> You need to speak for a minimum of *1 minute/2 minutes.*
>
> At the end of this section the examiner will *ask you a simple question/comment on your performance.*

2 Read the information in the box below. In Part 2 you have 1 minute to prepare a **1–2** minute talk on a topic. You can make notes if you wish.

> **Part 2**
>
> Describe a particular situation or event in which you were successful, eg an exam, a sporting event, a competition, etc.
>
> You should say
>
> What the situation/event was
>
> When and where it happened
>
> What preparation was involved
>
> You should also say how you felt about achieving this success.

3 Take it in turns to speak for **1–2** minutes on this topic. When the time is up, ask one of these questions:

> Do you think you will achieve more success in the future?
> Would you like to achieve more success in the future?

> Give feedback to your partner on their performance.

3 Part 3

1 Read the information in the box below and <u>underline</u> the most suitable answer.

> **Part 3 tips**
>
> This section will *focus on a new topic/be related to the topic in the previous section.*
>
> This section will be more *personal/general.*
>
> You are expected to give *one word/more extended answers.*
>
> *You may need to talk about the past, present and future/you will only be talking about the future.*
>
> You will need to *ask questions about the topic/give opinions on the topic.*
>
> *Ask/do not ask* the examiner for your band score at the end.

2 Work in pairs. Ask each other these Part 3 questions.

How is success measured in today's society?
How important do you think it is to have a good job?
Do you believe successful sportsmen and women earn too much money?
Can you name a successful person you admire and say why?

Do you think money equals success?
Do you think there is too much pressure on young people to pass exams?
Do you believe pop-stars earn too much money?
Can you name a successful person you admire and say why?

Then give feedback to your partner on their performance.

☆ Top tips for the IELTS Speaking module ☆

- Greet the examiner.
- Be polite, friendly and relaxed.
- If you don't hear something, ask the interviewer to repeat it.
  eg *'Sorry, could you repeat that please.'*
- If you really don't understand something, it is probably better to be honest rather than give incorrect information.
  eg *'Sorry, I don't quite follow.'*
  'Sorry, I don't understand.'
- It is better to be simple and clear rather than complicated and unclear.
- Practise the Speaking module with your friends or in class.
- At the end of the interview say *'Thank you'* and *'Goodbye'*.

Writing 1

Task 1

1 Read this Task 1 question. Does any of the data surprise you?

The pie chart below shows the origins by continent of all students who came to England from abroad to study in 2001. The bar chart shows the numbers of students coming to England from seven Far Eastern countries in the same year.

Write a report for a university lecturer describing the information below.

Time: 20 minutes   Write at least 150 words.

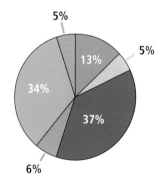
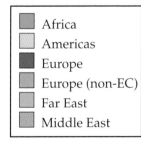
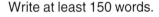
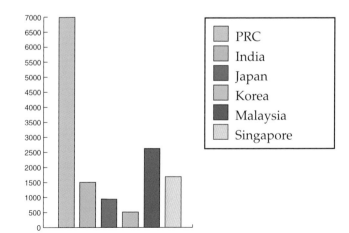

☐ Africa	
☐ Americas	
☐ Europe	
☐ Europe (non-EC)	
☐ Far East	
☐ Middle East	

☐ PRC	
☐ India	
☐ Japan	
☐ Korea	
☐ Malaysia	
☐ Singapore	

IELTS Task 1 Writing checklist

- Read the instructions and the question carefully.
- Make sure you understand the data in the diagram.
- Think about how to group the information – are there any significant trends over time or significant patterns in the data?
- Write the report, remembering not to copy the wording in the question.
- Begin your report with a general statement about the data.
- Do not use repetitive statements about the data.
- Leave a few minutes to check grammar, vocabulary, spelling and punctuation.

Now write your report.

2 Read this sample report and then answer the questions.

The pie chart below shows the percentage of all students who studied in the UK from abroad in 2001. The students from Europe (EC) and from the Far East were the most (37% and 34% respectively). The number of students who came from Americas, Europe (non-EC) and (i)<u>Middle East</u> were very (ii) <u>samiler</u> and very low (5%, 6% and 5% respectively). (iii)<u>Africa</u> student accounted for 13% of the (iv)<u>all</u>.

The bar chart (v)<u>illustrate</u> the numbers of students from seven different areas and countries who studied (vi)<u>at</u> UK in 2001. China had the largest number of (vii)<u>the</u> students about 3,900. The second and third largest number of students come from HK and Malaysia, both over 2,600. The follows were the students from Singapore, India and Japan, the number from 1700 to 900. The last number of students was those who (viii) <u>come</u> from S. Korea about 500.

---

1 Does the content of the report include

1 all of the data in the chart and graph, including all of the exact numbers?
2 most of the significant information in the chart and graph, including some of the figures, which may have been approximated?
3 information from the chart and graph, but also extra information that is not relevant?

2 The examiners will be looking for these features in a written answer.

1 a full and relevant answer to the question – presenting and comparing data
2 organization, including appropriate linking devices, sentence structure and grammar
3 a range of vocabulary

What do you think are the strengths of this report?
What do you think are the weaknesses of this report?

3 Check your work.

1 Make the corrections to the numbered points in the report.
2 Now carefully check the answer you wrote in exercise 1.

    a Does it answer the question?
    b Is it well organized?
    c Does it have a range of vocabulary?
    d Have you checked it for grammar and spelling?
    e If necessary, redraft it to improve these areas.

Writing 2

Task 2

1 Read this question.

Many people judge success solely by money and material possessions. However, success can be achieved or measured in other ways.

What are your opinions on this topic?

Time: 40 minutes   Write at least 250 words.

IELTS Task 2 Writing checklist

- Read the instructions and the question carefully.
- Think about what the writing task requires.
- Brainstorm ideas (and any relevant vocabulary).
- Make a rough essay plan organized by paragraph headings.
- Write the essay.
- Leave a few minutes to check grammar, vocabulary, spelling and punctuation.

2 Read this sample answer and then answer the questions.

In the world many people were successful as they took high risk at that moment. They fail many times but they didn't give up until they were success. Most of the time success is not got easily and people have to work hard for it. Some people believe money and material possessions mean success. I think that's a big mistake.

There are many ways to achieve success. Firstly you must to worked very hard. Don't be lazy! Especially like students, if you want go to university, you have to spend more time on study.

Secondly you must brave. Sometimes you are lucky. But you will have sometimes problems. Some students have problems and don't know how to do. What a pity! To be the successful businessman you have to take many risks.

Thirdly, you should not give up, this is the most important step. Also you see people who are famous and successful. But do you consider how much time and hard work it took?

How to achieve success you decide, nobody can help you, just yourself. In particlar, work hard, brave, don't give up and trust yourself that you will be success.

(193 words)

1. In general, is the content of this essay relevant to the question?

   A No, not really.
   B Yes , it is a satisfactory answer.
   C Yes, but only some of it.

2. The examiners will also be looking for these features in a written answer:
   Organization
   Arguments/ideas/opinions and evidence
   Communicative quality – is the essay easy to follow and understand?
   Sentence structure – grammar
   Vocabulary

   What do you think are the strengths of this essay?
   What do you think are the weaknesses of this essay?

3 Now write your own answer to this question.

☆ Top tips for the IELTS Writing module ☆

Read the information in the box below and <u>underline</u> the most suitable answer from the choices in italics.

IELTS Task 1 Writing checklist

1. Focus on developing *your own personal/an academic writing style.*

2. If you have particular grammatical weaknesses, aim to improve *your grammar in general/those specific areas.*

3. Always read the question carefully and keep your answer relevant to the *topic/task.*

4. Spend a *little/lot* of time planning your answer.

5. Make sure your writing is clearly organized in paragraphs and that you use *appropriate/numerous* linking devices.

6. *Write as much as you can within the time limit/Leave enough time to check your work carefully.*

On the day of the exam:

Keep calm and don't panic.
Arrive in plenty of time, so you don't feel rushed.
Listen carefully to any instructions.
Read the questions carefully.
Be strict with your timings during the exam.

How to revise effectively

1 What advice would you give to these students who are having some problems revising for IELTS?

1 'I try to memorize any good essays I've written word for word.'

2 'I have a lot of other responsibilities and I'm just too busy to revise.'

3 'I'm spending all my spare time revising and I already feel exhausted!'

4 'Whenever I start to revise I seem to drift off into a daydream. It's so boring.'

5 'I always seem to end up leaving it until just before the exam and then working all night.'

6 'I don't know where to start!'

2 Look at the pieces of advice below and match them with the problems you looked at in exercise 1.

A Use bits of spare time that you would usually waste – such as when you're waiting for a bus.

B You need to plan when you're going to revise. Make sure it's a sensible plan, with short breaks built in. If you plan to do more than you can really do, you will become demotivated.

C You need to prioritize. If you're not sure which area you need to work on most, ask your teacher.

D It is very unlikely that exactly the same question will come up, and you will simply end up not answering the question properly. Instead, learn useful phrases and vocabulary connected to key topics such as the environment, health, jobs and so on.

E Set yourself small, achievable goals and vary the methods you use. Try new methods, such as mind maps. Or try revising with your friends.

F Don't keep promising yourself you'll start tomorrow. Start today! Even if you only do twenty minutes this will help you feel more motivated. Reward yourself for each revision task you do.

Find these words in the unit. Then check their meaning in your dictionary and record them.

factor p.139	irrelevant p.140	strategy p.141
status p.140	inadequate p.140	respectively p.146
concept p.140	relative p.140	numerous p.148

Grammar

Unit 1 Forming questions

If there is an auxiliary verb *be/ have/* or a modal verb, reverse the order of the subject and the auxiliary.

eg He [is] happy.

   [Is] he happy?

If there is no auxiliary, use a 'dummy' auxiliary *do/does/did*.

eg He [likes] milk.

   Does he [like] milk?

0 You can swim   *Can you swim* .... ?
1 You have been to England.   Have ....
   .... ?
2 She is living in Hong Kong.   Is ....
   .... ?
3 Peter has been to Australia before.   Has ....
   .... ?
4 He writes books.   What ....
   .... ?
5 He came to school by bike.   How ....
   .... ?
6 We should eat dinner before we go out.   Should ....
   .... ?

Unit 2 Subject-verb agreement

Some phrases are always followed by singular verbs, some by plural verbs, and some can be followed by both.

Underline the best alternative.

0 Everyone *live/lives* between 2 and 10 miles from the college.
1 Most of the teachers *travel/travels* to college by car.
2 None of the teachers *cycle/cycles* to work.
3 Some teachers *travel/travels* to work by bus.
4 One of the teachers *use/uses* the train.
5 Nobody *is/are* late for college.
6 Every member of staff *has/have* a car park permit.

Unit 2 Present simple vs. present continuous

1 What is the difference between these pairs of sentences? Check your answers on page 23.

1 The sun rises in the East.
   The sun is rising in the East.
2 He lives with his mother.
   He is living with his mother.
3 I start work at 9 am.
   I am starting work at 9 am this week.
4 I read a lot of books in English.
   I am reading a lot of books in English.

2 Are these sentences right or wrong? Correct them if necessary.

0 Degrees are often requiring full-time study.
   Degrees often require full-time study.
1 I usually arrive early for class.
   ....
2 Temperature is increasing with pressure.
   ....
3 He is knowing Toronto very well.
   ....
4 Come on. We wait for you.
   ....
5 I am agreeing with you.
   ....
6 He constantly interrupts me when I'm speaking.
   ....

Unit 3 Articles

Complete the gaps using an appropriate article.

Articles are often **0** ....*a*.... difficult area for students of English as **1** .... foreign language. **2** .... most important thing to remember is that **3** .... definite article is used where both people in **4** .... conversation know what they are referring to. For example, **5** .... first time something is mentioned, there is no shared knowledge, so we use the indefinite article **6** ..../........... **7** .... second time something is mentioned, however, both people have shared knowledge of it, so we use **8** .... definite article **9** ....

This is true when **10** .... noun is unique, eg **11** .... *sun*, or **12** .... *Taj Mahal*. As there is only one of these things, both people know which one they mean, so we use **13** .... definite article **14** ....

There are **15** .... few other rules. The indefinite article is used in some fixed expressions such as **16** .... lot and **17** .... few, and to mean 'per', eg *70 miles* **18** .... *hour*.

Another common use of the definite article is in superlatives, eg **19** .... *best tea in the world*.

Finally, be careful with geography. Most place names and names of people do not need an article, but expressions like **20** .... Republic of Indonesia, that follow the pattern of 'The Republic/Kingdom/State, etc. of…' need **21** .... definite article.

Unit 4 *-ing* form and infinitives

Some verbs are followed by an infinitive, some by a gerund and some can be followed by both.

Underline the best alternative.

0 I would like *to do/doing* VSO next year.
1 Do you mind *to help/helping* me with my homework?
2 I enjoy *to learn/learning* new words.
3 He avoids *to do/doing* his homework if he can.
4 He decided *to take/taking* the exam early.
5 Two months before the exam, she began *to study/studying* hard.
6 Did you remember *to lock/locking* the door?

Unit 5 Future plans and arrangements

There are four common ways to express the future in English: *going to*, *will*, the present continuous and simple tenses.

Remember:
- Use *going to* for plans.
- Use *will* for predictions, promises, threats and for decisions made at the time of speaking.
- Use the present continuous for arrangements. It is very similar to *going to*, but usually sounds more fixed and unchangeable.
- Use the present simple for timetabled or regular events.

Underline the best alternative. If both are possible, what is the difference in meaning?

0 If Wednesday's a problem *we'll meet/we're meeting* on Tuesday.
1 I am *going to take/taking* the IELTS exam in June.
2 You are *going to fail/failing* your exam, unless you start working harder.
3 Online shopping *increases/will probably increase* in popularity over the next decade.
4 Can you open the window? Actually don't worry, *I'll do/I'm going to do* it.
5 *I'll try/I'm trying* not to be late for class again.
6 The exam *starts/will start* at 2 pm. Don't be late!

Unit 6 Defining relative clauses

Relative clauses give extra information about a person or thing in the main clause. They come immediately after the noun that they describe.

Defining relative clauses give information which is essential to the meaning of the main clause.
- No commas are needed at the beginning or at the end of the clause.
- *That* can replace *who* for people or *which* for things.
- If the relative pronoun refers to the object, it can be left out.

Underline the best alternative. 0 = no relative pronoun

0 The results *0/that/who* were published were later called into question.
1 The statistics *who/which/0* the government used were inaccurate.
2 People *who/which/whose* lives were negatively affected by the new factory numbered 350.
3 The percentage of adults *who/that/0* had two jobs halved the following year.
4 The amount of air pollution *who/that/0* was recorded in Los Angeles decreased slightly during that period.
5 There was an increase of 5% in the number of visitors to Canada *which/that/0* came from Germany.
6 Men *which/who/0* were still unemployed five months after leaving university numbered less than 500.

Unit 7 Non-defining relative clauses

Non-defining relative clauses give extra information about a person or thing in the main clause. This information is **not** essential to the meaning of the main clause.

- Commas are required before and after the relative clause.
- *That* cannot replace *who* for people or *which* for things.
- The pronoun cannot be omitted.

Combine the two sentences using a relative clause.

0 The computer virus has caused millions of pounds worth of damage. The computer virus is believed to have originated in Texas.

   The computer virus, which is believed to have originated in Texas, has caused millions of pounds worth of damage.

1 Oxford University took first place in the 'Times Good University Guide 2002'. Oxford University is the oldest university in the English-speaking world.

   ....
   ....
   ....
   ....

2 Nurses are vital to the health service. Nurses are not well paid in my country.

   ....
   ....

3 Reflexology is increasing in popularity in the West. Reflexology is dismissed as ineffective by some doctors.

   ....
   ....

4 Sweden has an active bilingualism policy. Sweden was ethnically homogenous until the 1930s.

   ....
   ....
   ....

5 The Prime Minister has resigned. The Prime Minister has been in office for seven years.

   ....
   ....

6 Email has made communication much quicker. Email is widely available in the UK.

   ....
   ....

Unit 7 The passive

There are three main reasons why the passive form is used.

- The emphasis of the sentence is on the action, event or process, which is seen as more important than the agent, eg *IELTS is taken by many students all over the world*.
- The agent is obvious – it does not need to be stated because everyone knows who it is, eg *The man was arrested (by the police)*.
- The agent is unknown, eg *The university library was built in 1876*.

The passive is often used in academic writing because it sounds more formal.

Complete these sentences using the appropriate form of the passive.

0 The memo ......*was passed*...... (pass) to me this morning.

1 It .... (announce) today that interest rates have gone up.

2 Five men .... (rescue) from a burning house two days ago.

3 Computers .... (probably/use) more in primary schools in the future.

4 My college .... (inspect) every year by the British Council.

5 A new drug .... (currently/ developed) to combat AIDS.

6 The film .... (direct) by Tarantino.

Unit 8 Conditionals

Real conditionals

A real conditional is used to talk about a possible situation and its likely result. The *if* clause and the main clause can be any combination of these structures.

If clause (possible situation)	Main clause (result)
If + present continuous,	*will* + infinitive
the population is increasing,	*housing will become a problem.*
If + present simple,	modal expressing possibility + infinitive
the population increases,	*housing may/might/could become a problem.*
If + present perfect,	present simple
the population has increased,	*housing becomes a problem.*

Grammar

We can replace *if* in conditional sentences with:
unless – meaning *if…not*. *I won't go unless he comes too.*
provided – when the situation is necessary for the result. *I'll go provided he comes too.*
when – meaning something always happens. *I forget things when I'm tired.*

Unreal conditionals

An unreal conditional is used to talk about an unlikely or imaginary situation and its result. The *if* clause and the main clause can be any combination of these structures.

If clause (unlikely or imaginary situation)	Main clause (result)
past simple	*would* + infinitive
people worked from home,	*we would not need so many new roads.*
If + past continuous	*might* + infinitive
people were working from home,	*we might not need so many new roads.*

1 Are these sentences real or unreal conditionals?

0 If I get a good score in IELTS, I may go to Cambridge University. .... *Real*

1 If the government does not do something about pollution, our health and our children's health will suffer. ....

2 If I had more time, I would be able to study more. ....

3 The population will continue to grow if nothing is done to prevent it. ....

4 It might be possible to increase profits if we didn't spend so much on advertising. ....

5 If you haven't been to the immigration office yet, you should go this afternoon. ....

6 If traffic were not increasing at such a rapid rate, the government's road building programme might be more successful. ....

2 Rewrite the real conditional sentences above using *unless* instead of *if*. Make any necessary changes.

eg 0 *Unless I get a good score in IELTS, I won't go to Cambridge.*

Unit 9 Present perfect and past simple

The present perfect links past events and situations with the present. It is usually used:

● to talk about past experience in a general way, eg *I've eaten crab.*
● to talk about recent events, eg *Three children have been rescued from a river.*
● to talk about actions or situations which began in the past, but continue to the present, eg *I've known him for a year.*
● with time expressions such as: *ever, recently, yet, for* and *since*.

The past simple is used to describe events or situations which:

● are complete and which happened at a specified time, eg *I left home in 1998.*
● are complete and happened over a period of time in the past, eg *I went to the gym every day for 10 months.*

Where a specific point in time is mentioned without *since*, eg last week, in 1998, three weeks ago, etc. the past simple should be used.

Underline the best alternative. If both are possible, what is the difference?

0 I *completed*/*have completed* my English assignment last night.
1 I *didn't go*/*haven't been* to America yet.
2 I *have lived*/*lived* here since 2001.
3 I *graduated*/*have graduated* from Harvard University in 1989.
4 I *studied*/*have studied* in Beijing for six months.
5 I *have taken*/*took* a lot of extra courses last year.
6 My teacher *has given*/*gave* me an 'A'!
7 I *have been*/*went* to Singapore many times.
8 My brother *has lived*/*lived* here for two years.

Unit 9 Countable and uncountable nouns

● Countable nouns are nouns which can be counted, eg *one pencil, two pens…*
● Uncountable nouns are nouns which cannot be counted, eg *love, salt, advice…*

Correct the mistakes in the following sentences. Why are they incorrect?

0 An amount of people reject the idea.
   A number of people reject the idea. 'Amount' is used with uncountable nouns.
1 I have a pens in my back pocket.

   ....
   ....

2 There have been a lot of price rise in the last few years.

....

....

3 Every advice I get just makes me more confused.

....

....

4 I don't have much dollars in cash, but I can write you a cheque.

....

....

5 Can you bring my luggages, please?

....

....

6 Oh, no! Not more homeworks!

....

....

Unit 10 Expressing the future

Rearrange the words to make sentences.

0 hope to doctor a I become
   I hope to become a doctor.
1 to in a I finish studies year aim my

....

2 might do I PhD eventually a

....

3 course will my soon I new start

....

4 to some day I my would like in father's company work

....

5 my hope gradually I improve English to

....

6 I go home I year but could won't next probably

....

....

Unit 11 Modals of obligation and prohibition past and present

● *must* and *have to* are interchangeable in most cases. *Have to* can be used to express obligation from a third party, eg *I have to get to work early, or my boss will give me the sack.*
● *should* and *ought to* have the same meaning, but *should* is much more common. *Ought to* can sound slightly more formal.

Rewrite these sentences in the past.

0 The world's resources should be more equally distributed.
   The world's resources should have been more equally distributed.

1 People must be treated equally regardless of gender.

....

....

2 You don't need to hand in your essay until after the summer.

....

....

3 You don't have to book your train seat in advance.

....

....

4 You have to arrive at least an hour before your flight.

....

....

5 Higher taxes shouldn't be imposed on those with lower incomes.

....

....

6 People ought not to throw litter on the street.

....

....

Vocabulary

Unit 1 Adjectives ending in *-ing/-ed*

Adjectives can have two forms:

To describe how we feel
I am confused.
To describe the effect something has on us
This is confusing.

<u>Underline</u> the correct alternative.

0 He was *amazing/<u>amazed</u>* that the university had accepted him.
1 Living abroad is really *exciting/excited*!
2 He was really *frustrating/frustrated* that he couldn't understand the Australian accent when he first moved to Perth.
3 After a while I felt more *relaxing/relaxed* about being in a foreign country.
4 He was so *boring/bored* during the lecture that he actually fell asleep.
5 She tried to explain the difference between the two words, but I still felt *confusing/confused*.
6 Learning a new language is really *fascinating/fascinated*!
7 I felt really *annoying/annoyed* by his behaviour.
8 That book was really *interesting/interested*. I'll lend it to you.
9 I was really *shocking/shocked* to hear his news.
10 I'm sorry you didn't pass your exam. You must be really *disappointed/disappointing*.

Unit 1 Noun phrases

Rewrite these phrases as noun phrases.

0 dropped steadily   *a steady drop*
1 fell slightly
2 decreased sharply
3 climbed slowly
4 fluctuated briefly

Unit 2 Collocation

Words that are often used together are called collocations.

Complete the gaps using the words in the box.

~~accident~~ safety heavy lights ~~works~~ fumes
air jams main rage users ~~busy~~

Check you know if the word comes before or after the word in the box.

1 *Traffic accident*   2 *Busy road*   3 *Road works*

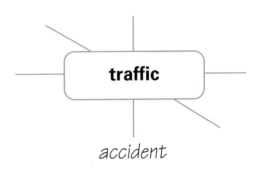

accident

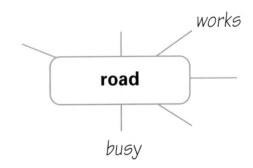

works

busy

Unit 3 Synonyms

1 Look at the words in the box. They all have a similar meaning to trip but are used in slightly different ways. Match the words with the definitions.

> voyage   flight   drive   tour   crossing
> expedition   outing

0   A short trip across water.   *crossing*

1   A long trip to a distant place, possibly with some danger, often for a scientific reason.   ....

2   A trip by car.   ....

3   A trip by plane.   ....

4   A long trip either by sea or in space. ....

5   A short trip (usually for the day) made by a group of people.   ....

6   A trip to a series of different places. ....

2 Now replace *trip* in the following sentences with a more specific word. Remember to change the article if necessary.

0   They went on a trip to the science museum.
   They went on an outing to the science museum.

1   Did you have a good trip? No, I hate flying.
   ....

2   The rough weather made her seasick for the entire trip.
   ....

3   He's trying to raise money for a trip to the Sahara Desert. They're going to look for a new species of desert cactus.
   ....

4   It's quite common for stressed-out executives to take up to a year off to do a world trip.
   ....

5   My trip to work only takes 20 minutes, provided the traffic isn't too bad.
   ....

6   Dennis Tito's trip into space was the most expensive holiday in history.
   ....

Unit 4 Dependent prepositions

Complete the sentences with a suitable dependent preposition.

> on   with   of   about   into   for

0   I believe we should wait ....*for*.... a resolution to world poverty before pouring money into space exploration.

1   The UN did not approve .... the President's decision to delay negotiations.

2   The ability to be patient .... their students is a key quality for a teacher.

3   The government became increasingly unpopular, and it seemed that no one was satisfied .... their decisions.

4   The company planned to diversify, and concentrate .... new areas and innovations within medicine.

5   The spokeswoman stressed that continued research .... cancer and its causes was absolutely vital.

6   Despite admitting that there had been difficulties, the CEO refused to accept the blame .... the company's poor turnover.

7   The President remained optimistic .... his re-election, in spite of poor indications at the polls.

8   The university has a good reputation .... supporting overseas students.

Unit 5 Suffixes *-ful* and *-less*

These suffixes are used to combine with nouns or verbs to form adjectives.
   eg   pain – painful – painless

-ful and *-less* are not always used to make opposites.
   eg   beauty – beautiful – ~~beautiless~~

Complete the table with adjectives using *-ful* or *-less* where possible.

Noun/Verb	-ful	-less
harm	*harmful*	
use		
peace		
tact		*tactless*
skill		
home		
care		
hope		
success		
power		

Unit 6 Collocations

Look at the possible collocations with crime and use the phrases to complete the sentences below.

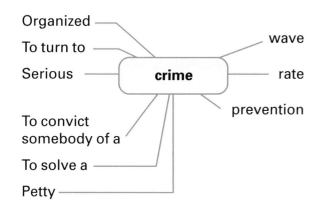

Organized — crime — wave
To turn to
Serious — rate
To convict somebody of a — prevention
To solve a
Petty

0 The court _convicted her of a crime_ she hadn't committed.
1 Rather than building more prisons, we should focus on ....
2 Young people who cannot get work may .... in desperation.
3 The blackout in the city caused a .... as criminals took advantage of the confusion.
4 The FBI has a large section dedicated to fighting ....
5 The government insists that the .... is falling as a result of its policies.
6 The police need to spend less time on .... , such as shoplifting, and more on ....
7 Regardless of what is shown in detective films, it usually takes the police less than 24 hours ....

Unit 7 Verb + noun collocations

Complete the sentences with a suitable verb from the box below.

reach   do   make   cut   earn   go   take   put
~~lose~~

0 Many shops ...lose... business due to poor service.
1 It is difficult for farmers like the Menzas to .... a profit.
2 It was a pleasure to .... business with you.
3 The two sides finally .... an agreement.
4 They decided to .... into business together.
5 Competition from cheaper imports forced them to .... their prices.
6 Loan sharks .... advantage of the desperate farmers.
7 She doesn't .... much money, but she enjoys the work.
8 He .... all his money into the business.

Unit 8 Dependent prepositions

Complete the paragraphs with suitable dependent prepositions. Use a dictionary to help you.

Many people see therapies such as acupuncture as a sensible alternative 0 ...to... conventional medicine. People who are allergic 1 .... pollen, for example, may suffer 2 .... allergy symptoms for several months of the year. They prefer not to take drugs for this length of time and believe that acupuncture provides a cure 3 .... most of their symptoms.

Others disagree 4 .... this view. According to Professor Ernst, there is no scientific support 5 .... most of the claims made by alternative therapists. 'I'm not convinced 6 .... the so-called scientific explanations therapists give. When the therapies work it's simply because people believe 7 .... them.'

Unit 9 Synonyms

These verbs are all synonyms of 'make', but have a more specific meaning.

> manufacture   invent   develop   create   design

Use your dictionary to answer these questions.

Which word(s):

1   can be used to describe things made in factories?
....

2   are often used to describe making something new, or making something for the first time? (2 words) ....

3   can also mean to improve something?
....

4   often includes the idea of deciding how something will look as well as how it will work?
....

Unit 9 Spelling

Underline the correct spelling of these words from the unit.

0   There has been huge improvements in robot *tecnology/technologi/technology* in recent decades.

1   Asimo's capabilities were *demanstrated/demonstrated/demonsated* at a conference in New York.

2   *Communicasion/Comunication/Communication* has grown increasingly important in today's world.

3   Many of the *dewelpments/developments/developmants* in computer science over the last twenty years have been essential for business.

4   The Internet was a very *significant/significent/signiphicant* recent advance in technology.

Unit 10 Homonyms

Homonyms are words with the same spelling, but different meanings (though the meanings may be related).

1   Look at these nouns from the text on pages 114 and 115 and match them with two meanings: the original meaning, and the new, computer-related meaning.

> document   memory   drive   web   file

2   What other meanings can you find in your dictionary for these words?

> file   post   save   key   mouse   click   screen

Original meaning	New computer-related meaning
1 Something that you remember.	a All the websites that people have created on their computers for people to look at using the Internet.
2 Energy and determination, a big effort.	b The part of the computer in which information is stored.
3 A net of thin threads that a spider makes, or a complicated set of related things.	c A computer file that you can write in.
4 A box or container in which papers are kept together.	d The part of a computer that reads and stores information.
5 A piece of paper or a set of papers containing official information.	e a set of information that is stored on a computer and given a particular name.

Unit 11 Prefixes

Choose a prefix from the box that will go with ALL the words in each group.

re   under   well   over   dis   micro

1   ....weight/ ....seas/ ....hear/ .... crowded
2   ....name/ _____consider/ _____build/ ....write
3   ....advantage/ ....belief/ ....similar/ ....loyal
4   ....second/ ....phone/ ....wave/ ....film
5   ....developed/ ....ground/ ....stand/ ....value
6   ....off/ ....cooked/ ....known/ .... made

Unit 11 Suffixes

-ate and *-ise* are typical verb endings.

Find verbs with these endings from the reading text on pages 128 and 129 which have a similar meaning to the definitions. The first letter and the number of missing letters is given in each case.

0   To try to persuade people to buy a product by announcing it on television, in newspapers etc.
   A _d v e r t_ ise
1   To know what something is (or who someone is) because you have seen or heard it/them before.
   R _ _ _ _ _ ise
2   To examine something very carefully.
   S _ _ _ _ _ _ ise
3   To change, improve or make additions to something.
   R _ _ise
4   To express an intention in an indirect way.
   I _ _ _ _ ate
5   To take in an idea or information and make it part of your knowledge.
   A _ _ _ _ _ _ ate
6   To recognize the difference between things.
   D _ _ _ _ _ _ _ _ ate

Unit 12 Collocations

All these words can collocate with the word exam. Use them to complete the word map.

paper   oral   pass   ~~take~~   practical   set   sit   do   fail   mark   final   nerves

Three similar words
1 *take* ....
2 .... an
3 ....

Two things an examiner does
1 ....
2 .... an

Three different types of exams
1 ....
2 ....
3 ....

Two opposite words
1 ....
2 .... an

exam

Two phrases where 'exam' is used as an adjective
1 ....
2 ....

Writing

Unit 1

Model answer for Writing 1 on p12

The graph shows how many students were studying five different subjects at university level between 1996 and 2001. According to the chart some subjects became more popular over this period, while others dropped in popularity.

There was a slight increase in the number of students taking Medicine and Dentistry, from just under 40,000 in 1996 to nearly 50,000 in 2001, although this remained the least popular subject of the five. Biological Sciences showed a steady increase over the five-year period, from 80,000 to over 90,000 and there was a sharp increase in the popularity of Computer Sciences, especially between 99/00 and 00/01 when numbers increased by nearly 30,000.

In contrast, there was a slight fall in the number of students studying Physical Sciences, and Engineering and Technology showed a steady drop in popularity, from nearly 140,000 to just over 120,000. However, together with Computer Sciences, Engineering and Technology was still one of the two most popular subjects in 2001.   (159 words)

Comments

This answer begins with a clear opening statement that is not exactly the same as the description in the question. The second sentence tells the reader generally what happens in the chart (…some subjects became more popular …). After this general point the descriptions become more specific (…from just under 40,000 in 1996 to nearly 50,000 in 2001). Phrases describing change are varied and accurate (… showed a steady increase …). The answer is well organized and clear.

Model answer for Writing 2 on p15

The chart shows the numbers of recent graduates who found full-time work within a four-month period after graduating. In general, employment levels have risen during the six-year period for both sexes, but the percentage of women in work was consistently lower than it was for men, except in 2001.

In 1995, just over 80% of recent male graduates were working. There was a steady overall increase during the six-year period, with sharper rises in 1996 and 2000, followed by falls. This was especially marked in 2000, when there was an increase of around two per cent to a peak of just over 84%, which dropped to 83% the following year.

The trends were similar for female graduates, with a steady overall increase from 78% in 1995 to 83% in 2001. As for men, there was a sharper rise in 1996. In contrast to male graduates, numbers for women remained constant from 2000 to 2001, and in the final year employment figures were equal for men and women.   (169 words)

Comments

The opening statement has been rephrased. There is a general comment on the overall trend in the data (In general, employment levels have risen …). Specific data is given (In 1995, just over 80% of recent male graduates …). There are a good range of expressions to describe change (…sharper rises …to a peak …remained constant). The answer includes the most significant points from the data, and is clearly structured and concise.

Unit 2

Model answer for Writing on p25

There is no doubt that in recent years the number of cars on the road has increased significantly. This has led to numerous problems such as a rise in air pollution, a higher accident rate and, of course, far more traffic congestion. Some argue that if public transport played a greater role, then some of these problems might be reduced. However, the current situation is unlikely to change dramatically in the near future unless certain actions are taken.

There are two important changes that the government would need to make in order for people to use public transport more. Firstly, prices would have to be reduced – travel by train, in particular, is not cheap in this country. Secondly, the quality and frequency of public transport services would need to be improved. Many types of public transport are uncomfortable, unreliable or simply infrequent. In addition, more dramatic changes, such as higher car taxes or congestion charging, might put some individuals off driving, particularly if there was a better public transport service.

Yet even if these changes were implemented, I still believe that the attraction of the private vehicle is too powerful these days. Most people prefer to travel in their own car because it is convenient and gives almost total independence.

To sum up, it is important that the government aims to increase the role of public transport in order to encourage individuals to use it more. As a result, traffic-related problems might be reduced. Nonetheless, these aims may not be fulfilled as long as the car remains such a powerful influence in the modern world. (265 words)

Comments

This answer tackles the question satisfactorily. It has been well-planned and is organized into 4 clear paragraphs with an introduction, main body and conclusion. There are ideas about problems (pollution, accidents, congestion) and possible solutions (more public transport, higher car tax). A good range of structures, vocabulary and linking words are used accurately (Firstly, Secondly, In addition). The answer ends with a concise paragraph in which the writer's views are clearly expressed.

Model answer for Writing: further practice on p27

Many countries of the world are currently experiencing problems caused by rapidly growing populations in urban areas, and both governments and individuals have a duty to find ways to overcome these problems.

Overpopulation can lead to overcrowding and poor quality housing in many large cities. Poorly heated or damp housing could cause significant health problems, resulting in illness, such as bronchitis or pneumonia. Another serious consequence of overcrowding is a rising crime rate as poor living conditions may lead young people in particular to take desperate measures and turn to crime or drugs.

In terms of solutions, I believe the government should be largely responsible. Firstly, it is vital that the state provides essential housing and healthcare for all its citizens. Secondly, setting up community projects to help foster more community spirit and help keep young people off the street is a good idea. For example, youth clubs or evening classes for teenagers would keep them occupied. Finally, more effective policing of inner city areas would also be beneficial.

Naturally, individuals should also act responsibly to address these problems. If the measures described above are put into place by the government, then it will encourage people to have more pride in their own community and improve the situation.

Therefore, it is clear that the problems caused by overpopulation in urban areas are very serious. Yet if governments and individuals share a collective responsibility, then it may well become possible to offer some solutions. (243 words)

Comments

The answer has been clearly organized and has relevant content backed up by reasons and examples. The introduction does not repeat the description in the question but is rephrased, paragraph 2 describes problems, paragraph 3 offers solutions, paragraph 4 suggests the role of government is very important. The conclusion states that 'collective responsibility' for governments and individuals is the key to the solution. A range of structures are accurately used (If the measures described above are put into place …).

Unit 3

See Writing task on p38

Unit 4

See Writing task on p48

Unit 5

See Writing 1 on p62

Model answer for Writing 2 on p64

The information in the pie charts shows the relative importance of different types of employment in two very different countries.

In Tanzania, agriculture employs by far the most people. Nearly four out of five (79%) work in this sector, whereas only two per cent of Irish people are in agriculture. In Ireland, the largest employer is the service sector, where over 70% of the population work. In Tanzania, the figure is only 14.2%, despite the fact that Tanzania has a significant tourist trade, and this is included in the services figure.

Although manufacturing is quite significant in Ireland, employing over a fifth (21.5%) of the population, not many people are employed in this sector in Tanzania. Other industries are not very significant in either country. Construction, for example, is less than 5% in Ireland, but is even less important in Tanzania, with only a very small number of people (0.6%) employed in this industry. There is also some employment in the energy and water industries in Ireland. However, this is not mentioned in the Tanzanian data. (174 words)

Comments

There is a clear opening statement that emphasizes a contrast between these two places (two very different countries). The text compares and contrasts the data by focusing on the most important sectors first (…agriculture employs by far the most people…), providing specific details (Nearly four out of five – 79%…) and using linking devices to show differences (whereas, although, etc.).

Unit 6

See Writing task on p71

Model answer for Writing: further practice on p74

One of the most serious problems existing in society today is the rising crime rate among young people. The number of offences committed by teenagers, which is usually higher in urban areas, includes crimes such as joy-riding, vandalism, theft and mugging. However, I am not convinced that simply giving heavy punishments is the best approach. Tackling crime among young people, who may be as young as eight, should involve a combination of new strategies, improved social facilities and better education.

In recent months, new measures to address this issue have included getting young offenders to meet their victims. As a result, youths see the harm or damage they have caused which may put them off re-offending. Another method, the electronic tagging of young offenders, which has been piloted in England and Wales, also has benefits. It means that movements and behaviour are monitored. Consequently, it is more difficult for them to commit crimes.

A different approach, which many feel is a better solution, would be to provide better social facilities such as youth clubs or local sports facilities. If young people have activities to occupy them, they are less likely to offend.

Finally, I strongly believe that education is more important than tough measures. Therefore, parents, teachers, social workers and police officers all have a responsibility to raise awareness of the serious consequences of crime.

To sum up, I would recommend a number of strategies to lower crime rates among young people. Indeed, I feel that there is not always one simple solution but different approaches depending on each particular situation.   (261 words)

Comments

In the introduction, the writer challenges the statement (I am not convinced that simply giving heavy punishments…) and then signals three preferred approaches (…new strategies, improved social facilities and better education). There is clear progression in the text as the three suggested approaches are discussed in detail in the following three paragraphs that make up the main body. The essay backs up statements with factual knowledge of recent developments (offenders meeting victims, electronic tagging) and a wide range of topic-related vocabulary is evident (vandalism, mugging, offender, crime rates, etc.)

Model answer for Question 7 on p75

Although the number of crimes committed by young people keeps growing each year, the government is not doing enough to cut crime. Every year they promise an improvement. It never happens because they don't take tough enough measures.

I would agree that young criminals are not frightened of the consequences of their actions because they do not seem to mind the punishments they receive. These punishments are too light, so they commit more crimes.

Light punishments such as community service do not work. Therefore, young people should be punished more severely. This will make them think more carefully about what they do.

Unit 7

See Writing task on p86

Model answer for Writing: further practice on p87

This diagram shows the process of extracting sugar from sugar beets. First, the sugar beets arrive at the plant and are unloaded from the trucks. They are dirty because they have come straight from the farm, so they are shaken in order to remove the dirt and then washed in a machine called a beet washer.

Next the beets are cut up into small pieces, which are called cossettes. After this, sugar is drawn from the beets using hot water, which makes a kind of sugar 'juice'.

As this juice may still be dirty, milk of lime is added in order to clean it. The mixture is then filtered so that the milk of lime can be removed.

Following this, the sugar juice is heated several times, which evaporates the water. This results in a purer sugar solution.

Finally, the sugar is boiled and spun in a centrifuge to create crystals.   (148 words)

Comments

There is a clear introductory sentence describing what the diagram shows. Sequencers (Firstly, next, after this), connectors indicating purpose (… in order to …) and reason clauses (…so that the milk of lime can be …) are used correctly. The passive voice is employed appropriately to show the process (… they are shaken … the sugar juice is heated …) and to keep the text impersonal and factual.

Unit 8

Model answer for Writing on p96

Alternative medicine is not new. It is accepted that it pre-dates conventional medicine and it is still used by many people all over the world. I am unconvinced that it is dangerous, and feel that both alternative and conventional medicine can be useful.

The conventional medical community is often dismissive of alternatives, as there is little scientific evidence to support the claims of their supporters. However, it is widely accepted that they can be effective. Furthermore, people often try such treatment because of recommendations from friends, and therefore come to the therapist with a very positive attitude, which may be part of the reason for the cure. Moreover, these therapies are usually only useful for long-term, chronic conditions. Acute medical problems, such as accidental injury, often require more conventional methods.

On the other hand, despite the lack of scientific proof, there is a lot of anecdotal evidence to suggest that these therapies work. In addition, far from being dangerous, they often have few or no side effects, so the worst outcome would be no change. One of the strongest arguments for the effectiveness of alternative therapies in the West is that, whilst conventional medicine is available without charge, many people are prepared to pay considerable sums for alternatives. If they were totally unhelpful, it would be surprising if this continued. Finally, looking at a problem from a different perspective must be beneficial.

I strongly believe that conventional medicine and alternative therapies can and should coexist. They have different strengths, and can both be used effectively to target particular medical problems. The best situation would be for alternative therapies to be used to support and complement conventional medicine. (277 words)

Comments

The writer introduces the topic in the opening paragraph and puts forward a clear view on the issue (I am unconvinced…and feel…). The essay has a well-balanced argument. The second paragraph expresses some doubt about alternative therapies (…little scientific evidence …only useful for long term…), but in the third paragraph the writer takes a different view (On the other hand…) and examines the benefits (…few side effects). The writer's concluding paragraph offers a strong opinion (I strongly believe…) and sums up the fact that both types of treatment are valid today. There is also a good range of grammatical structures (If they were totally unhelpful, it would be…), and connectors (despite the fact, in addition, finally).

Unit 9

Model answer for Writing 2 on p111

A sports hot air balloon consists of a large bag attached by steel ropes to a basket, in which usually up to four people stand. The balloon itself is made of rip proof nylon, so as to be light and very strong. A quick release rope is attached to a vehicle and the balloon is inflated by fans blowing cold air. A crown rope is also attached so as not to launch the balloon before the pilot is ready. A propane gas heater sends powerful jets of flame upwards into the balloon. This heats the air inside the balloon in order to lift it. When the air is hot, the balloon rises.

When the balloon is flying, its speed and direction are determined by the wind which varies at different altitudes. However, the pilot, who needs to wear a safety harness, can maintain or change the height using the blast valve. This controls the flow of gas to the burner. (160 words)

Comments

The first sentence explains what the object consists of. Relevant vocabulary from the diagram (rip-proof nylon, propane gas heater) is used in the description. Infinitives of purpose show what components are used for (… in order to lift it … so as not to launch …). There is a good range of tenses and both the active and passive voice are used to describe how the object works. The text also progresses logically.

Model answer for Writing: further practice on p112

This fire extinguisher is a strong metal container filled with water used to put out fires. Inside this is a cartridge containing a compressed gas such as liquid carbon dioxide. Near the lever of the extinguisher, there is a safety pin, which prevents the handle being depressed accidentally.

In order to use the extinguisher, first the safety pin must be removed. Secondly, the lever is pressed. This pushes a rod into the valve of the cartridge and opens it. The carbon dioxide is then released at high pressure from the cartridge into the main container, putting pressure on the water within it. This pressure causes the water to be forced up the siphon tube and out of the nozzle. If the handle is released, the rod will move upwards. This closes the valve on the cartridge of gas and removes the pressure on the water. Therefore the water will stop rising up the siphon and out of the nozzle. (159 words)

Comments

The opening sentence explains what the object is and what it does. Parts are identified (a safety pin) and the function (which prevents the handle being depressed accidentally), location (inside this is a cartridge) and what happens in the process are described using a range of structures (if the handle is released, the rod will move upwards). The description is clear, simple and follows the sequence shown in the diagram.

Unit 10

Model answer for Writing on p122

The last two decades have seen enormous changes in the way people's lives are affected by IT. Twenty years ago few people had access to a computer whilst today most people use them at work, home or school and use of email and the Internet is an everyday event.

These developments have brought many benefits to our lives. Email makes communication (particularly overseas) much easier and more immediate. This has numerous benefits for business, commerce, and education. The World Wide Web means that information on every conceivable subject is now available to us. Clearly, for many people this has made life much easier and more convenient.

However, not all the effects of the new technology have been beneficial. Many people feel that the widespread use of email is destroying traditional forms of communication such as letter writing, telephone and face-to-face conversation. With ever increasing use of information technology these negative elements are likely to increase in the future.

The huge size of the Web means it is almost impossible to control and regulate. This has led to many concerns regarding children accessing unsuitable websites. Unfortunately, this kind of problem might even get worse in the future at least until more regulated systems are set up. Yet perhaps the biggest threat to IT in years to come will be the computer virus – more sophisticated or more destructive strains are almost inevitable.

In conclusion, developments in IT have brought many benefits, yet I believe developments relating to new technology in the future are likely to produce many negative effects that will need to be addressed very carefully. (265 words)

Comments

The introduction talks in general about the increasing use of IT. The following paragraph mentions the present benefits of these developments, but the opening sentence in the third paragraph is a qualifying statement (However, not all the effects ...), so the writer can now focus on the negative elements. The fourth paragraph provides two other negative examples (lack of regulation, viruses). Both paragraphs suggest that these problems will continue in the future. The essay

concludes with a clear opinion that agrees with the statement. Overall, it is a well-balanced text that mentions the present situation (…this has made life…) but importantly, also refers to the future of IT (…likely to increase… , might get worse…).

Unit 11

Model answer for Writing on p134

There is no doubt that advertising dominates the world we live in today. Adverts appear on television, on the World Wide Web, in the street and even on our mobile phones. However, many of the strategies used to sell a product or service can be considered immoral or unacceptable.

Indeed, the fact that we cannot escape from advertising is a significant cause for complaint. Constant images and signs wherever we look can be very intrusive and irritating at times. Although we expect adverts in numerous situations, it now seems that there are very few places we can actually avoid them.

A further aspect of advertising that I would consider unethical is the way that it encourages people to buy products they may not need or cannot afford. Children and young people in particular, are influenced by adverts showing the latest toys, clothing or music and this can put enormous pressure on the parents to buy these products.

In addition, the advertising of tobacco products and alcohol has long been a controversial issue, but cigarette adverts have only recently been banned in many countries. It is quite possible that alcohol adverts encourage excessive consumption and underage drinking, yet restrictions have not been placed on this type of advertising in the same way as smoking. Many people consider this to be unacceptable and I tend to accept this view.

It is certainly true to say that advertising is an everyday feature of our lives. Therefore, people are constantly being encouraged to buy products or services that might be too expensive, unnecessary or even unhealthy. In conclusion, many aspects of advertising do appear to be morally wrong and are not acceptable in today's society. (281 words)

Comments

This text is organized into five clear paragraphs, contains relevant ideas related to the topic and is well expressed. Focusing on the language and structures in particular, the essay starts with an appropriate introductory sentence (There is no doubt ...). Linking words are used accurately (However, In addition, Therefore). Phrases that signal opinions are evident (A further aspect of advertising that I would consider unethical…) backed up by reasons (…encourages people to buy products they may not need or cannot afford) and examples (Children and young people in particular, are influenced by adverts). In general, many other useful phrases are used, indicating a good control of language (It is quite possible… Many people consider… It is certainly true to say…).

Unit 12

Model answer for Writing 1 on p145

Students come to the UK to study from all over the world, and the pie chart shows their distribution by continent for 2001 entry. The two most significant areas are the Far East and the European Union countries. Between them, they account for over 70% of the total. Thirteen percent of the students come from Africa, with the remainder coming from the Americas, the Middle East (5% each) and non-EU European countries (6%).

Considering the student numbers from the Far East in greater detail, the largest number comes, unsurprisingly, from China. In 2001, almost 4,000 students applied to study. Large numbers of students also came from Malaysia, (2,623). The next most important group numerically was from India and Singapore. Slightly more than 1,500 Indian students applied to study, and almost 1,700 Singaporean, while numbers from Japan and South Korea were much lower, at around 1,000 and 500 respectively.

(148 words)

Comments

The writer has chosen to organize the text by describing the pie chart in the first paragraph and the bar chart in the second. The answer begins with a clear opening statement giving general information about the data in the pie chart. The most significant facts are highlighted (the two most significant areas…). More specific details from Asian countries are then considered and information is compared using superlatives and comparative forms (the largest number…were much lower…). Relevant words and phrases are used (the remainder, respectively).

Model answer for Writing 2 on p147

If a person appears to be relatively wealthy, perhaps owning an expensive car, living in a nice house and generally enjoying a high standard of living then most people would say this person is successful. This may indeed be true but there are certainly numerous other ways, in my view, in which success can be achieved or measured.

First of all, in terms of education, passing exams or completing a course can be considered successful activities. If A levels, a diploma or a degree are attained then this is recognized as a successful achievement, yet qualifications such as these do not necessarily lead to riches.

Another type of success can be achieved in work situations simply by doing one's own particular job effectively. Furthermore, job satisfaction and career fulfilment are also indications of success, yet do not necessarily mean being in highly paid employment. For example, a voluntary worker for an aid agency in a developing country who has helped to construct buildings or to improve local facilities has been part of a successful project.

I also believe that success can be achieved in domestic life such as raising and supporting a family. On a personal level it might also simply mean putting up shelves for the first time or winning a local sporting competition.

In conclusion, there is no doubt that in today's society people often regard success purely in terms of wealth or materialistic values, but in my opinion this does not account for the variety of other ways that success can be achieved. Ultimately, measuring success might depend on a individual's personal goals.

(266 words)

Comments

The essay has been organized into five paragraphs with a clear introduction, main body and conclusion. In terms of opinions, the three central paragraphs on different types of success (education, work, family) are introduced with a topic sentence (I also believe that success can be achieved in domestic life … .) followed by evidence and examples to support the main idea. The text is easy to follow as linkers and relevant phrases are used accurately (First of all… Another type of… I also believe… .). The writer has also used some complex sentences (If a person appears…) and has a wide vocabulary range (attained, aid worker, materialistic).

Tapescripts

1 Studying abroad

 01

(AO = Admissions Officer; LC = Li Cha)

AO: Hello Li Cha, I'm Susie Shaw, the Admissions Officer.

LC: Hello, pleased to meet you.

AO: I'd just like to talk to you to find out a little more information to give your new tutor, Stephen Ennis.

LC: OK.

AO: How old are you, Li Cha?

LC: I'm eighteen.

AO: OK. Now your start date is next Monday, that's the 14th of February. And you're in class 2B.

LC: Sorry, 2D?

AO: No 2B. B for Bravo. And do you know when you're finishing? October or November?

LC: I'd like to go home and see my family in November.

AO: Finishing at the end of October then, the 29th. We need a contact number here and one in China, Li Cha. Do you live with your parents?

LC: No, I live with my grandmother and brother, Shao, in Hong Kong. Their telephone number is 8731 4591. And my mobile number here is 0825 701 6924.

AO: Obviously you've studied English before. How long have you been studying?

LC: About three years.

AO: Is that all? You must work hard! I thought you'd been studying for at least five years. Do you have any other hobbies?

LC: Well, I like playing table tennis. I also spend a lot of time emailing friends. Oh, and I like reading. I read in English sometimes too.

AO: Great, that's probably why your English is so good. Now, you want to take IELTS, don't you? Why's that?

LC: Well, I want to go to the University of Sydney. I'd like to study IT and computing.

AO: Really? Would you like to get a job in IT in the future?

LC: Yes, I'd really like to work with computers, there are just so many possibilities.

 02

Hello everyone. Thanks for coming this evening. I've been invited here tonight by the International Student's Society to talk a bit about culture shock. For many of you who have recently arrived from your home countries, life here in New Zealand must seem quite strange and different to you in many ways. Because of my work as an anthropologist, I've had the opportunity to work in quite a number of different countries with quite diverse cultures, so I've had my fair share of culture shock and know exactly how you might be feeling at this time.

Tonight, I want to talk a bit about my own experiences of culture shock and then go on to give you a few hints on how to minimize the effects.

I first left New Zealand when I was only 22 to do some research work on the island of Sumatra in Indonesia. I was interested in learning all about the country and the people, but I was particularly fascinated by the architecture.

In the part where I was working, the buildings have beautiful, curved roofs that I had never seen before and I loved them!

Life in Indonesia is very different from life in New Zealand, and at first I found it very difficult to adjust. The worst thing was looking different to everyone else. I'm about average height in New Zealand, but in Indonesia, I was much taller than most people, and it made me feel very uncomfortable. One of the best things, though, was the food. A change in diet can be one of the biggest problems of moving to a new country, but for me Indonesia was not difficult from that point of view. I'm very keen on spicy food, and there is an Indonesian chicken curry called 'Rendang' that is out of this world!

Climate can be another thing that people find it difficult to adjust to. I found working in Egypt very difficult because of the extreme heat. In contrast, living in Finland was hard because during the winter months the days are so short. Where I was, in the North, it was only light for about four or five hours a day in December. By the end I was pretty good at cross country skiing, though!

Language is often one of the biggest barriers when you're settling into a new country, but I'm quite good at learning them and this hasn't usually been a problem for me. However, Japan was quite different. I had learnt some spoken Japanese before I went, but I hadn't tried to learn to write, so initially, I was a bit nervous about going to a country where I couldn't read anything. This did make life a lot more difficult for me. I couldn't read the destinations on buses, or menus in restaurants, or even road signs.

Sometimes it can be very small things that you're not used to that can make you feel the most homesick. For me, in China, it was connected with eating again. I really love Chinese food, but I found it very difficult to eat with chopsticks. I did learn eventually, but I still prefer a fork! One of the best things about my stay in China, though, was the Professor I was working with at the university. He was really enthusiastic about his work, and that made my job very satisfying.

OK, well enough about my experience. Having mentioned some of the problems I faced, I want to look a bit more generally at how you can adapt to culture shock ... (fade)

 03

... so this afternoon we've been talking a bit about culture shock and your experiences of culture shock so far in adjusting to life in this country. Maybe this hasn't happened to you and you're thinking it won't because you're from Europe, or you've done a lot of travelling before. But it is important to understand that culture shock can hit you whatever culture you come from and however well travelled you are. It's a perfectly normal experience, if a little worrying when it does happen to you.

There are some things you can do, however, to help yourself get through it. First of all, do keep in touch with home. Aki, on student reception, can help you to buy a phone card to make cheaper calls home, and you can always email friends and family from the Resource Centre. If you haven't brought any photos of friends and family, get them to send you some, so you can feel at home.

Make sure you eat well – not just crisps and chocolate! And it's a good idea if you can eat some familiar food. Other students from your country will probably be able to help you find shops which specialize in food from your country. And you need to exercise too – not only for your health. And it's a good way of meeting people.

Make some new friends. Get to know the other international students, whether from your own country or others. They will understand something of what you're feeling and their experience may be able to help you. And, if you can, try to make friends with the local home students. That way you can really learn about this new culture – and they can learn about yours.

Let us help you! You're here at the orientation programme, which is a good start, but we also offer a drop-in centre with a student advisor available daily, and personal counselling. You might not use such a service at home, but remember that you perhaps don't have the same support networks of friends and family here, and these services can provide you with some support. The most important thing is to find someone who will listen uncritically and with understanding, rather than isolating yourself.

You need to remember that culture shock is entirely normal and usually unavoidable. It's not a sign that you've made a mistake or can't manage. In fact, it can be a significant learning experience, making you more aware of aspects of your own culture as well as the new culture. It will give you valuable skills which will be part of the benefit of an international education.

04

(L = Lecturer; J = James)

L: ... and today James is going to give us his presentation on household waste disposal. James, are you ready?

J: Yeah, thanks. Well, when I was deciding what to do for this presentation, this topic really attracted me, because it's such an important issue, and it's going to become even more important in the near future when new European law comes into effect. Um ... if you have any questions as I go along, please feel free to ask, and I'll do my best to clarify things.

OK. I think the facts and figures speak for themselves: on average we produce 30 million tonnes of solid household waste every year or around half a tonne per person which is a tremendous amount if you think about it, and obviously it's vital that waste is minimized and disposed of in a way that protects our environment and our health.

We're talking about waste food products, packaging, newspapers, glass, garden waste and so on. In fact some studies have shown that almost two-thirds of our waste is biodegradable; food, paper, natural textiles for example and glass makes up about 10%.

L: Sorry, sorry to interrupt, but can I just ask you if those figures are for the UK only, or are the proportions the same in other countries?

J: No, that's fairly universal, at least in the developed world, but different countries do have very different levels of recycling. In Britain for example, we bury in the region of 25 million tonnes of biodegradable waste; this is known as landfill. I'm sure you can imagine that this is a limited option, particularly in a country with a small amount of land. As well as this, 2.5 million tonnes is burned to produce electricity, which is better, but still has environmental problems associated with it, and 2.5 million tonnes is recycled or composted.

L: This is the current situation in the UK?

J: Yes, it is. However, new European law requires us to reduce amounts of waste, and by 2020 we will only be able to send 10 million tonnes of this for landfill and the rest will have to be recycled, burned or treated in a different way. So clearly things are going to have to change, and everyone is involved in this issue in some way ...

L: So what exactly is being done?

J: Well, the policy of the government and of environment agencies is firstly to reduce the amount of waste we create to begin with, and secondly, to reuse the waste that is created. Obviously some disposal is necessary but the aim is to limit this as much as possible. What we need to do is to conserve raw materials, like tin and aluminium, while still protecting the environment and public health.

L: Yes, but what does this mean in reality?

J: There are quite a few things that are being done, mostly by local councils. They're responsible for household 'dustbin'

collections, or taking away all the rubbish you produce in the home. In recent years many more sites have been set up to collect waste separately for recycling. There are often containers in car parks or outside supermarkets for people to put bottles in: clear, green and brown bottles are separated. Also newspapers and magazines can be recycled as well as tins made of aluminium. One of the problems of this, though, is that most people are not bothering to take their rubbish there. To overcome this, some local councils also provide special containers, often called 'recycling bins' for residents to collect glass and paper in. They put these outside their houses at the same time as their rubbish, and they are collected and recycled.

L: I see. So are you saying that recycling is more important than actually reducing waste?

J: No. Nowadays, many products are increasingly being designed with reuse or recycling in mind and I think, in general, people are far more aware about these issues. In some countries, like Switzerland for example, they have put a tax on black rubbish bags, so that people are encouraged not to just throw things straight in the bin, and to reduce their rubbish. Having said that, I think it's still absolutely crucial for the government to continue raising peoples' awareness of the importance of waste management and disposal. Overall, the situation has improved over the past 25 years, and this is mainly because of new laws with tighter controls and higher standards. Even so, individuals and businesses still need to work very hard to reduce and reuse waste as much as possible.

L: Thank you very much. That was a very nice presentation. Does anyone have any further questions? ...

 05

1. If you ask **me**, keeping animals in zoos is **really cruel** because they're taken away from their natural habitats and have far less space than they do in the wild. I **honestly** think that animals should remain in their original environments.

2. I can't **stand** the fact that cars are still allowed in many city centres – they cause so much noise and pollution. I **much** prefer city centres that are pedestrianized, where people can walk around with no worries about too much traffic.

3. I guess I'm quite **lazy** really as I don't bother recycling much except newspapers. I know we should try and reuse our resources if possible, but sometimes it's just not convenient. I'm **convinced** that more people would recycle stuff if there were better facilities, and it was generally easier.

3 Out of this world

 06

Hello. Can I just have your attention for a minute? Thank you. My name is Mary Golding, some of you may recognize me – I used to be a teacher here at the college, but I changed jobs last year, and I now work as the

Student Officer. OK, well, I'm in today to tell you about a trip that we've got going to er ... Paris. Well, this'll be a good chance for those of you who haven't been to France before to have a look at another country, and Paris is very beautiful. I think those of you who come will thoroughly enjoy it. The trip is going to be for five days, from the 31st of March, which is a Saturday, to the 4th of April, the following Wednesday. We'll be leaving pretty early in the morning, seven o'clock, from college, so you'll have to set your alarm clocks, and we'll be going through the Channel Tunnel on the train, so no ferries or coaches for those people who get seasick or travel sick! We'll be back again on Wednesday about ten o'clock at night.

 07

So, what will we be doing when we get there? If you look at the diagram of Paris that I've given you, you can see that we're going to be staying in a small hotel near the centre of town. It's actually in the area called Montmartre. The accommodation will be shared, so you'll be in a room with one of your friends – you can obviously choose who you'd like to share with. On the first day we're in Paris, we'll be going on a boat trip, up the River Seine and up the Eiffel Tower, the famous monument in the middle of Paris. There should be a good view from up there. Both of these things are included in the cost of the trip, so you won't need to worry about spending extra money. On the second day, we'll be going to Notre Dame, which is a large cathedral with beautiful stained glass windows. There's no admission charge for this, but there are lots of souvenir shops around, so you might need some money for those! There will be lots of time for having a look around on your own, and doing some shopping – I know that some of you are very keen on that! On the third day, our last day in Paris, you'll be free to do whatever you like. You could go to an art gallery, for example the Louvre is a very famous one, where you can see the 'Mona Lisa'. You'll have to pay to get in there, but it's not expensive. The biggest problem is that the queue to get in is often very long. The cost of the whole trip is a hundred and twenty pounds, which includes all of the transport, the hotel, and breakfasts. You'll have to buy other food yourself, so you'll need more money for that. It's a really popular trip, we've had real success with it before, I'm sure those of you who come will really enjoy it.
If you'd like to go, can you sign up on this form on the student noticeboard by Friday. It'll be first come, first served, so do try and sign up as quickly as you can. Thank you very much, I hope to see some of you on the trip.

 08

(TEP = Tele-enquiry person; S = Student)

TEP: Hello, National Train enquiry line. Can I help you?

S: Yes, please. I'd like to find out about times and prices of trains to Edinburgh.

TEP: Fine. And which station will you be travelling from?

S: Birmingham.

TEP: And when would you like to travel?

S: Umm. Friday March the 4th .

TEP: Will that be a Single or Return?

S: Return please.

TEP: Standard or First class?

S: Standard.

TEP: And what time of day would you like to travel?

S: In the morning, please, um, round about 8.00.

TEP: Right, well, there's a train which leaves Birmingham New Street at 8.05 arriving in Edinburgh at 12.38.

S: OK, let me write that down … leaving at five past eight and getting there at … what time?

TEP: 12.38.

S: 12.38. Thanks. Do I have to change trains?

TEP: No, it's direct.

S: And what about the one after that?

TEP: The next one is at 9.15, arriving Edinburgh at 14.35, with a change at Stockport.

S: OK, leaving 9.50, arriving 2.35.

TEP: No, 9.15

S: Oh. OK. And what about coming back?

TEP: What time would you like to leave?

S: Late afternoon, please.

TEP: Right. There's one at 16.45 which is direct and gets to Birmingham at 20.21, and the one after that leaves at 18.05 arriving at 21.57 including a change at Manchester.

S: Oh, would that be Manchester Oxford Road?

TEP: Erm, no it's Manchester Piccadilly.

 09

S: Right. And how much is the cheapest ticket?

TEP: Well, it depends. If you can leave after 9am, it's cheaper. There's an Apex Super Saver which you have to book at least 14 days before you want to travel. That costs £33.50.

S: Thirty three … ?

TEP: Fifty.

S: OK. And what happens if I want to leave before 9am?

TEP: If you can book seven days in advance, then you can buy an Apex Peak Saver. That costs £41.30, but if you can't do that, the next cheapest ticket is the Standard Saver which costs £54 return.

S: So it's £41.30 if I book seven days in advance.

TEP: Yes.

S: And £45 if I don't.

TEP: No, it's £54 for the Standard Saver.

S: Oh, OK.

TEP: If you can travel on a different day of the week, then we have the Off Peak Saver at £38.

S: But I can't travel on a Friday for that fare?

TEP: That's right.

S: Fine. Thanks very much for your help.

TEP: You're welcome.

S: Bye.

TEP: Bye.

 10

(IDP = Information desk person; S = Student)

IDP: Hello, can I help you?

S: Yes, I hope so. I've just come here by bus, and I'm trying to find my way around the train station. Can you tell me where the ticket office is?

IDP: Yes, of course. Look over there, to your right, the ticket office is to the right of the cafe as you look at it.

S: Oh yes. Thanks. And are those the platforms straight ahead of us?

IDP: Mmmm – which one do you need?

S: I think I need platform 15.

IDP: Yes – platform 15 is in the far corner.

S: Sorry, I can't see it …

IDP: Just there, behind the flower shop.

S: Oh yes. Great – just one more thing – can you tell me where the toilets are?

IDP: Sure – they're over there, on the left, behind the newsagent's.

S: Thanks for all your help.

IDP: No problem.

4   All in the mind

11

(A = Announcer; JG = John Gregory)

A: As part of our series of study skills talks, John Gregory is going to talk to you today about the theory of multiple intelligences, a way of discovering more about how you, as an individual, may learn best.

JG: Hello. I'd like to start off today by giving you a little background information on the theory and then look at what these multiple intelligences are and how you can learn to make the most of your strengths in different areas.

The traditional view of intelligence, as measured by IQ tests, tends to focus on just two sorts of intelligence – Linguistic and Logical Mathematical, or in other words being good with words or with numbers and logic. In his book, *Frames of Mind*, Howard Gardner suggested that there were in fact other ways of being intelligent, that were not always recognized by the school system. He suggested seven different intelligences, which we will look at today, though he has since increased the number to eight, and thinks there may be more still.

So, what are the types of multiple intelligence? Firstly, those already mentioned. Linguistic and Logical Mathematical. People with linguistic or verbal intelligence are good at communicating with others through words. They will learn languages easily and enjoy writing and speaking. They tend to think in words rather than in pictures. They will be good at explaining and teaching and persuading others to

their point of view. Not surprisingly, they will often become journalists, teachers, lawyers, politicians and writers.

12

Those who are strong in Logical Mathematical intelligence are good at seeing patterns and making connections between pieces of information. They reason well, can solve problems effectively. They're the kind of student that asks a lot of questions! They make good scientists, engineers, computer programmers, accountants or mathematicians.

Then there are the Personal Intelligences – Interpersonal, meaning between people, and Intrapersonal, meaning within yourself. Those of you with good Interpersonal intelligence have the ability to see things from other people's points of view, understanding how others feel and think. You encourage people to co-operate and communicate well with others, both verbally and non-verbally. You'll make good counsellors, salespeople, politicians and managers.

Intrapersonal intelligence is more about being able to understand yourself, recognize your own strengths and weaknesses, and your inner feelings. If you're strong in this area you'll make good researchers, theorists and philosophers.

If you tend to think in pictures rather than words, you may be strong in Visual-Spatial intelligence. You enjoy drawing and designing as well as reading and writing. If you tend to doodle on your notes in class, that may be a sign of this intelligence. You'll have a good sense of direction and find graphs, charts and maps easy to understand. A good job for you might be a designer, an architect, a mechanic or engineer.

Bodily-Kinaesthetic intelligence is about the ability to control body movements and handle objects skilfully. Athletes, dancers, actors will be strong in this area. Sometimes physical skills are seen as something entirely separate from intelligence, something which Gardner strongly challenges by including this intelligence.

Finally, Musical Intelligence. If you have a good deal of musical intelligence you'll often play an instrument, but not necessarily. If you often find yourself tapping out rhythms in class, this may be a sign that you're learning through your Musical intelligence. Not surprisingly you'll make a good musician or songwriter.

13

If you're aware of where your strengths lie, you can use this information to help you study more effectively. For example, if you have high Linguistic intelligence you'll learn well through group discussions, listening to lectures and reading, whereas if you're stronger in Logical Mathematical intelligence you may learn better through problem solving activities. Those of you with strong Visual-Spatial intelligence will respond well to videos, diagrams and charts. You'll probably find it helpful to learn vocabulary through using mind maps.

If you are interpersonally intelligent, try working in groups or pairs or teaching someone else what you're trying to learn. Your good communication skills mean that you'll also learn well through listening to others. Or, if you're more intrapersonally intelligent, it may be better for you to do some studying alone, setting yourself goals.

If you have high Bodily-Kinaesthetic intelligence you may find it easy to study while walking around – though perhaps you shouldn't try this in class! The Musically intelligent may learn well through songs, or with background music on while they study.

It is important to recognize that everyone is a combination of all the intelligences, just in different strengths. For many tasks and jobs you need to use a combination of strengths. So, what does the questionnaire you've completed tell you about how you learn? (fadeout)

 14

Good morning everyone. We'll start the lecture in a moment, but first I have a few notices. The trip to the City Museum and Art Gallery in Bristol tomorrow has had to be postponed. Mr Struthers is in bed with the flu and no one else is able to take it. I'm told he should be back soon though – if not tomorrow, then the next day, so you should talk to him about the new date. So that's the first thing, the second, is next week is of course the Christmas ball. The venue we're using is brand new and I've been reliably informed that in addition to the usual dinner and dancing, there'll also be ten-pin bowling. There will, however, be a charge of nine pounds for this per team, so why don't you get together with some friends to split the cost. Plus, don't forget it's fancy dress. I expect to see some marvellous costumes! I myself am currently creating something that'll be even better than my Tin Man from the Wizard of Oz of last year.

 15

(DW = Dr Williams; S = Sian)

DW: Hello there, Sian.

S: Hello Dr Williams – I'd like to talk to you about my assignment please.

DW: Fine. Come on in and have a seat. Have you started work on it yet?

S: Yes, I have – I've started doing some reading around and I've roughed out an outline of what I want to do, but I wanted to just check with you that I was going in the right direction.

DW: OK, good. So what have you decided to look at?

S: What really interests me is the idea of 'nature vs nurture' with regard to intelligence and looking at whether a child is just born clever, or whether their parents, teachers, friends – people like that influence them. Do you think that this is a suitable subject for me to focus on?

DW: Well, it's a big topic for a 2,000 word assignment. People have been debating that for years, and there's still no definitive answer.

S: Yes, I know. I've been researching in the library, though and I've found several

studies that have tried to compare the effects of genetic factors and environmental factors on children.

DW: Well, there's no shortage of literature on this subject, that's for sure!

S: Yes! And that's my main problem at the moment. For every study that shows that genetic potential is the most important factor, there's another to show the opposite!

DW: The best thing to do is to choose a selection of research that shows a similar pattern, and compare that in relation to one or two studies which don't follow the same trends. Then try to analyse why the results might differ.

S: OK. Another question I wanted to ask you was whether I should include my own opinion?

DW: It's fine to do that, but be careful not to make your writing sound too personal, that is make sure that you back up any statements with clear reasons or evidence and don't forget to make reference to where you found that information.

S: What do you mean, exactly?

DW: Well, for example, if you say that in Australia fewer children from lower income families go to university, even though that's a fairly well known fact, you need to mention the source of that information.

S: You mean find a study that has shown that?

DW: Yes, and include the reference in your bibliography at the end of your assignment.

S: The bibliography – should that include all of the books I've used for reference?

DW: No, only the ones that you've directly cited in the essay. Put them in alphabetical order according to author – not in the order that you use them in the essay. Remember: you were given a handout on this topic at the start of term.

S: Yes, that's right. Right – thanks for your time. I'll go and get on with it!

DW: OK – goodbye. If you have any further questions or points you want to discuss, then we can cover these in your next tutorial.

S: Great. Thank you for your help. Bye.

DW: Cheerio.

5 A career or a job

 16

(S = Sally; J = John)

S: Hi John, how're you doing?

J: Oh hi Sal, not so bad, I'm just looking at this poster, have you seen it?

S: No, what's it about?

J: It's a careers talk next week – now that Christmas is over, I'm starting to realize that it won't be very long before I have to start looking for a job!

S: It's only the first week of the Spring term.

J: I know, but think how fast the last two years went – we'll be finished before we know it.

S: I suppose you're right, it's a bit scary, isn't it? Do you know what you want to do? Are you going to be a singer in a band all your life?

J: No, I'd like to be, but my Dad would kill me … With a degree in Business, I've got quite a few options, but I think I'd like to go into marketing.

S: That'd be interesting – you'll make good money too, won't you?

J: I could do, but that's usually after you've worked your way up a bit. What about you – do you know what you're going to do?

S: I really want to try and get a job overseas – my sister and her two kids live in Australia, and I'd like to go out there …

J: Really, that'd be great! I'll come and visit you!

S: Yeah, OK. Apparently, there's a big demand for medics Down Under. I need to get more hospital experience before I can be a GP, though. The main trouble is I'm not really sure how to go about finding a job. I mean, I know I'll have to look through the adverts, but I'm not sure where the best place to look is, or how to sell myself properly.

J: So, what are you doing on Wednesday? Shall we go to this talk?

S: Who's the speaker, then? Mmmm, oh no, it's Professor Davis. I had him for a lecture once and he went on and on and never seemed to make any relevant points at all!

J. No, that can't be right. Are you sure it was the same man? Professor Davis is thin and quite bald.

S: Oh no, this guy was fat and he had a moustache.

J: That's Mr Davidson – you're right, his lectures aren't the best, but apparently he does important research, and gets a lot of money from industry for the university.

S: Oh, as long as it's not him – I don't think I could stand two hours of that, again!

J: No, Professor Davis is from my department and he always talks sense. So what do you think. Shall we go?

S: Maybe – what's he going to talk about?

J: Umm, let me see – it says here that the lecture will cover looking for work and writing applications, including tips on how to impress your potential employers. It says that there'll be time for questions as well.

S: That sounds perfect, actually. What time does it start?

J: Says 7 o'clock here.

S: OK, I'll meet you here, outside the main hall just before seven. We can go in together.

J: Why don't we make it a bit earlier – say half six, and we can go and have a quick drink in the bar first.

S: Great! Listen, I've got to go, I'm meeting Tariq in ten minutes. I'll see you in the bar at 6.30 on Wednesday, then.

J: OK – see you then.

 17

Hello everyone, it's good to see so many of you here. This is an important time in your lives – your first job is an important step into the world, and although it's not irreversible, it's important to try to make sure that you find a job that suits you and that you enjoy.

My talk tonight is going to be divided into two main parts: firstly, looking for a job and secondly, writing applications. Another important area is interviews, but they'll be discussed in a separate talk. There'll be time for questions afterwards, so if you could wait until then to ask anything, I'd be grateful.

Right – looking for a job. There are four main ways that you can look for work. The first, and traditionally the best, is newspapers and magazines. Papers will often run adverts for different types of job on different days, for example, The Guardian advertises educational posts on a Tuesday. Find out which day is applicable to you for each paper. Another useful source of adverts for work are magazines, for example, specialist industry magazines. If you don't already know what's available for your subject area, now is the time to find out! Where you want to work will also influence where you look. If you can be flexible and move house for a job, then use national newspapers and magazines. This will give you more choice about jobs. If you don't want to move, or have a certain place in mind, it might also be a good idea to look in local papers or in local editions of the bigger papers. In some areas, especially the bigger cities, London, Birmingham and so on, there are magazines of local job advertisements that are distributed free, often outside railway stations and major supermarkets. The second place to look for work is through an agency or a job centre. This can be very efficient, as you're actually letting someone else do some of the job searching work for you. Mostly, agencies will get a fee from your prospective employer, so you won't have to pay anything, either. Another place to look for work is the Internet. This is becoming more and more popular, and many companies will also encourage you to complete on-line application forms. There are lots of sites that advertise jobs, I'll be giving you a list of sites later. You can usually search for the kind of work and location you want. Finally, if there is a particular company that you're interested in, you could also contact them directly and enquire about vacancies.

So, you've found a job that you want to apply for. What next? Usually, you phone the company and ask for an application form and a job description. The advert will often have a reference number, so make sure you have that handy when you call. Read the job description carefully – is this the job you want? Could you do it? OK, you have the form in front of you – either a paper copy or on your computer – what next? Some good advice is to take your time and make sure that the information you give is specific to this job and not just general. Remember that this is the first impression that an employer will have of you, and they will probably have a lot of applications – if it is messy, or filled in incorrectly it will go straight into the bin! Unless it specifically asks you to handwrite it – and some will – then word process it and make sure that there are no spelling or grammar mistakes. Fill in all parts of the application form – if you think it doesn't apply to you, write n/a, which means 'not applicable', but don't leave blanks. After you've completed the form, most applications will also ask you to include a covering letter. This is your chance to shine. Think carefully about the job and why you're the best person for it. Why are your experience and qualifications relevant and what personal qualities do you have that would benefit the employer? Don't be modest here, but don't lie – if you say that you speak fluent Spanish, and you can actually only say hello and goodbye, you're asking for trouble! Finally, it's always a good idea to get someone you trust to look at your form before you post it, maybe a friend, a tutor, possibly even one of your parents. They might spot something that you haven't! If it's all OK, then send it off, giving plenty of time for the post to get it there before the deadline. The main thing to remember is that the perfect job for you *is* out there – if you don't get the first one, just keep trying.

Right, has anybody got any questions?

6 Crime and punishment

 18

(P = Presenter; R = David Renshaw; L = Lorna Coates; J = Jennifer Simpson)

P: Today on 'Burning Issues' we are going to discuss the issue of school absenteeism or truancy. It's been in the news a lot recently because of the woman from Oxford who was jailed because she didn't make sure her two daughters were going to school regularly. First of all, let me introduce my guests, David Renshaw, a government spokesperson, Lorna Coates from The Crime Reduction Charity and Jennifer Simpson, a mother of three from Oxfordshire. Let me start with you, Mr Renshaw. What is the government doing about truancy?

R: Good morning. Well, obviously, children need to go to school. Truancy damages education, of course, but can also lead children to a life of crime.

P: But aren't the new laws about putting parents in prison rather tough?

R: Well, we have introduced imprisonment in some cases, and some people think this is too hard, but it does seem to work. Even the mother who was jailed said that it was a good thing for her children because they now realize how important it is to go to school. It's not the only measure we have, though. Something else we are thinking about is 'weekend' prison sentences. This means that the parent would only go to prison at the weekends, but could still keep their job in the week. We're also considering heavy fines.

P: OK. Thanks for that. Lorna, maybe you could tell us why you think children play truant.

L: Well I must say that I think the government isn't looking at the reasons why children play truant – they just want a quick answer, and I don't think it'll be successful. Children miss school for many reasons. For example, they might be unhappy at home, or they might have friends who play truant and encourage them to do the same. Peer pressure like this is very strong in teenagers, particularly. Bullying is another common reason. Children who are bullied at school will often avoid going. I strongly believe that more research needs to be conducted into this problem.

P: That's all very well but can you be more specific?

L: Well, for a start, I don't think punishing the parents will have long-term benefits. Everybody needs to work on this together – parents, children, schools, the government and social services. It shouldn't be just the government sending parents to prison.

R: We are obviously trying to make that happen, but it's very difficult. For example, in the spring, there were over twelve thousand youngsters absent from school, and a lot of these were with their parents. Now, if children are missing school with their parent's consent, then the government needs to take tough measures.

L: Yes, but it's not always as simple as that, is it? What I'm saying is that we need to look at the reasons why this is happening.

P: Right. Let's look at it from a parent's point of view. Jennifer, you live in Oxford and have three teenage children?

J: That's right.

P: So how do you feel about this issue? Do you think that the parents are responsible for children playing truant?

J: Well I think Lorna's right that it is a very complex issue and I tend to agree that you can't punish the parents for the child's behaviour. If a parent is sent to prison or fined heavily, this isn't going to help us to understand the main reasons why their child is missing school. If the child is unhappy or depressed about something at school, this isn't going to help, is it?

P: A good point Jennifer. So what would be better?

J: I think the emphasis should always be on the child. You need to find out why he or she is missing school. Then you can make decisions on that information about what to do.

L: Jennifer's right and can I just add that this is the approach that our charity would advocate too.

P: Counselling is another effective option. Wouldn't you agree, Lorna?

L: Well, it's certainly a possibility.

P: Do you have anything else to say, Mr Renshaw?

R: I can assure you that the government is considering all of these points and I should add that nothing is definite yet – we are still at the proposal stage.

P: OK. Thank you all very much for contributing to this discussion. And on tomorrow's programme …

19

It's very nice to see so many of you here tonight. I'm Constable Moore and I'm the Crime Prevention Officer for this area. I'm here tonight to talk about 'Neighbourhood Watch'. Can I ask how many of you have been involved with this before? Oh yes, a few of you – that's good. Well, for the rest of you, Neighbourhood Watch is a scheme set up between the police and local people and I'd like to tell you a bit about how it operates.

Basically, it's just common sense and community spirit. Fifty or a hundred years ago, people tended to live in the area that they grew up in and they didn't move around very much, so most people would have known their neighbours. They probably knew each other's habits – what times they came home, who their friends were – that kind of thing, and so it was very obvious if something abnormal was happening. If a stranger was hanging around, or if someone was moving things out of a house, usually someone in the area would see what was happening and would call the police, or take some kind of action. In these days where people move around the country so much, you lose a lot of that community spirit. We don't tend to know our neighbours very well, and we feel a bit embarrassed to get involved.

Imagine this scene. One day, you see a large van outside your neighbour's house and some men carrying things out of the house into the van. Without any knowledge or information about your neighbour, most of us would feel too embarrassed to do anything. Meanwhile, your neighbour's house is being burgled and all of his possessions are being stolen in broad daylight!

Another example is vandalism – people might see someone smashing a telephone box or spraying paint on a wall, but usually they don't want to get involved or call the police.

These kinds of things happen every day. A Neighbourhood Watch scheme aims to bring back a bit of the 'nosy neighbour' in us all, so that we'll know if we see something suspicious, and feel as if we can contact the police.

How much you do is really flexible. It might be as simple as keeping an eye on a neighbour's home while they are away on holiday, or keeping a look out for suspicious things going on in your road. If you have time, you might want to take a more active role as a committee member, or volunteer to write, print or distribute newsletters. It's really up to you.

Another major benefit of being in a watch programme is that often insurance companies will lower your premium on your house insurance. Talk to your insurance company to check the details on this, sometimes you have to fit suitable locks on your windows and doors first – but this is a worthwhile thing to do, anyway.

Right – has anyone got any questions …

7 Globalization

 20

In the first part of today's lecture I would like to introduce you to the topic of globalization. I will start by considering what globalization is. Secondly, I will explain something of its history. Finally, I intend to look at who the main players in globalization are, both for and against it, and briefly summarize their arguments.

So, let us begin with what may seem an obvious point. What exactly is globalization? A lot of people think it is mainly about economics, or increased global trade. However, it can also be seen as increased cultural and technological exchange between countries. Examples might be McDonald's in Calcutta and Japanese motor technology in Britain. Now let us look a little at the history of globalization. There is no agreed starting point, but it could have been about 100 years ago. Certainly, there was a big expansion in world trade and investment then. This was put back considerably as the capitalist world came up against the First World War and then the Great Depression in 1930.

However, the end of the Second World War set off another great expansion of capitalism in 1948 with the development of multinational companies. These were companies interested in producing and selling in the markets of countries all around the world. Finally, globalization really took off when the Soviet Union collapsed.

It's important not to forget the importance of air travel and the development of international communications. The telephone, the fax and now computers and email have all encouraged the progress of international business.

 21

Turning now to the main players involved in globalization, we find that there is a clear division between those who are pro-globalization and those who are anti-.

The main organizations against globalization are the environmental organizations, such as Friends of the Earth and Greenpeace, who put forward the belief that globalization harms the environment.
In general, they blame global corporations for global warming and the depletion of natural resources. The most obvious is oil and gas, but there are others such as tropical rainforests, which are cut down for timber, and the resources of the sea, which may be affected by pollution.

Organizations which represent developing countries, including international aid agencies such as Oxfam, are also against globalization. They are concerned that the global organizations, such as the International Monetary Fund and the World Bank, are not doing enough to help the poor and, indeed, may be adding to their problems. Some are critical of the World Trade Organization. They argue that the WTO is making it difficult for poor countries to protect and build their own industries.

Many companies in rich countries also oppose globalization because they are worried that competition from imports will cost them money. A good example is companies that make clothing and shoes. These are among the few industries in which poor countries can provide effective competition with imports of cheap goods, because wages are so much lower than in America or Europe.

Lastly, some trade unions oppose globalization too. They say it leads to a lowering of wages and conditions of work in the developed and the developing world.

 22

Having looked at some of the anti-globalization arguments, let's now consider those in favour. There are, of course, many organizations in favour of globalization. Perhaps the most important one is the World Trade Organization, or WTO. This was set up in 1995 and has 123 member countries. It administers the rules of international trade agreed to by its member countries. The WTO's rules make it difficult for a country to favour their own industry over imports from other countries.

The WTO argues that the growth of trade between countries increases the wealth of everyone. Trade allows those who can produce goods most cheaply to do so, thus giving everyone the best possible price.

Another pro-globalization organization is the International Monetary Fund or IMF. This was established after World War II in 1946. It aims to promote international cooperation on finance and provide temporary help for countries suffering financial problems. The IMF has 182 member countries.

Finally, the United Nations, which was established after the Second World War, has become a promoter of globalization. It aims to promote a shared set of values in the areas of labour standards, human rights and environmental practices between the UN and the business community.
So, we've seen that there are powerful arguments and important players both for and against globalization. I'd now like to move on to look at some of the key issues for debate. Let us begin by considering the question of global inequality.

23

I'm going to talk about a company which is called Honda. It's a Japanese company and they sell a range of vehicles such as small family cars, estates and sports cars. They also produce motorbikes. It's a very good company and is well known all over the world. I'm sure Honda products are common in most countries but I've heard that they are especially popular in Asia and Europe.

There are many reasons why Honda is successful but I think one of the main ones is because it produces a new range of models every year. I expect the company has teams of skilled professionals who design and create cars using modern technology, which means new models have many of the latest features. Another reason for Honda's success is that the models are often more economical than some of their competitors – in both price and petrol consumption. Honda also makes expensive luxury cars too and some of these are designed to be very fast. This shows that Honda products appeal to a wide range of people.

The company is also successful because parts for these cars are usually very cheap and easy to get in most countries.

As far as I know, Honda advertises new cars on TV quite a lot and these advertisements often look quite stylish. I've also seen their products advertised in newspapers and on large billboards by the side of the road.

In my country you see many Hondas on the road but these have been imported from overseas as we don't really have much of a car industry.

 24

Well, there are clearly different ways of looking at it. Cheaper flights mean that more people can afford to travel. This has to be a good thing in that more people can experience different cultures and places. On the other hand, more flights cause more pollution and some tourist destinations have too many tourists and not enough clean water supplies, and so on. As far as I'm concerned though, the benefits outweigh the disadvantages.

8 What's the alternative

 25

(See p. 94.)

 26

(S = Student; L = Lecturer)

S: Hello, you wanted to see me?

L: Hi, yes, I just wanted to see how you're getting along with your assignments this term.

S: I'm doing fine. I've finished the first assignment and I'm working on the second one now.

L: Good. Are you managing to find enough material?

S: Yes, I've been using the college library, the department library and the Internet.

L: Fine. And you're managing to work to the deadlines?

S: Yeah, and I've been told that if I need an extension, I can ask for one.

L: OK. Good, you seem to be on the right track, then.

 27

(See 26 above.)

 28

(L = Lecturer; B = Barry; R = Ron; A = Alice)

L: OK, Barry, thank you for your very clear presentation on human cloning. I'd like to start the discussion by asking you this. Even though, as you said, therapeutic cloning could be used by hospitals to fight and cure disease, whereas reproductive cloning is growing an entirely new human, do you think that ethically there is really any difference between the two?

B: That's a good question, and I'm not really sure that I know the answer. Reproductive cloning is often the one that people fear. If you ask me, the idea of making a new

person who is identical to someone who is living, or has lived, is a bit too close to science fiction.

L: What do you think, Ron? You look as if you have something to say.

R: Yeah, Barry's right. People think of armies of clones, all the same, non-thinking machines, almost, who could be used in an attack by some mad dictator. There are so many books and films on this theme that people seem to imagine that it could really happen.

A: And couldn't it?

B: No, of course not, Alice. Just because you have the same genes as someone doesn't mean you're a robot. If that were true, then every set of identical twins would be doing exactly the same thing all the time, and that doesn't happen, does it Ron – you have twin brothers, don't you?

R: Yes, I do, and although they look the same, they have quite different personalities. So, equally it's unrealistic to think that clones would behave in the same way.

A: So is there a positive side to reproductive cloning? I mean, would anybody benefit?

R: Childless couples. As I see it, they'd have the chance to try for a baby, even though they were infertile.

L: That's a very good point, but we haven't touched upon therapeutic cloning yet. What does anyone think about that?

A: The possibilities are fascinating. Can you imagine being able to grow a new heart for someone who needed a transplant, or a new kidney, or a lung? We have the technology already to transplant these things, but often the problem is finding an organ. Usually you have to wait for someone who wants to donate an organ and who has the same blood and tissue type, to die. Didn't you do some research into this, Ron?

R: Yes, I *was* reading about this, and apparently it could also be used for some degenerative diseases – you know, like Parkinson's, that get worse as you get older.

L: So, are we playing God, here? What do *you* think, Barry?

B: As far as the ethics go, I think that that therapeutic cloning is easier for most people to accept. You're only talking about making a part of a human being, and not a whole one, that can think, and feel and talk back.

9 Gadgets and gizmos

 29

In today's lecture I want to give you a brief overview of the history of robotics, from ancient times up to the present day. We can then look at some of the key inventions in more detail over the next few weeks.

You may have wondered when I mentioned ancient times. Aren't robots a modern invention? Well, technically, yes, but ancient civilizations had very similar ideas, for example, there was the story of Talos, a man made from bronze, who guarded the island of Crete, in Greece. Then in Roman mythology the god Vulcan made two female robots out of gold to help him walk.

However, by 1774 myth had become fact, and two French brothers, Pierre and Henri Louis Jacquet-Droz were creating very complicated automatons, such as a boy robot, which could draw and write messages. They also created a robot woman, which could play a piano. Another example was a mechanical duck, which quacked, flapped its wings and pretended to eat and drink. This was invented at about the same time, by a man called Vaucanson. That's V.A.U.C.A.N.S.O.N.

In the next century robots started to be designed which were not so much toys, but had more practical, industrial uses. The industrial robots used in factories today have their origins in these early automated machines.

A good example is Joseph Jacquard's Textile Machine, invented in 1801 which was operated by punch cards.

Then, in 1834, Charles Babbage designed one of the first automatic computers, the Analytic Engine. This also used programs on punched cards to carry out mathematical operations. It had a memory capable of one thousand 50 digit numbers. The project was never finished, but it provided an excellent model for later developments.

 30

The 20th century was a time which saw huge development in the science of robotics, particularly after the computer had been developed in the mid-forties. George Devol designed the Universal Automaton in 1954, which was the first programmable robot. The name was later shortened to Unimaton, which became the name of the first robot company.

Unimaton Inc sold designs to General Motors, who, in 1962, installed the first industrial robot on a production line. The 'Unimate' robot was used in a car factory to lift and stack hot pieces of metal.

In 1970, a computer controlled robot called Shakey was developed. On one occasion Shakey was asked to push a box off a platform. It couldn't reach the box, so it found a ramp, pushed the ramp against the platform, rolled up the ramp and pushed the box to the floor. Doesn't that seem like intelligence?

 31

Since then hundreds of robots have been designed and developed for a variety of uses: assembling small parts in factories, providing the handicapped with artificial limbs, carrying out household chores and even carrying out surgical operations.

In 1967 Japan imported its first industrial robot from the United States, which was, at this time, about ten years ahead in robot technology. However, within a very short time, Japan started to catch up and then take over. Japan is now a world leader in robotics. Sony's Aibo robot dog was the first sophisticated robotic product to really sell well to the public. Now Honda have created Asimo, who has been made two-legged, in order to look more human. He is designed as 'a partner for people', or to work in the home. Asimo became the first non-human to open the New York Stock Exchange. Asimo will continue to be developed and, in the future, its power may come from hydrogen fuel cells, a technology whose only waste product is water. This may mean that Asimo will have to go to the toilet!

If these plans work out then society in the future could be very different. In fifty years time, perhaps, no home or workplace will be without one.

 32

Today I'm going to briefly outline the trends in world music sales from the late sixties to the present day as shown on this graph. From 1969 to 1978, there was a steady rise in sales from about $2 billion to $10 billion. This increase was caused by new developments such as the introduction of stereo LPs and later audio cassettes. From 1978 to 1980 sales remained steady, but in 1981 there was a slight drop in sales to about $8 billion. This probably resulted from the global economic downturn. By 1984, figures were around the $10 billion mark again. After this date there was a sharp increase in world music sales which reached a peak of $40 billion in 1993. This was largely due to the introduction of the CD. America, in particular, experienced a tremendous growth in sales, but other European countries, for example, Britain and Germany also sold millions of CDs.

Surprisingly, sales dropped slightly in the nineties. By 1996, world music sales were about $37 billion. The following year there was a slight rise, but after this sales decreased and in 2001 they dropped to $34 billion. These fluctuations are probably a result of free or cheap music being downloadable from the Internet. It may also be connected to the increased availability of hardware to copy music, for instance, CD burners.

From the information shown on the graph, it can be concluded that …

 33

Now if you could look at the following data: this pie chart shows that in the year 2000 CDs dominated the market and accounted for 67.7% of sales. Cassettes still had a healthy slice of the market with 21.8% and singles made up 10.1%. In terms of LPs, the percentage was 0.4% and sales of mini-discs produced an even lower figure of 0.02%, an amount that is likely to increase in the future. In fact there may well be new formats to take into account. From the data shown on this pie chart, it is clear that …

 34

The bar chart illustrates the percentage of Internet and mobile phone users in different regions of the world by the end of the year 2000. The area with the highest proportion of Internet users was the USA with 57%. Western Europe and Japan had similar figures of 27% and 28% respectively, but in China only 2% of the population were using the Internet.

The proportion of mobile phone users, however, was slightly different. For example, Western Europe had the most owners with 62%, followed by Japan with 46% while in the United States not even 40% of the population used mobile phones.

Looking at the figures for the whole world, it seems that the percentages were quite low in the year 2000, with only 7% of the people on earth using the Internet and 12%, or just over one in ten of the world's population, using mobile phones. There is little doubt that these figures are likely to have changed dramatically by now, especially in countries like China, where the percentage is certain to have risen significantly.

 35

(T = Tutor; S = Student)

T: OK, if you can just make a note of the following books that you're all expected to have copies of for next term. The first one is by David Royce, that's R.O.Y.C.E. It's called Understanding Economic Markets, and it's by David Royce. This is a really useful book, which covers all the core ideas we explore in the first few weeks. Please make sure you've finished reading Understanding Economic Markets before the start of term. Then, Microeconomics: an introduction, by Bill Harris and Sarah Tarnley, T.A.R.N.L.E.Y. As it says, an introduction to microeconomics, so you should find this quite easy to follow, even though the ideas may seem a little complicated at first. Hopefully your lectures will make things clearer.

S: Sorry, could you repeat the name and authors of the second book, please?

T: Yes, Microeconomics:an introduction, by Bill Harris and Sarah Tarnley, that's spelt T.A.R.N.L.E.Y, and Harris is H.A.R.R.I.S. OK? Finally, if you can all also get hold of Economics Today, by Julie Bond please. That's Julie with an 'e', J.U.L.I.E, Bond, B.O.N.D. OK?

 36

(AV = Automated Voice; C1 = Caller 1, etc.)

AV: You have four new messages. First new message, received at 9.29 am today. Beep.

C1: Hi, Steve, this is Paula. I'm in Manchester on business today and I was hoping we could meet for lunch to discuss that new contract. If you get this message in time, could you call me on 07790 765456? That's 07790 765456. Cheers.

AV: Second new message, received at 10.10 am today. Beep.

C2: Mr Wilkes? I don't know if you'll remember me, my name's Joe Fuller. I came in for an interview last week for a job. It's just that I haven't heard anything yet. Would it be at all possible for you to ring me? I'll be at home all day. It's 01923 7766892. Thank you very much. Perhaps I'd better say the number again. It's 01923 7766892. Thank you again.

AV: Third new message, received at 11.30 am today. Beep.

C3: This is a message for Stephen Wilkes. We'd just like to remind him that he has an appointment here with the dentist at 9 am tomorrow morning. If there's any problem he could ring the dental surgery on 01923 4567622.

AV: Fourth new message, received at 3.10 pm today. Beep.

C4: This is Paula again. It's now some time after 3.00 and I need to be getting back, so I'm just ringing to say I guess we'll have to meet up some other time. Never mind. You could email me. My address is p dot reece (R.E.E.C.E.) @ somers (S.O.M.E.R.S.) dot co dot uk. Hope to speak to you soon, one way or the other.

10 The future of computing

 37

(G = Graham; J = Julie; M = Mark)

G: … there have been a lot of interesting sites that have come up on the Internet, recently, but one of the ones that's getting a lot of publicity is one called 'FriendsReunited'. The idea, like all good ones, is very simple – it's essentially a database of schools that you can add your name to and contact other people who went to the same place – people you've lost contact with accidentally or otherwise. This morning in the studio, I have two guests: Julie McDonald, a journalist who has been looking at the site for us, good morning to you, Julie and welcome to the programme, and Dr Mark Jones, a psychologist who has done several studies into how and why we form and maintain friendships. It's nice to see you again, Mark. Julie, can you start by telling us a bit about the site?

J: Yes, Graham. It's actually quite compulsive. I hadn't really expected to be very interested by it, but it's amazing how seeing a few familiar names can change that – it took me back to my teenage years so easily— I stayed on the site for about an hour looking up old friends. The site itself is fairly straightforward – you have to log in, which just really means giving a few details such as your email address, and your name. Of course, you have to give your former name, too (the one you were known by in school) if you've got a different name now. You might have got married for example, and people wouldn't recognize your new name. Then, if you want to, you can also write a short note about what you're doing at the moment, what's happened to you since you left school – that kind of thing …

G: Do most people do that?

J: No, actually a lot of people don't bother. It's really annoying, too, when you find someone that you remember and they haven't written anything!

G: So what happens after you've logged in?

J: Well, then you find your school – you can look up your primary school, secondary school, even your workplace. The school part, is great – you find your school, as I said, and then you can look down a list of all the other people who were in your year, or at least, who left in the same year, and access the information that they've provided.

G: And then get in touch with them …

J: Well yeah, but it's at that point that it stops being free.

G: Ahhhh.

J: Well, I guess that they have to make some money out of it somehow and it's not very expensive. You have to pay seven pounds fifty a year and for that you can send unlimited emails to people you know. When I first saw the price, I thought it was for one contact, but it's not, you can contact as many people as you like, so I thought it was pretty reasonable.

G: And did you? Was there anyone there that you knew?

J: Yes, there were – in fact, a lot of names that were familiar, apparently, they have over 5 million registered users, so there were likely to be one or two I recognized, but no, I haven't contacted anyone yet. I can imagine I might do in the future, though.

G: Thank you – and so, Dr Jones, we've heard a bit about this website – can I ask you, what do you think the attraction is of this kind of link up?

 38

M: I think that there are probably three main reasons why people are interested in a site like this. Julie put her finger on one reason earlier. Curiosity. That plays a big part. The Internet has a very voyeuristic character to it, that can be very attractive – we can see in, but other people can't necessarily see us watching. It's almost the same kind of motivation that makes soap operas so addictive – we have an involvement with the characters because we've seen their history, and so we want to know what happens next, too. On this level, I think it's quite normal and healthy.

G: So you think there are other ways in which it isn't normal and healthy?

M: Well, for some people, those who feel that they've been successful in life, especially if they didn't do very well at school, it can be used to show others what they've done. For example, the businessman who left school with no qualifications, but now has a company worth several million pounds. These kind of people often feel quite insecure and want to prove themselves.

G: Is this a bad thing?

M: No, it doesn't have to be, but it is important for people to understand that other people's opinions of them aren't so important.

J: It's difficult though, isn't it? We all like other people to think we are successful.

M: Yes, of course, and that's OK as long as it doesn't become too necessary.

G: And are there any other ways that the site could be a bad thing?

M: Yes, in fact, the biggest problem I think it could cause is for people who have not been successful or even particularly happy in their adult lives. These people may look back nostalgically and think that everything was perfect when they were at school.

G: Mmm, looking back can be a dangerous thing, can't it?

M: It can be. It's easy, to think that the girlfriend or boyfriend that you had was perfect, for example, and compare them to your husband or wife now, especially if you're not very happy with your current partner. The truth is that life was probably just much easier then – no bills, no job, not so much responsibility.

G: So do you think this kind of website is a bad thing?

M: No, of course not – for most people it's harmless fun, but it is worth realizing the possible down sides, too, for some people. If it's a bit of curiosity that's motivating you, fine, but if you're at a particularly insecure part of your life, then be aware that this might not help.

G: Well, I'm not feeling very insecure, so I'm going straight home to log on to my computer and see who I can find! Thank you to my guests. Join us again next week for …

11 The art of advertising

 39

(S = Student; T = Tutor)

S: Can you explain what the problem was with my assignment on advertising standards?

T: Well, to begin with, you really should have read the question more carefully. The question asked you to compare and contrast the rules applied by advertising standards agencies around the world and you only wrote about your own country.

S: So, I ought to have given more examples?

T: Yes, and you were also supposed to compare and contrast them, or say how they're different or similar.

S: Oh, I didn't understand that I had to do that. OK. Was that the only problem?

T: I'm afraid your handwriting wasn't very good either. You didn't need to word-process it, but it would have helped me to understand what you wanted to say. Having said all that, you did have some very good ideas about …

 40

Advert A

(YC = young child; A = Adult)

YC 1: Um … here's a good idea for you. If you want to set up your own business, you should be at least … um, at least twelve. I think that you can sound grown up on the phone, then you should …

YC 2: I'd set up an office at the top of Mt Everest. I'd set it up in the middle of nowhere, so that I had lots of peace and quiet to get on with my work.

YC 3: My daddy says you have to pay for a lot of taxis when you have a business, but I'm not sure why, cos he's got his own car …

A: For grown-up advice about starting your own business, call the Business Helpline on 0800 501 5001 or visit businesshelp.org. We're here to help you!

Advert B

Interest free credit, and you don't have to pay a penny for a whole year! – that's the fantastic Summer Sale offer at Harold's, but it must end this week. Save up to 70% on lounge, dining and bedroom furniture. You want leather furniture? We've got it! You want beds, carpets and curtains? Look no further! You can spread the cost over three years, without paying a penny in interest and if you spend over £200, you don't even have to pay a deposit. Ask for written details.

There's big savings, no deposit, no payments, no interest and no catch, but you'll have to hurry. The amazing Summer Sale must end at 5pm this Sunday at Harold's, Stratford Rd Shirley and the Kingfisher Centre.

Advert C

(A = Woman 1; B = Woman 2; M = Man)

A: What are you up to this weekend?

B: I'm trying to get a washing machine.

A: Ah, so you'll be looking for a 'Super mega deal', then, or a 'Price Slasher', or a 'Red hot Summer Sale'? Or maybe a 'Special £10 off voucher – ask in store for details'?

B: No

M: At Star, we check thousands of prices at other stores every week, so you don't have to. You can rest, safe in the knowledge that our price guarantee is what it says. If you can find the same thing cheaper, we'll match the price AND give you £20 in cash. You can trust us, because we care about prices.

A: What about a Blazing Saver?

B: NO!

 41

(T = Tutor; A = Adam; B = Betty; C = Charlie)

T So, you've all had a chance to study the adverts, who'd like to start us off by talking about the first one?

A: I thought this one was quite interesting. It's not a commercial organization, is it?

T No, it isn't. It's a government body.

A: So, arguably it's different from the other two, it's not actually selling something, it's offering a service to people.

B: I thought that, too, but when I actually stopped to consider the implications, it's not so different, is it? In the commercial sector and the government sector, the aim of the advert is to persuade. Whether that means persuade people to buy something, or persuade people to use something isn't very important.

A: That's a good point, but I think there is a difference. It's less difficult to persuade someone to use something if the thing you're offering isn't going to cost them any money. Am I right in thinking that the service is free?

T Yes, I think that would be a fair assumption, Adam. I do think, though, that you can classify this advert according to the criteria we are looking at. In my opinion, it uses simple information to persuade. It's a service that many people won't have heard of and it's probably unique. They are working on the principle that if they say what they are offering, and make it a little bit entertaining with the children's voices, then that will be enough.

C: Don't you think there's a certain amount of repetition in there, too? They said the name about three times at the end, in quick succession.

A: Yes, but that's the same for almost every ad, isn't it?

C: I guess so. It was certainly true for the second one.

T Do you think that was the main technique in that case, then?

C: No, the main thrust was definitely the half price/special offer method. The whole advert was centred around what a great deal you could get, how little it would cost, how you could get interest free credit, et cetera, et cetera. They mentioned that the offer would finish that Sunday, too. I suppose that making it seem as if you can get a great bargain, but only if you act quickly is a good way of selling things, too.

T So, how about the final advert, Betty, can you take us through that one?

B: Yes, this one is quite interesting, especially after the furniture store advert. That was so much about selling a special deal, for a limited time only, and then the last one was completely opposite. I thought it was absolutely fascinating, the way they used language like, 'a blazing saver' or a 'Super mega deal'. We hear this kind of thing on adverts all the time, telling us how 'absolutely amazing' the product is, but here it was used sarcastically, by a woman who obviously felt very doubtful about these special offers and the language used to sell them. It's almost like putting the advertiser on the same team as the potential buyer – they both dislike the way many products are sold.

A: So you think that kind of ad is very effective?

B: Well, it probably wouldn't work for a long series of adverts – it's kind of like a joke – it wouldn't be funny if you heard it too often. I do think, though, that that kind of anti-advertising approach is so different, and still quite unusual, that it makes you listen.

A: And that's what advertisers want, of course.

B: Of course.

T So, of the three ads, which do you all personally think is the most effective? There's no right or wrong answer, here, I'm just interested in your opinions.

B: I like the last one – it's the only one that was different enough to make me actually listen.

C: Yes, I'd agree – although I don't think any of them were very good. The second one might interest me if I wanted to buy furniture – we usually want to believe what we are told, even if on some level we know it's not true.

A: I actually liked the first one, but I'm not sure if it's fair to compare it with the other two, for the reasons we talked about earlier.

T OK, good. Right, now can we turn our attention to the next question, then …

12 IELTS preparation

42

(A = Announcer)

A: Good afternoon. It's very nice to see so many of you here for our Open Day. I hope that you've enjoyed looking around the campus and have been able to get any questions you have about courses answered. We open this afternoon with a short talk from one of our success stories. Ali Khan is a former student of the university who we are very proud of. He is here this afternoon to tell us a little about his career and how his studies here have helped him. I hope that he will be an inspiration to you.

Ali: Thank you very much and good afternoon. It's very nice to be back to visit the university. I have many happy memories of my time here – although I have to admit that the best of these are of social occasions rather than lectures!

I first came from Pakistan eleven years ago to study here. I think that the main reason was the reputation that England has. So many English universities have such a strong reputation for academic excellence and a great academic tradition. Also, to be frank, a good British degree is a passport to a higher position and a good job in Pakistan and it has certainly worked that way for me. I'm quite sure I wouldn't have done so well if I hadn't studied here.

I originally came to the UK wanting to study Economics and did so here for the first year, but then I found that actually I was much more interested in Politics. I never wanted to become a politician, in my country most people think that they are only a step away from criminals, but I was really fascinated by the way that government functions and the effects that this can have on ordinary people. I wish I had realized this earlier, as it cost me a year's study. When you're choosing your field of study, I think that it's very important to balance what you think will make you employable, with what you're interested in. In my case, as my parents were supporting me, the balance also included what they wanted me to do! Luckily, they were very sympathetic!

When I graduated in Politics, I went back to Pakistan and began looking for work in the public sector. As I said, I had no intention of becoming a politician, but I felt as if I wanted to do something positive to help my country to develop. I applied for work in the Ministry of Education. The competition for jobs like this is fierce but the fact that I had a good degree from a well-regarded British university made a huge difference. Partly this was because of the standard of education, but I think that there were other reasons why employers favour graduates who have studied overseas. Language, of course, is a major one. Even in Pakistan, where all educated people speak English and the standard is generally high, if an employer knows that you've studied in English to a tertiary level, it gives them confidence in your abilities. It's not only language, though.

To have had the experience of studying overseas gives you a lot of independence and flexibility. You definitely need to be flexible in order to cope with all of the cultural differences of a different country. Employers value that, I think.

So, I got the job I wanted and worked for six years in the Education sector, before coming back to England to get a Masters degree in Development Studies. I was actually sponsored to do this by the Ministry, and when I finished, last year, I went back to take up a new position of Director of a project to improve technical education in one region of the country. It's an important post and a very interesting one. I suppose that it would be too strong to say that I owe it all to this university, but the education I received here has certainly been a major factor in my success.

43

Well, everyone, your IELTS test is next week, so I just want to give you a few final hints on the Listening test – I know that some of you are a bit worried about that part. Remember that there are four parts to the Listening test, and they get more difficult as they go through, but before each section you'll have a short time to look at the questions. This time is really important to you – the first thing to do is to read the instructions carefully so that you understand the task type – is it a multiple choice? is it a table? how many words can you use in the answer? – that kind of thing. As you're doing that you also need to think about trying to predict the context – what do the questions tell you about what you're going to hear? It's not really a good idea to predict answers to questions before you've heard the tape, but something that you can usefully do is to read the questions carefully so that you know the kind of information that is being asked for. For example, is it a place name, or a number, or a date? This is a lot to do in the short time you have, but it'll make listening a lot easier. While you're listening to the tapes, write down your answers as quickly as you can, but while you're writing, stay focussed on the tape. If you don't hear something very well and you're not sure about the answer, try to note down a possible answer. You might be able to guess it later. Finally, in the last 10 minutes, transfer your answers very carefully, making sure that all the numbers match up, and don't hang around – get the answers on the answer paper and then quickly check your spelling. Remember that you'll lose marks unless the spelling is correct.

Macmillan Education
Between Towns Road, Oxford OX4 3PP
A division of Macmillan Publishers Limited
Companies and representatives throughout the world

ISBN 1 405 01392 3

Text © Rachael Roberts, Joanne Gakonga and Andrew Preshous 2004

Design and illustration © Macmillan Publishers Limited 2004

First published 2004

All rights reserved; no part of this publication may be reproduced, stored in a retrieval system, transmitted in any form, or by any means, electronic, mechanical, photocopying, recording, or otherwise, without the prior written permission of the publishers.

Design and page make-up by Mike Cryer, eMC Design; www.emcdesign.org.uk

Illustrated by Phillip Burrows, Celia Canning, Stephen Dew, Richard Duszczak, Roger Fereday, Phil Garner, Roger Goode, James Holderness, Bill Houston, Jeffy James, Janos Jantner, Mark di Meo, Mike Phillips, Simon Rumbles, Tony Wilkins

Cover design by Andrew Oliver
Cover photograph by Taxi/Getty

The authors would like to thank their long-suffering spouses Chris, Jack and Jo for their constant encouragement, help and incredible patience. We could not have done this without the support of our families. We also want to thank our children Sam, Kinuthia, Mwathi, Laura and Eleanor for providing regular distractions and entertainment throughout this project.

Thank you to the many students at Solihull College who trialled material and provided sample answers and valuable feedback.

And finally, thanks go to Sarah Curtis, Joe Wilson and all the team at Macmillan, whose faith in us and whose months of hard work helped to make the idea a reality.

The publishers would like to thank all those who participated in the development of the project, with special thanks to Peter Birch, Liz Hunt, Susan Hutchison, Edwina Johnson, Paula Nelson, Denley Pike, Lorraine Sorrell, Merlin Thomas, Sarah Varney-Burch, Olyvia Wilson.

The authors and publishers would like to thank the following for permission to reproduce their material:

UKCOSA: The Council for International Education for extracts from 'International students and culture shock' from *Guidance Notes for Students 2003*; AusAID for diagram 'W-Curve: Stages of adjustment experienced during orientation' taken from *Orientated for Success* edited by M Barker (Australian International Development Assistance Bureau, 1990); Joanna Walters for extract from 'Car-crazy Britain driving itself to complete gridlock', copyright © Joanna Walters 2001, first published in *The Observer* 08.04.01; N I Syndication Limited for extracts from 'First space tourist grins down on planet Earth' by Mark Franchetti and Tom Rhodes, copyright © Times Newspapers Limited 2001, first published in *Sunday Times* 29.04.01; The Ecotourism Association of Australia (EAA) 1997 for extracts from *www.bigvolcano.com.au/natural/nattract.htm* (03.01.02); Bureau of Tourism Research for extracts from *www.btr.gov.au/service/datacard/datacard_action.cfm*;

New Scientist for extracts from 'Crow reveals talent for technology' by Stephanie Pain taken from *www.NewScientist.com*; Earth Trust for extracts from 'Project Delphis' taken from *www.earthtrust.org/delphis.html*; Guardian Newspapers Limited for extracts from 'Family matters' by Tim Radford and Stephen Moss, copyright © The Guardian 2003, first published in *The Guardian* 21.05.03; Susan McRae for table from *Mother's Employment and Family Life in a Changing Britain* by Susan McRae (Oxford Brookes University, Oxford); Centre for Families, Work and Well-Being for extracts from *www.worklifecanada.ca/compendium20011.pdf*; Victim Support Organisation for information on the charity; Victim Support Organisation for information based on their 'Burglary leaflet' 2003; Macmillan Publishers Limited for definition from *Macmillan English Dictionary For Advanced Learners* copyright © Bloomsbury Publishers Plc 2002 and Cafod for extract from 'What is globalisation?' taken from *www.cafod.org.uk/schools*; N I Syndication Limited for extracts from 'What's the alternative?' by Sanjida O'Connell, copyright © Times Newspaper Limited 2002 first published in *The Times* 16.07.02; Focus Magazine (www.focusmag.co.uk) for extracts from '100 years of gadgets' by Caroline Elliott first published in *Focus* Magazine March 2001; New Scientist for extracts from 'Software aims to put your life on disk' by Ian Sample taken from *New Scientist* 20.11.02; Advertising Standards Authority Inc for extracts from 'Code for advertising to children' taken from *www.asa.co.nz/codes/children.htm*; Guardian Newspapers Limited for extracts from 'Should our children be spared Ronald?' by Helen Sleaford and Rupert Howell, copyright © The Guardian 1999, first published in *The Guardian* 22.11.99; Hodder & Stoughton for extracts from *Marketing: An Analytical and Evaluative Approach To Business Studies* by Ian Swift (Hodder & Stoughton, 2000); How To Books for adapted extracts from *Passing Exams Without Anxiety* by David Acres (How To Books Ltd, Oxford, 1998).

The authors and publishers would like to thank the following for permission to reproduce their photographs:
Alamy pp6(b), 8, 22, 30(c), 66, 110, 135, 148; Corbis pp6 (t-Ariel Skelley), 90(l-Thom Lang), 102(l- Alain Le Garsmeur) (c-Ray Juno)(r- Haruyoshi Yamaguchi/ Corbis Sygma), 122(Ariel Skelley); Getty pp18, 30(l,r), 34, 46, 47, 54, 90(r), 114, 119, 127, 138; Sally and Richard Greenhill p73.

Picture Research by Pippa McNee

Whilst every effort has been made to locate the owners of copyright material in this book, there may have been some cases when the publishers have been unable to contact the owners. We should be grateful to hear from anyone who recognises copyright material and who is unacknowledged. We shall be pleased to make the necessary amendments in future editions of the book.

Printed and bound in Spain by EDELVIVES.
2008 2007 2006 2005 2004
10 9 8 7 6 5 4 3 2 1